METAPHOR AND IMAGINAL PSYCHOLOGY

Metaphor and Imaginal Psychology: A Hermetic Reflection provides the first full-length exploration of the significance of metaphor in post-Jungian psychology. Its portrayal of the mythological figure of Hermes as a personification of metaphor marks an original contribution to the field of metaphor studies.

After a 2,500-year exile from philosophy and related areas of study, beginning with Plato's ejection of the poets from the ideal city-state, metaphor is today experiencing a season of renewal. Among the fields where its significance as a way of seeing, thinking, and feeling has been especially prominent is archetypal psychology, perhaps the most philosophically attuned of psychological disciplines.

Approaching the work of James Hillman and other key archetypal psychologists from a poststructuralist perspective, *Metaphor and Imaginal Psychology* draws insightful comparisons between archetypal psychology and the deconstructive philosophy of Jacques Derrida, a principle theorist of metaphor's philosophical resurgence.

By linking two disciplines that might at first appear as strange bedfellows, *Metaphor and Imaginal Psychology* underscores the influence of metaphor in reason and emotion, and makes a compelling case for the Mercurial ethos of our postmodern world. Aside from representing essential reading for therapists and theorists working in post-Jungian studies, the book will appeal to readers, students, and scholars of literary criticism, psychology, philosophy, and mythology.

Marc Slavin is a writer living in Oakland, California. He studied archetypal theory at the California Institute of Integral Studies, San Francisco, where he was awarded a PhD in Philosophy and Religion in 2014.

METAPHOR AND IMAGINAL PSYCHOLOGY

A Hermetic Reflection

Marc Slavin

Routledge
Taylor & Francis Group
LONDON AND NEW YORK

First published 2018
by Routledge
2 Park Square, Milton Park, Abingdon, Oxon OX14 4RN

and by Routledge
711 Third Avenue, New York, NY 10017

Routledge is an imprint of the Taylor & Francis Group, an informa business

British Library Cataloguing in Publication Data
A catalogue record for this book is available from the British Library

Library of Congress Cataloging-in-Publication Data
A catalog record for this book has been requested

ISBN: 978-1-138-64987-3 (hbk)
ISBN: 978-1-138-64988-0 (pbk)
ISBN: 978-1-315-62565-2 (ebk)

Typeset in Bembo
by Swales & Willis Ltd, Exeter, Devon, UK

To
Gerald M. Slavin
and
Constance Halter Slavin
in memoriam
and to
Mark Alan Heltemes
with lasting admiration

CONTENTS

ACKNOWLEDGMENTS

My heartfelt appreciation to the faculty, administrators, and staff of the California Institute of Integral Studies in San Francisco, and in particular to the innovators in the Philosophy, Cosmology, and Consciousness program for fostering the unique interdisciplinary environment in which I formulated the ideas in this book. I am especially grateful to Robert McDermott and Richard Tarnas for their unflagging encouragement and sound guidance.

I would also like to thank the following scholars and friends for invaluable dialogue and for thoughtful comments on earlier versions of the manuscript: Michael Vannoy Adams, Gustavo Beckman, John Beebe, Patricia Berry, Edward Casey, Clive Cazeaux, Tom Cheetham, Steven Goodman, Gale Lipsyte, Gregory Mengel, Rod O'Neal, Kirk Pillow, Susan Rowland, Richard Shapiro, Giuseppe Stellardi, Gay Walley, and Sylvester Wojtkowski. All errors, of course, are my own.

My thanks as well to Susannah Frearson at Routledge for her confidence in this project.

. . . as if the fullness of the soul did not sometimes overflow in the emptiest metaphors, since no one can ever give the exact measure of his needs, nor of his conceptions, nor of his sorrows; and since human speech is like a cracked kettle on which we hammer out tunes for bears to dance to when what we long for is to move the stars. (Gustave Flaubert, *Madame Bovary*, 1856)

INTRODUCTION

A book about metaphor should invoke suspicion. Metaphor sows the disciplinary ground with ambiguity and paradox. It unceremoniously places into question the absolutes of any literalism. Yet it is our identity as subjects in a kingdom of the literal that lends coherence to our lives. Within a taxonomy of the self and its objects, we appear as a species of the literal. To look past the seemingly natural categories that give us a fix on the world in search of their ideational provenance is to invite an existential threat, or, what amounts to the same thing, to engage in philosophy. In an irony largely lost on two millennia of philosophers, metaphor turns out to be quintessentially philosophical. Their incognizance began to give way with Nietzsche's insolent approach to the age-old problems, and from there made steady concession. As it becomes increasingly revenant in philosophy and its related disciplines, metaphor—the word stems from the Greek *metapherein*, meaning "to carry over or across"—sets about to ferry the soul of literalism over its flat, positivist horizon to depths of post-objectivist meaning. Now into its vital season, metaphor is able to claim sufficient empirical and theoretical research in its name to make up for the generations lost to its creative repression (see, e.g., Ortony, 1979 and 1993, and Gibbs, 2008). Still, it continues to cut an intrinsically unsettling figure as it materializes at the doors of perception.

The style of a metaphorical epistemology is not to lock in absolutes, but, as we will see, to sow impossibility and allow for the wavering of truth. This book maps metaphor's sinewy path in the post-Jungian field of imaginal, or archetypal, psychology. Metaphor's role there is a principal instance of what James Hillman (1983b) called "destructuralizing" (p. 57). The term, occurring in an interview, is an apparent conflation of two related philosophical movements, poststructuralism and deconstruction. It suggests a philosophical purpose for imaginal psychology, that of taking up, from the precincts of psyche, the poststructural enterprise to question the assumptions of objectivism in an extended consideration of the principle of difference.

The freshness of imaginal psychology is in its aesthetic approach. Its guiding premise is that the psyche, or soul, functions not literally, but figuratively, expressing itself on a poetic basis. The focus is not on analysis, but on image. In Hillman's (2004a) words, "the soul is primarily an imagining activity" (p. 18). The basic idea is expressed by a term of art, *seeing through*, which Hillman identifies as the very act of psychologizing. Seeing through means that what we see is often a function of how we see. It means that we see the world in terms of, or *via*, our ideas about it, and that we do well to cultivate a critical eye toward those ideas, seeing not solely, and insistently, the *world* they make manifest, but as well the *worldview*, or presuppositions, that produce it.

Imaginal psychology's most comprehensive treatment, Hillman's 1975 *Re-Visioning Psychology*, proclaims the central role of seeing through in its title. Re-visioning constitutes an engagement with the psyche's refractory tendency to bend events to point of view. Imaginal psychology draws out the implications of Jung's classic statement of equivalency (a metaphor), "image *is* psyche" (CW 13, par. 75). It de-literalizes image, which ceases to be an object pictured by the senses, and instead becomes, in Edward Casey's (1974a) formulation, a way of knowing that discerns or envisions the symbolic content "present at *every* level of human experience," physical, psychological, and spiritual (p. 20). Imaginal psychology therefore enacts a revisionary epistemology. "By re-viewing, re-presenting and re-visioning where we already are," Hillman (1975) wrote, "we discover the psyche speaking imaginally in what we had been taking for granted as literal and actual descriptions" (p. 127). Employing italics, he added, "*Through psychologizing I change the idea of any literal action at all—political, scientific, personal—into a metaphorical enactment*" (p. 127). Hillman's emphasis indicates metaphor as the Archimedean lever with which archetypal psychology would move the world.

The philosophical space wrought by a re-visioned psychology is one of incommensurability. With insights that derive not from the reductive techniques necessary for analytical theorizing, but from the symbolic mode of the Romantic imagination, it reflects the uncanny encounter in which epistemology arrives at the explanatory frontier of objectivity only to find itself meeting the gaze of subjectivity. It is within these perspectival borderlands that we can discover metaphor's significance. In her study of the importance to literary theory of Ludwig Wittgenstein, who famously underwent an epistemological shift from Russellian logic to a self-described mysticism, Marjorie Perloff (1996) says of re-visioning that it is a function of "the feints and ruses of language" (p. 66). In a comparable manner, the metamorphosis in perspective imminent at objectivity's limits was described by Thomas Nagel (1974) in terms suggestively metaphorical. "The fact that an organism has conscious experience *at all* means, basically, that there is something it is like to *be* that organism," Nagel said. "We may call this the subjective character of experience" (p. 435). With this insight, Nagel adequated ontology to likeness.

Although metaphor loosens or dissolves the semantic petrifaction in which fundamentalisms adhere, it works both sides of the literalist divide. We employ metaphors to understand and experience our world, yet in so doing, we establish them as the world itself, so much so that the metaphors appear not to be ways of knowing, but the actual thing known. Let us take examples of this concretizing phenomenon drawn somewhat at random from the work of George Lakoff and Mark Johnson (1980), leading proponents of the cognitive school of metaphor studies, which asserts that metaphor structures the way we think. Each example presents a metaphor for how we understand ideas followed by some of its common uses.

1. IDEAS ARE FOOD. What he said *left a bad taste in my mouth.* All this paper has in it are raw facts, half-baked ideas, and warmed-over theories. There are too many facts here for me to *digest* them all. I just can't *swallow* that claim.
2. IDEAS ARE PEOPLE. The theory of relativity *gave birth* to an enormous number of ideas in physics. He is the *father* of modern biology. Whose *brainchild* was that? Look at what his ideas have *spawned.*
3. IDEAS ARE PLANTS. His ideas have finally come to *fruition.* That idea *died on the vine.* That's a *budding* theory. It will take years for that idea to *come to full flower.*
4. IDEAS ARE PRODUCTS. We're really *turning (churning, cranking, grinding) out* new ideas. We've *generated* a lot of ideas this week. He *produces* new ideas at an astounding rate. His *intellectual productivity* has decreased in recent years.
5. IDEAS ARE COMMODITIES. It's important how you *package* your ideas. He won't *buy* that. That ideas just won't *sell.* There is always a *market* for good ideas.

Lakoff and Johnson's work is replete with numerous other examples. Each consists in the relation of two interactive words or phrases variously known by theorists as *tenor* and *vehicle*, *focus* and *frame*, or *source domain* and *target domain.* In the examples, IDEA is the target domain onto which are mapped the concepts from various source domains. The basic interaction conceives knowing as an integrally responsive process among linguistic components. Yet it evinces not only perspectives, but perspective itself. Herein lies metaphor's duplicity. It reveals fresh vistas of meaning, but each entails the potential to become a fixed point of view, another of literalism's absolutes. Paradoxically, however, in its positing of literalisms metaphor offers no absolution. It is, if anything, amoral. *Any* transitive figure implicates a direct object. Metaphor enacts ways of seeing, and it appears unconcerned whether the sight it engenders is so bright as to be blinding.

Two of the oldest metaphors in Western culture, said the writer and translator Alberto Manguel (2007), come to us from Homer. The *Iliad* and the *Odyssey* serve as extended treatments of the conceptual metaphors Life is a Battle, and Life is a Journey (p. 2). (The words "battle" and "journey" are the frame, vehicle, or source domain of the metaphor, lending semantic inflection to "life," which is the focus, tenor, or target domain.) These ways of experiencing are no less real for being metaphorical; life can indeed seem to be a battle or a journey. Yet to say so is to risk the error of the *is*, mistaking predication for identity. The distinction points to metaphor's implicit *like.* Although life can resemble a battle or a journey, when we confuse predication, seeing *in terms of*, with identity, seeing *that*, we reify perspective, fixing metaphor's polytheistic (Homeric) provenance in monotheistic insistence. We *lose sight* of the fact that at all times we see through the transpersonal forces of nature effecting what Spinoza (1996), who was, after all, a lens grinder, called "the eyes of the mind" (§5P23s), and so we deny ourselves the critical ability to change the idea of the literal. As Jung said, "a positively overwhelming importance attaches to the little word 'like'" (CW 5, par. 203).

With apologies in advance to archetypal theorists and poststructuralists alike for an inevitable rounding off of the distinct complexities of scholarship in each discipline, this book will be an attempt at a metaphorical transposition, or a *seeing through*, in which each school of thought might be understood in terms of the other. Standardly, the concern with archetypes has to do with the identification of formal structures that can account for cultural manifestations. The concern with varieties of poststructuralism has to do with circumstances that escape the boundaries of any structural order, appearing irreducibly situational. Poststructuralisms ask how we account for the anomaly, and to what extent we can consider any occurrence, any event, any linguistic or cultural expression, human subject or human body, to be non-anomalous. In a sense, the two fields seem demarcated. What I wish to do is transgress their boundaries, seeing each from the perspective of the other.

I invoke transgression as a fundamentally metaphorical gesture. Metaphor occurs at the intersection of incommensurables, a theme Hillman addressed in *The Myth of Analysis* (1978b), where he opened a chapter on psychological language by noting the "necessity of the human psyche to tell two kinds of tales about the nature of things" (p. 117). Our dualisms go by many names, rational and irrational, mythos and logos, subject and object, truth and opinion, mind and body, *res extensa* and *res cogitans*. Though dualism can be reduced to opposition, it is generated at intersection and crossroads. Understood analytically, any binary "would sterilize metaphors into abstractions" (p. 121). The displacement of "the metaphorical drive" from poetic to analytic articulation transposes "stands, positions, gestures, styles" into the ubiquity, indeed the basic human condition, of psychopathic behavior (p. 123). The transgression, seeing one thing in terms of another, is primary. It is a given. The pathologizing occurs when the figure, the image, or metaphor, that idea through which we see, literalizes into the concept. As Nietzsche noted, the concept is necessary to the living of life, which would otherwise give forth in an uncontained flood of Dionysian sense impressions. The concept is inevitable, as is the fundamentalism that adheres to it. When the duality inherent in any perspective, any *seeing as*, fixates, each pole defends against the other, giving rise to dualism. Conceptual dualisms are metaphorical duplicities. Each concept starts as a fiction. Born in pathos, or sense impression, it harbors pathological tendency. The making of truth from lies, literalization, instantiates pathology, tragedy, and transgression as the fundaments of life. I hope in what follows to traverse the space of transgression "itself," in its poststructural and archetypal expressions, mapping metaphoricity as primary ontological fact. From a transgressive space between two disciplinary fields I want to suggest the *inter vivos* nature of metaphor. Archetypally, to take interstice as a living force is an invocation of the mythological figure of Hermes. Under his aegis I propose to gather duplicity, transgression, linguistic structure, and the trick of conjuring the literal from the metaphorical. I will unfold the Hermetic attributes of each topic as the narrative proceeds.

The book's first part relates a history of metaphor in philosophy. It is not "the" history of metaphor, for other versions may be written; it serves as a necessary threshold into an understanding of the role of metaphor in imaginal psychology. "History," Hillman (1978b) said, "is only a doorway into further reflection; its value for psychology lies in exposing archetypal patterns" (p. 7). This part is an attempt to take metaphor on its own terms as an archetypal peculiarity whose sufferings need not be subjected to the cure of the rational mind. It follows metaphor's riverine habitat in the margins of philosophy as it seeks its own level, surfacing as the formal element in Kant's third *Critique* and rising to floodtide in the work of Nietzsche. The section examines the cognitive turn that inaugurated the current apotheosis with a look at the work of Max Black and other theorists of the modern view. It explores the contributions of Paul Ricoeur and Jacques Derrida for insights into metaphorical thought as the "other" of conceptual determinism. Each chapter is a dispatch of sorts from the field of metaphor studies, reporting on the theories of one or more leading scholars, importing their insights into imaginal psychology. For an explication of the pre-Kantian period and the emergence of metaphor into critical awareness in the mid-twentieth century, the period of the cognitive turn, I rely on the work of Mark Johnson, whose partnership with George Lakoff has produced perhaps the most influential of contemporary approaches to metaphor. The examination of Kant is based principally in the work of Clive Cazeaux and Kirk Pillow, whose intricate readings bring out the latent metaphorics in Kant's critical project. The chapter on Nietzsche derives from a classic study of his relation to metaphor by Sarah Kofman, a leading formulator of deconstruction. For the comparison of Derrida and Ricoeur, I draw upon the work of another theorist of deconstruction, Giuseppe Stellardi. This part is by no means a comprehensive treatment. Metaphor theory extends to many disciplines and covers multiple approaches; the contents are selected for what they add to the argument for the metaphorical basis of imaginal psychology.

The second part examines that metaphorical basis. It considers the archetypal concepts of *soul*, *image*, *personifying*, *psychologizing*, *pathologizing*, and *dehumanizing*, all formative of Hillman's work, for what they might contribute to a depth psychological, and specifically imaginal, theory of metaphor. This part draws principally upon the foundational text of Hillman's school of study, *Re-Visioning Psychology*. Both parts of the book rely as well on the work of leading theoreticians of imaginal psychology, including Patricia Berry, Tom Cheetham, Edward Casey, Paul Kugler, Rafael López-Pedraza, Susan Rowland, and Richard Tarnas. Readers familiar with post-Jungian scholarship may note that I have not drawn from the work of Wolfgang Giegerich, with whom Hillman had a rich series of exchanges on rhetoric, metaphor, and history (see, e.g., Hillman, 1994), which, though they do not appear here, are catalysts for further exploration of the topic. This book was inspired and informed by the ideas of Michael Vannoy Adams, in particular his comparative essay on Hillman and Derrida (Adams, 1992). Throughout, I draw upon overlapping themes from poststructural philosophy and imaginal psychology to read for the possibility of a poststructural archetypology.

TOWARD A POSTSTRUCTURAL ARCHETYPOLOGY

The question of which this book is composed, whether imaginal psychology is a psychology of metaphor, arises along what Paul Ricoeur (1978) called "the boundary between a semantic theory of metaphor and a psychological theory of imagination and feeling" (p. 141). I approach metaphor as a boundary phenomenon of the psyche, a faculty of mind functioning interpretively among *poietic* frames of reference (in the classical sense of *poiesis*, meaning "to make") so as to cultivate, in William James's (1996) ironic formulation, a "pluralistic universe." I hope to bring out the ambi-valent quality in metaphor's nature, or in its "temperament," that, following Rafael López-Pedraza (2003), can be said to mark it as a "child of Hermes." Archetypally, the ancient god can be understood to be a "cunning" (Brown, 1990, p. 6) personification of contingency. He heralds circumstances that are disorienting in their deviation from a final cause. The tug of events toward a determinate outcome finds a compensatory phenomenon in Hermes, who qualifies as a strange attractor, describing a turbulent route to the unknown that leads through paradox, *masa confusa*, and alterity. His manipulation of rationally wrought distinctions muddles the divine with the human, the dead with the living, and the self with the other. In C. G. Jung's distinctive peopling of the psyche, Hermes is the avatar of *enantiodromia*, in which each thing is also, unavoidably, its opposite. He is a culture hero whose influence, propitious and otherwise, is felt cross-culturally. With allowances for distinctions, he is Coyote in much Native American lore (Kokopelli among the Pueblos of the Southwest), Hanuman in the Vedic tradition, Loki in the Norse tales, and Susa-nö-o in Shinto mythology (Hyde, 1998). My theistic concern is not with the "next" world, but with this one: summoning Hermes to guide Priam into the enemy camp so the Trojan King may treat with Achilles to reclaim the body of Hector, Zeus lauds Hermes' "delight in befriending mortals" (Homer, 2011, bk. 24, line 334). The human world, as influenced by Hermes, said Mircea Eliade (1978), is "by definition open, constantly in process of being formed," to which he added in a Hegelian vein, "that is, of being improved and exceeded" (p. 276). The world as *poietically* open is what James Hillman (1975), borrowing from Keats, called "the vale of soul-making" (p. xv). "You make soul," Hillman said, "by living life, not by retreating from the world into 'inner work' or beyond the world in spiritual disciplines and meditation removes" (Hillman & Ventura, 1992, p. 50). The vale invoked by this motto is not, Hillman said, "simply utilitarian," a place of "obstacles, pitfalls, monsters to be met in order to make one's interior soul" (p. 51). We "go through the world," he said, not solely for our "own sake, making our own soul," our own *anima*, but equally for the *poiesis* of the *anima mundi*, the soul of the world. Soul-making extends beyond the redemption of our personal sufferings to that of "the plight of the world, the suffering of its oceans and its rivers, its air and its forests, the ugliness of its cities and depletion of its soils" (p. 51). I associate this *poietic* imperative with the trickster god, whom, said Lewis Hyde (1998), "makes this world."

My invocation of Hermes stems in part from a re-visioning through two sometimes incongruent frames of reference—poststructuralism and archetypal theory—for the ways in which each may illuminate (or adumbrate, deepen) the nature and logic of metaphor. I regard them as compensatory *vocabularies* in the sense that Richard Rorty (1999) used the term, to designate "alternative tools" (p. 11) rather than contradictory beliefs (p. 12). Each of these philosophical modes, and indeed every other metaphysic, can be said in a poststructural vein to amount to a style of writing intended to gain a provisional purchase on human experience. In their interrelation I seek a Hermetic form. Perhaps the result is a convergence "from utterance to utterance" of ships in the night, or "passing theories," a term Rorty took from Donald Davidson (Rorty, 1979, p. 14). The two theories book passage on one another to an uncertain destination. The omega point cannot be known in advance because the grammaturge "is typically unable to make clear exactly what it is that he wants to do before developing the language in which he succeeds in doing it" (p. 13).

This book is an attempt to write "the tension of metaphorical truth" (Kurzweil, 1980, p. 107). It threads a path between two fields, the paradigmatic haunt of the god who took his name from the *hermaion*, the "heaps of stones . . . found on the edges of traveled ways" onto which, as with these pages, "every passerby threw a stone" (Eliade, 1978, p. 275). Though the relevance of any mythological figure to archetypal theory is obvious, in particular the relationship of Hermes to depth psychology, likened by Helena Shulman Lorenz (2004) to "a psychology of the margin . . . always about the pull of the future, about what has not yet found expression" (p. 235), the application of Hermes to poststructuralism may require explanation.

The central concern of poststructuralism is the *thinking* of difference. In various formulations, principally Nietzschean, Marxist, feminist, or postcolonial, the poststructural purpose is to question the seemingly natural givens of identity. My use of the word "central" is already problematic. Centrality, in terms of fixity, is precisely the concept that poststructuralism puts into question. The need for an absolute beyond the range of the metamorphic, whether ideational or organic—minds or bodies—is the very kernel of metaphysics that poststructuralism seeks to crack. In my admittedly, and perhaps unavoidably, reductive approach throughout this book (I am already slipping between the poststructural and the archetypal), I will want to understand poststructuralism's extension of the metamorphic to the absolute in terms of metaphor, and to understand metaphor in terms of Hermes.

Metaphor presented its speculative value at the turn of the twentieth century, increasingly asserting itself into the discourses of philosophy as the century unfolded. Ever the symptom, it encountered dissection at the hands of Anglo-American philosophy of language, and a characteristically more holistic treatment in hermeneutics and phenomenology, especially in their poststructural variants. The destabilizing intellectual climate of late-stage Enlightenment in which "long-established certainties" (Tarnas, 1991, p. 355) were cast into doubt, including the bulwarks of material progress, religious faith, and the supremacy of the rational mind, made possible, or coincided with, the reappraisal of a means of knowledge long derided by rational thought as anti-philosophical. To express the point post-structurally and archetypally, we might say metaphor became the rising sign of an era that witnessed the decadence of conceptual idols. "Perhaps," Hillman (1978c) said of the historical moment, "the Age of Reason had reached its last borders: the borders of reason itself" (p. 137). The forensic aim of any poststructuralism is the cross-examination of truth claims for the possibility of contra-diction, and thus of inabsolute grounding. Poststructuralism, said Christina Howells (1998), "asserts that truth claims are ultimately dependent on the discourse or conceptual scheme from which they emanate" (p. 2). Metaphor's formal efficacy made it a touchstone for the structuralist and poststructuralist concern with the instability of meaning.

This unsettling contradictoriness, what Niall Lucy (1995) called "errancy, contamination, metaphoricity, excess . . . both potentialising and limiting all-or-nothing concepts" (p. 29), enables a concatenation of poststructuralist insight and the mythological Hermes. The application of metaphorics to metaphysical truth in particular puts Hermes in play. Unthinkable in the philosophical sense without conceptual critique, metaphor qualifies as an estrangement of literal thought, but in the empirical effects of its displacements and transpositions, it manifests as an avatar of the *uncanny*. For Nietzsche (1967b), the *unheimlich* was the element of nihilism within every value harboring its potential undoing. Hermes, said Walter F. Otto (2014), has his "essence" in the uncanny (p. 112). As commissar of the crossroads, from which aporetic *topos* he ferries souls to Hades, it is Hermes' habit to make a problem of material progress. His influence can be felt in the problematics of subjectivity that marked the advent of structuralism.

Structuralism attained its apex in the 1950s and 1960s, but it began to emerge as a school of thought in the first decades of the twentieth century. The sociologist Emile Durkheim (1858–1917) was the first to import the architectural term *structure* into the humanities, associating it with the nascent enterprise of the social sciences then striving for legitimacy against the academic hegemony of the classical humanities (Dosse, 1997). Structuralism was from the start a form of protest from below. In his sweeping study of the history of structuralism, Francis Dosse notes the tenor of the time:

> [S]tructuralism demonstrated an extreme sensitivity to everything that had been repressed in Western history. Indeed, it is no accident that the two leading sciences of the period—anthropology and psychoanalysis—privilege the unconscious, the nether side of manifest meaning, the inaccessible repressed of Western history. (p. xx)

The importance that the structuralist paradigm shift in the humanities holds for a study of metaphor's emergence into philosophical awareness rests to a significant degree on the sense in which structuralism made it philosophically respectable to doubt the linear causality underlying the two dominant conceptions of human purpose: reason and religion. Though the Enlightenment was in large measure a liberation of the thinking subject from religious dogma, it retained the essential Christian idea of the perfectibility of "man," the heroic trajectory of the human species toward a culminating revelation. Whether that revelation lay in divine grace or scientific beatitude, in either case we are slouching toward Bethlehem. Archetypally put, what structuralism, and the intensification of the differential in poststructuralism, allow us to see is that although we may as a culture pray at the altar of a defied temporality, whether in rational or religious guise, we need not also profess that time will deliver us from our basic nature, that is, our grounding in multiple, and differential, structures—replete with shadow manifestations. As with every Idea, temporality would have us adopt its full salvational doctrine. De-cathecting from the temporal catechism, we disgorge all the other gods. The structuralist "moment" unfolded in the wake of the First World War and, a generation later, in the Holocaust, twin horrors of a technological age that deeply disturbed faith in human progress. Against the backdrop of such depredations, and (as it has been put) the incommensurable teleologies of the Cold War, it became untenable to conceive of Western "man" as the triumphal subject of a progressive historical narrative. The meaning of time was thrown into question. Underlying historicity, the diachronic progress of humanity into a positive and positivistically realized future, structuralism *posited* (in a persistence of the scientistic predilection) a synchronic counterweight, the existence of purely formal linguistic relationships within which cultural forms took shape. These were understood by structuralist investigations into mind and culture to be entirely beyond the subjective ken, serving to dislodge the knowing subject from its own intentionality.

Synchrony, to apply a phrase of Hillman's, distinguished "history as a story from history as cause" (Hillman & Ventura, p. 17). The epistemological orientation of every epoch was understood to be built not on the overcoming, through time, of prior advances, but, said Dosse (1997), on the "discontinuous succession of different structures" (p. 356). In a Nietzschean environment of the "eternal recycling of different configurations of the past" (p. 356), time became relativized by space, a question of positioning. The notion of an epochal arrangement of cultural forms enabled meaningful associations to be constructed or discerned independently of any assertion of origin or *telos*. The self-reflective *cogito* found to its dismay that formal influences operating at a depth of remove unsettled its developmental pretenses. To employ a phrase of Michael Ventura's, the meaning of progress shifted "from fixity to flux; from clarity to paradox" (Hillman & Ventura, 1992, p. 111). Structuralism, said Dosse, "transformed man as the subject of his history into an object of history that he could not understand," in other words, a history beyond his manifest intention (1997, p. 357). The riddling of the present "offered a hermetic horizon" to the idea of progress (p. 359). It served as a counterweight to a providential historicism, which, as Michel Foucault (1988) put it, "aims at dissolving the singular event into an ideal continuity" (p. 88). The incongruity might be thought archetypally as the binary opposition of Hermes and Chronos. The pretense of chronology (or, in linguistics, etymology) to be prime mover and limit condition gave over to the possibility that history might be seen through or re-visioned in terms of what Hillman (1978c) called "a concatenation of events, like a dream with many themes calling for interpretive understanding" (p. 126). In archetypal terms, the structuralist re-visioning takes Hermes as a depth phenomenon and the interpretive or hermeneutic imperative as primary.

With structuralism there came an appreciation for the in-between. The linguist Ferdinand de Saussure (1857–1913), the seminal figure in the turn to a structural perception, pioneered the theory that linguistic pertinence, as Jonathan Culler (1986) explained it, derives not from the "natural, inevitable, or necessary" (p. 34) designations of words to the seemingly pre-existing concepts that they name, but of arbitrary and "continually shifting" semantic "boundaries" that articulate the world in different ways (p. 32). "The history of languages," said Culler,

> is full of examples of concepts shifting, changing their boundaries. The English word *cattle*, for example, at one point meant property in general, then gradually came to be restricted to four-footed property (a new category), and finally attained its modern sense of domesticated bovines. (p. 32)

The structuralist field amounted to a clearing for the cultivation of contingency. Saussure invoked the arbitrariness of the relation of sounds to concepts, and of sound/concept formations, or *signs*, to objects by emphasizing the synchronic structure of language over its diachronic development as follows.

The sign, as Saussure distinguished it, consisted in a *signified*, a concept, designated by a *signifier*, the abstract form of a physical sound. Words themselves might be sounded variously within a single language by virtue of dialects and accents, and so it was not the physical sound that constituted the signifier, but the variation that distinguished the sound from other sounds in the pronunciation of the community of speakers. Meaning was a consequence of differential relations in an overall system. As Culler put it, "both signifier and signified were arbitrary divisions or delimitations of a continuum (a sound spectrum on the one hand and a conceptual field on the other)" (p. 39). The salience of signs, their meaning-making capacity, derived from the differences among them not, said Culler, from the possession of any essential property (p. 37). "In a language," said Saussure, "there are only differences *and no positive terms*" (§166).

Saussure's structural imperative displaced the traditional study of the evolution of language, the diachronic approach, with an ahistorical analysis, a synchronic approach, that emphasized the relationship of sound to concept that pertained in any given moment. Signifier and signified were seen as intrinsic to one another; they arose simultaneously, neither prior to the other. As Culler (1986) made clear, the synchronic emphasis of structural linguistics does not situate the sign outside of history, but, on the contrary, indicates that significance is a function of the quality of the time. This paradox in the nature of the sign is a factor of its arbitrariness. "Since the sign has no necessary core that must persist, it must be defined as a relational entity, in its relations to other signs. And the relevant relations are those which obtain at a particular time," Culler said (p. 46). Saussure further typified the synchronic structure as entirely internal to language. Already an arbitrary, and originary, relation of sound and concept, the sign in addition lacked an essential connection to the object it named. In a basic example, *The cat sat on the mat*, the significance of the words derives more from their contrasts than from identity with the concepts they invoke or the objects they name. As Niall Lucy (2005) explained,

> The fact that there are many languages, and that languages evolve, is because of the arbitrary or undetermined structure of the sign. What "cat" means in English, then, doesn't have anything to do with cats as such, but rather with the differences between "cat" and other English words. We recognize that "cat" refers to a cat because "cat" is not "dog," for instance, but also (more specifically) because it isn't "sat," "fat," or "bat" and so on. From this we can say that all signs signify by virtue of their relations to general differences ("cat" isn't "dog" or "philosophy") and specific differences or structural similarities ("cat" isn't "bat"). (p. 110)

Saussure distinguished the structure of the differential relation, that is, said Lucy, of the "conditions of possibility for signs generally" (p. 111), with the term *langue*. The vagaries of everyday usage, he designated as *parole*. *Langue* is the structure, *parole* the conforming particular. Saussure's *Course in General Linguistics*, assembled posthumously by his students, marked a turn to a general science of signs of which linguistics was to be a special branch.

Saussurean dichotomy followed linguistics in its mitotic division across the humanities. The rule of differential relation, synchrony, marked a shift of the locus of meaning from the subject to the system of latent distinctions of which it was constituted. These were variously seen in terms of unconscious infrastructure or social superstructure as language, economics, repressed or unrealized psychic contents, and constructed hierarchies of race and gender. As it populated other disciplines, said Annette Lavers (1982), the structural theory of language and its discontinuities provided the basis for an inquiry into "constants and variables" and the "syntax of transformations which allows one to pass from one to the other" (p. 8). Saussure's hope for a semiology of which linguistics would be but one branch turned out the other way around. In the science of signs that emerged, any latent structure of differential signifiers was understood to be *linguistic* in the sense that discourse, or text, was the environmental circumstance within which all explanatory and existential paradigms, or signifying systems, took shape. The idea of the internal or synchronic structure of the concept produced structuralist theories in anthropology (Lévi-Strauss), psychoanalysis (Lacan), the history of ideas (Foucault), literary criticism (Barthes), and Marxist studies (Althusser).

The hope for a universally applicable science of signs gave way in the transition to poststructuralism. Although structuralism shifted the focus of the humanities from content to form, it nevertheless retained an empiricist claim to detached, objective observation. The setting of the sign, as is natural, began at structuralism's height in the mid-1960s as the theory of formal patterns wielded by structuralists wheeled back upon structuralism itself making theory an object of theorizing. "The postmodern critique of the rhetorical foundations of Western epistemology," said Paul Kugler (1990), "led to the realization that all conscious knowledge, as well as our theories of knowledge, work through figurative structures that render them ambiguous and indeterminate" (p. 315). This poststructuralist outcome had been implicit in the conception of structure. Saussure's dichotomies, diachrony and synchrony, *langue* and *parole*, signifier and signified, event and structure, which grounded the idea of the linguistically determined subject, made inherent reference to the dynamics of dichotomy. The reference became overt in poststructuralism, resulting in the overturning of the binary opposition. Amidst an overgrowth of structural positivities, the interstice between the binaries now came into focus. Emblematic of this hitherto recondite discourse is the writing of Jacques Derrida. I will employ Derrida's work for the way in which it draws forth the fundamental metaphoricity of philosophy. It is my view that underlying the themes of writing, metaphysics, psyche, ethics, myth, religion, politics, language, and the many other critical issues on which both Derrida and Hillman deepened our understanding, there can be found an extended meditation on metaphor—even when metaphor is not the overt topic. Throughout their work one hears metaphor's autobiographical voice. It is the voice of what I. A. Richards (1981) called the "constitutive form" (p. 49) of "matter and its adventures" (p. 50). Derrida's lexicon provides a rich variety of terms that can be taken to describe the nuances of metaphor's constitutive action, including the following that concern us in this chapter: *play*, *trace*, *supplement*, *text*, and, not unique to Derrida, *bricolage*. Other concepts closely associated with Derrida, such as *logocentrism* and *differance*, will cross our paths in subsequent chapters.

At what was in retrospect the very culminating point of structuralism, the International Colloquium on Critical Languages and the Sciences of Man held in 1966 at Johns Hopkins University, Derrida (1978b) delivered (in every sense of the word as he was wont to assert) the *post*structural *enfant*. Structuralism, he said, stressed a "rupture" (p. 278) in conceptualization that began with Nietzsche and out of which the names of "invariable presence—*eidos*, *archē*, *telos*, *energia*, *ousia* (essence, existence, substance, subject), *alēthia*, transcendentality, consciousness, God, man, and so forth" (p. 279) were emerging not in the traditional form of "a fixed locus but a function, a sort of nonlocus in which an infinite number of sign substitutions came into play" (p. 280). Despite Saussure's assertion of this very effect, that in the play of signification positivities fall away, structuralism harbored an insistence on an absolute of its own, the *phoneme*, the vocalized sound, an ultimate presence in which language became fully transparent to itself. It repeated the suspensive move of metaphysics by placing beyond the ludic field a fixed point, an ontotheological referee, to which all play is referred, or by which all play is determined. Indeed, it is impossible, Derrida believed, for any philosophy not to countenance the reflection of such a locus of certainty because even critical appraisal of the metaphysical tradition inevitably partakes of its thematics. Nonetheless, the rupture of metaphysics, the appearance of a breach where all had appeared seamless, revealed the plasticity of the metaphysical absolute, putting it in play, and remained a phenomenon to be reckoned with.

To "turn the page of philosophy" as the cultural moment appeared to be demanding, Derrida (1978b) said, is not to close the book on metaphysics, but to "read philosophers *in a certain way*" (p. 288). This reading, in the twilight of ultimacy, was to see the texts of metaphysics not as structuralist "science," but as mythopoesis. Yet philosophy cannot be *reduced* to mythopoesis. "The problem of the relations between the philosopheme or the theorem, on the one hand, and the mytheme or the mythopoem, on the other," Derrida said, counts as a "classic" question that "cannot be answered" (pp. 287–288). To read *in a certain way* thus becomes a matter of reading for the "unnoticed fault" in the terrain of philosophy, to interrogate "transphilosophical concepts" such as "sign, history, truth, and so forth" for their fault lines, the cracks just beneath the surface of their claims to epistemological ultimacy (p. 288). Such a re-reading would place the play of signification into "tension with history" (p. 290). The structuralist foregrounding of the historical moment is

> in complicity with a teleological and eschatological metaphysics, in other words, paradoxically, in complicity with that philosophy of presence to which it was believed history could be opposed. The thematic of historicity, although it seems to be a somewhat late arrival in philosophy, has always been required by the determination of Being as presence. (p. 291)

No less than other historicist readings, structuralism requires the fixed locus, either a priori or a posteriori, that escapes the basic *poietic* circumstance.

The mythopoetic reading, on the other hand, proceeds as a *bricolage*, or contingent assembly. The term, meaning "tinkering" or "do-it-yourself," was applied by Lévi-Strauss to indicate a quality of intellectual activity most apparent in the continual recombination of themes that distinguish myth-making. The *bricoleur*, Derrida said, uses

> the instruments he finds at his disposition around him, those which are already there, which had not been especially conceived with an eye to the operation for which they are to be used and to which one tries by trial and error to adapt them, not hesitating to change them whenever it appears necessary, or to try several of them at once, even if their form and their origin are heterogeneous . . . . (p. 285)

Not only, said Derrida, has *bricolage* been construed as "critical language itself," but "every finite discourse is bound by a certain bricolage" (p. 285), a boundary condition that permits metaphysics to be read "no longer from the standpoint of a concept of finitude as relegation to the empirical, but from the standpoint of the concept of play" (p. 289).

By *play*, Derrida (1978b) meant "the disruption of presence" (p. 292). In a poststructuralist reversion to Saussurean fundamentals, he said, "The presence of an element is always a signifying and substitutive reference inscribed in a system of differences" (p. 292). Derrida sticks with the signifier, the interpretive gesture of the differential process, that "tries to pass beyond" humanism and its dream of "full presence, the reassuring foundation" that "escapes play and the order of the sign" by "deciphering a truth or an origin" (p. 292). Such humanism, he said, "lives the necessity of interpretation as an exile" (p. 292). The rupture, the disruption, of the myth of fixed meaning, ushers in a homecoming both "nostalgic" and "joyous" (p. 292). An occasion of mourning for the "the lost or impossible presence of the absent origin," it is nevertheless also an

> affirmation of a world of signs without fault, without truth, and without origin which is offered to an active interpretation. *This affirmation then determines the noncenter otherwise than as loss of the center.* And it plays without security. For there is a *sure* play: that which is limited to the substitution of *given* and *existing*, *present*, pieces. In absolute chance, affirmation also surrenders itself to genetic indetermination, to the seminal adventure of the trace. (p. 292)

As a Derridean term of art, *trace* refers to a presence that is immediately absent, necessarily mediated. The term emphasizes that the defining characteristic in the play of signifiers is not the presence of contrasting elements, but the absence that defines the space among them. If each element depends for its significance upon a differential relation to other elements partaking of a field of distinctions, the other elements are both constitutive of and absent from the element in question. Within that element, these others leave their trace. This formal agency is exemplified by metaphor, which depends for its poetic and semantic power on the absence of the "like" or "as" that is overt in simile. We might say the "seminal adventure of the trace" names an existential condition of metaphoricity or inter-determinacy.

Derrida's (1997) primary invocation of the viewpoint expressed by the principles of the piece work of *bricolage*, the primacy of interpretation, and the recombinatory imperative of mythopoesis, occurs in the metaphor of "the world as a space of inscription" (p. 44). In his study of how the metaphysical tradition has construed the idea of writing, *Of Grammatology*, he expressed the central point with the declaration *il n'y a pas de hors-texte*, there is no outside-text (p. 158). Derrida's re-visioned metaphysics, said Susan Rowland (2006), is one in which "reality itself becomes textual; there is no representation, there is only the weaving of texts against and within each other" (p. 110). The familiar assertion is that metaphysical speculation reflects not a fixed locus of ultimacy that it merely represents, and in which it might come to closure, but that totality, wholeness, is an interpretive outcome. Just as the myths tell us that Hermes is the father of Pan, so too does philosophy's be-all and end-all stand not outside the play of signifiers as a referential presence to be re-presented by and in it, but in a dependent, even filial, relationship to interpretation, in Hillman's (1978b) terms, the "creative tensions" or "contestations . . . between [creative] modalities" that produce "position[s] of truth" (p. 48). "'Outside' is regarded as an effect of textuality," said Rowland, "not its precondition" (p. 111). A suspension of creative tensions, the closure of metaphysics, could be seen, Derrida thought, in the persistent description (a de-scription) of presence as speech, presumed unadulterated in its proximity to its maker, and the corresponding view of writing as a projected Platonic shadow of the Real. Derrida used *writing* to mean "absence" in his principal deconstruction presence/absence, metaphorized as speech/writing. By rigorously demonstrating that the argument from presence for the primordiality of speech presupposes the primacy not of speech, but of the opposition presence/absence, or speech/writing, Derrida turned the disdain for writing, and absence, against the metaphysical tradition. Contrary to intention, metaphysics institutes *writing* as a structural necessity of speech, absence as a condition of presence. A false hierarchy or moralization, that of speech and presence over writing and absence, is therefore subverted. The subversion is not Derrida's, but rather an unwitting outcome of metaphysics "itself," its inherent deconstructive tendency (the inverted commas serving to question a unitive identity). To make such a claim, to stake it, is not to drive a stake into the heart of metaphysics, to seek its destruction, but quite a bit more subtly, to seek out its deconstruction. To "make enigmatic what one thinks one understands by the words 'proximity,' 'immediacy,' 'presence'," Derrida (1997) said, is the "final intention" of a grammatology (p. 70).

Derrida's "making enigmatic" is an entailment of the turn in philosophy and the humanities toward language, a paradigm shift or changing of the gods in which the archetype of communication is the emergent factor. (All *turns* of theory are arguably Hermetic, but with reference to linguistics, Hermes has a particular salience.) The "linguistic turn" in philosophy manifests as structuralism in the continental school and as logical positivism and ordinary language philosophy in the analytical school. The efforts of analytical philosophers to explain metaphor will concern us in Chapter 4 on the cognitive turn. Derrida's assertion of textual imperative as a matter of enigmas suggests that the key to *textuality*, the meaning of *text* as employed to counter the trope of invariability in its many philosophical expressions, lies in the strangeness of an encounter with the unknown.

In a depth psychological sense, unknowability resides in the enigma with which Oedipus crossed paths, the objective psyche. "The problem of defining the unconscious," said Kugler (1990), "is difficult, if not impossible, because by definition the unconscious is the *not known*" (p. 307). Definition is problematized, perhaps, by the nature of the Mercurial archetype in which *text*, *language*, and *unconscious* intersect. Yet the indefinability of the unconscious begins to clarify in conjunction with the notion of textuality. As Kugler put it,

> To arrive at a knowledge of something unconscious, that content must first be psychically *represented* to consciousness as a word, an image, an emotion, or inscribed in the flesh as a psychosomatic symptom. These (re)presentations in consciousness constitute the textuality of our psychic life and are the primary focus of depth psychology. When reading and analyzing these psychic manuscripts we are, paradoxically, both author and critic of our own text. (p. 307)

Referring to Lacan, who, in similarity with Hillman, posited the *imaginary* as a domain of images and words representative of objective experience, Kugler drew the notion of *text* into the realm of the mediate: "By acquiring the ability to name an experience, the individual is able to symbolize himself or herself by replacing lived experience with a text . . . This process establishes a realm of representations that *mediates* experience" (p. 312). Applying Kugler's definition of language as "the psychic capacity for representation," we can understand *text* as psychization of experience, its metaphoric construction in word and image (p. 312). We can therefore take Derrida's claim that there is nothing outside the text to indicate the metaphorical nature not only of philosophical objectivity, but of psychological objectivity as well. In other words, there being no absolute answer to the question of who we are, in our existential indeterminacy we are metaphorically expressed.

The deconstruction of presence amounts to a question, and a questioning, of religion, *religare*, an already metaphorical ligature, or binding. It is an inquiry into the nature of foundationalism, the grounding of belief in an incontrovertable certainty—which, again, is not to say that certainties do not pertain, but that they stem from modes of perception, that is, *texts*, discourses, archetypes, metaphors. In perhaps the paradigmatic act of a founding, Abraham bound Isaac, and in so doing based a tradition on metaphorical substitution, Isaac for the ram. Always a "sacrificial substitution," as Derrida (2002) called the binding of Isaac (p. 415), metaphor is the ramification of meaning. It relinquishes the literal, reformulating presence as presence/absence, so that significance might flourish. The sacrifice of the bound son, from Attis to Jesus, would seem to instantiate the religious instinct as a boundary, a hermitage where the propitiation to a Hermetic paternity sustains a panoply of worldly significance. Yet the boundary phenomenon of the trickster archetype, if it is basic to human nature, is also supremely indifferent to human fate. The advent of significance just as easily sustains depredation as sublimity. The metaphorical imperative of our psyche, enabling us to see life and world in terms of meaningful ideas, may produce religious expression of great artistry and subtlety, yet—and here is where we are tricked—it may bind us to ideas in terms so unforgiving that we become nailed to a cross of fundamentalism. Our crosses, our absolutisms, whether spiritual, scientific, technological, economic, political, militaristic, racial (the list is long), are *religious* in the sense that we are bound to them, but they are irreligious in the sense that as fixed and frozen metaphors they lose the capacity for nuance that is necessary to sustain a sense of the sacred, of interconnection. "Metaphor," said David Punter (2007), "is the way in which we bind things together. These things can be bound together in helpful ways which will improve our understanding; but they can also be bound together in unhelpful ways" (p. 84). The expression of the boundary as bin(d)ary opposition can institute hierarchies that we convince ourselves are in the natural order of things, or it can, deconstructively, foster a sense of all things as *written*, as differential relation. Under the institution of the former, we establish ourselves with hubris *outside* the waywardness of worldly efflorescence; under the latter, we remain, with humility, within its horizon.

On the insufficiency of Saussure's semiology, its appeal to "the durable institution of a sign," to a phonocentric purity outside the play of signification, Derrida (1997) said:

> The very idea of institution—hence of the arbitrariness of the sign—is unthinkable before the possibility of writing and outside of its horizon. Quite simply, that is, outside of the horizon itself, outside the world as the place of inscription, as the opening to the emission and to the spatial *distribution* of signs, to the *regulated play* of their differences, even if they are "phonic." (p. 44)

The sacrifice of literalism, the outside of signification, upon the altar of *writing*, entails a tragic sense of the world, as immortalized by Omar Khayyám:

> The Moving Finger writes; and, having writ,
> Moves on: nor all thy Piety nor Wit
> Shall lure it back to cancel half a Line,
> Nor all thy Tears wash out a Word of it.
>
> *The Rubáiyát of Omar Khayyám*

It is not presence that endures, but the differential relation presence/absence. Derrida (1997) provides this elaboration:

> [T]here has never been anything but writing; there have never been anything but supplements, substitutive significations which could only come forth in a chain of differential references, the "real" supervening and being added only while taking on meaning from a trace and from an invocation of the supplement. (p. 159)

A supplement is an addition to that which already asserts self-sufficiency, and therefore might be regarded paradoxically, Derrida said, as "the mark of an emptiness" (p. 145). The *supplement* is the iteration that forecloses the purity of the origin and the propriety of the literal. Supplements viewed from the hierarchy identity/difference are categorically decorative, but upon deeper consideration can be seen as "a plenitude enriching another plenitude" (p. 144). *Supplementarity* in the deconstructive sense stands not for extraneous addition, but for the irreducible process of textual interplay, of interpretation, participation, or metaphoricity. The *supplement* problematizes that to which it refers in a duplicitous, Hermetic sense. Without it the referent is not whole, otherwise there would be no supplementary need, but as an addition it indicates itself as extraneous to a whole. Supplements "produce the sense of the very thing they defer: the mirage of the thing itself, of immediate presence, of originary perception" (p. 157). The elegy for presence expressed by Derrida's allusively metaphoric terms of art, *play*, *trace*, and *supplement*, is the Hermetic lament of *writing*.

With such Hermetic revaluations deconstruction becomes philosophy's identity crisis—its supplement—and so, too, does metaphor become the identity of the literal. Metaphor's *like*, born of differential relation, refuses to sacrifice strangeness to identity. It suffers literalist exile for its errancy, which Christopher Bracken (2007), explicating Nietzsche, called "greater or lesser intensities of illusion" (p. 7). I want to conclude these introductory remarks on the Hermetic quality in deconstruction, and preface our look into the deconstructive quality of imaginal psychology, by turning to Bracken for a distinction between *poiesis* and *mimesis*, and between the semiology of Saussure and of Charles Sanders Peirce. Bracken helps to establish the argument broached above, and pursued throughout this book, that metaphor bids fair as a description of nature's creativity. At the same time that Saussure was removing the referent from the play of signifiers, on the other side of the Atlantic, Peirce was re-inscribing it. Peirce's semiotics, as distinct from Saussure's, regarded the sign's formal agency not as distinct from the reality to which it referred, but as productive of it. For Peirce, said Bracken (2007), "Language was immanent in nature, and because nature was action, language was a form of action too" (p. 13). In this way Peirce re-construed philosophy's objectivist imperative. He maintained the relationship between sign and object, but saw the sign not as the representation of a given, but as its motive force. In other words, signs did not mimic reality, they instantiated it. As Bracken put it, "the sign produces a fact," and, citing Peirce, "A model of the universe that did not account for 'the power of representations [of signs] to cause real facts'" would be "futile" (p. 12).

Peirce's term for "the act of realization," Bracken said, is *interpretation*. Bracken wants us to see through the taboo of the interpretive universe. Most famously expressed by Freud (1955), the interpretive taboo is the prohibition against ascribing animate power to language. This mistaken view, Bracken (2007) points out, was attributed by J. G. Frazer in his classic work *The Golden Bough* to the inability of pre-modern peoples, in Frazer's words, "to discriminate clearly between words and things" (p. 2), which by no coincidence is the title (*Le Mots et les Choses*) of

Michel Foucault's study of the role of discourse in shaping experience, translated in English as *The Order of Things*. In what Bracken suggests is an instance of the cyclical view of history as *corso* and *ricorso* advanced by Giambattista Vico (1668–1744), the interpretive (hermeneutic) universe has come round again. The view is evident in theories that can be regarded as poststructuralist. Drawing on Walter Benjamin's notion of "magical criticism," in which the art critic does not "decipher the meaning of the artwork" but "brings it back to life . . . as if it were a living, self-conscious subject," Bracken said, "interpretation is . . . animation. Reading is resurrection" (2007, p. 17). "A sign that has 'sympathy' with an object," Bracken said, citing Novalis for a basic kabbalistic notion, "is a 'soul'" (p. 16). The fashioning of semiotics as interpretive *poiesis* rather than objectivist *mimesis* entails a discernment in the play of signifiers of what Bracken called "life, face, and voice" (p. 15). For Vico the motive force of signs was *prosopopoeia*, "a species of metaphor" (p. 15). To declare the universe interpretive, participatory, hermeneutic, or metaphoric does not, however, merely reverse the hierarchy animate/inanimate to insist upon the efficacy of signs. The interstitial logic of such a rendering requires of any absolute that it resolve into paradox. "Metaphorical animation," Bracken concludes, "affirms that the inanimate world both is and is not alive" (p. 15). The metaphoric universe is errant, it wanders, as Nietzsche had it, among intensities of illusion.

The foregrounding of paradox in the binary opposition is a move that suggests the trace of the trickster. Just as Hermes leaves his mark in Derrida's work, so, too, does deconstruction figure in imaginal psychology. As we explore the argument for mutual implication—for a poststructural archetypology—let us turn from the Hermetic quality in deconstruction to the quality of destructuring in imaginal psychology. Poststructuralism's Hermetic bent avails itself of insight in Hillman's (1983a) study of the poetic artifice of case histories, healing fictions. In a discussion of genre, Hillman distinguished the elements of a Saturnian discourse from those of a Hermetic one. The former involves an exposition of structures, the latter of "significances" (p. 22). Whereas "hermetic writing where connections do not close up but open and reveal" (p. 23) is concerned with "that precise image and its metaphorical implications" (p. 22), the "senex [Saturnian] style" is

> a question of instances exemplifying principles, images as allegories, scenes as enactments in time of eternal verities. In this genre of examining a case—and I say examining deliberately—the function of consciousness, represented by the writer-analyst, is that of seeing abstractions, a keen-sighted perspicacity into structures and laws. (p. 22)

In an appeal to the psychological efficacy of imaginal psychology's principal trope, that of sticking with specific, irreducible images that otherwise become gathered up by the analytical abstractions and reductions necessary to meld disparate experiences into self-same structures, Hillman ventures to assert the point of view of the anima, which: "would stay with images and fantasies themselves, never translating them or organizing them into narrative or through plot, but responding to them in a metaphorical style where consciousness is one of innuendo, reflection, echo, tone and elusive movements" (p. 23). In the mode of the anima there is a Hermetic concern with nuance, the telling detail that makes the occasions of experience undecidable (therein the trick), an ill fit for structural generalization. Hillman's destructuring move is to suggest that one might discern the point of view of an archetypal figure, reading Jungian structures for their specificity rather than for the general categories they bestow upon the analytical understanding.

The use of poetic figures (metaphors) such as Hermes or Saturn/Chronos as methodological tools is the principal move of *archetypology*, a term Hillman (1975) used in a Romantic sense to mean the application of "eternal actualities of the imagination" (p. 30) to the discernment of perspective. "By stepping back into the mythic, into what is nonfactual and nonhistorical," Hillman said, "the psyche can reimagine its factual, historical predicaments from another vantage point" (p. 30). Hillman referred to his work and that of affiliated psychologists concerned with the exploration of the cultural force of psyche as archetypal psychology or imaginal psychology. The former term furthers—and reimagines—one of Jung's (1979) central contributions, the principle of the archetype. Jung conceived of the Ideas or Forms of Platonism in a narrower Kantian sense as structures of mind, a priori categories unknowable in themselves, but evident in, and necessary to, the images of the imagination. In a late and partial turn toward a broader view, Jung suggested that the agency of the archetype might well extend beyond the psyche to the cosmos, serving to structure *psychoid* or psyche-like events that manifest as "synchronicities," or meaningful coincidences between event and perception that apparently surpass causal relations (CW 8). The term *psychoid* can be understood metaphorically as a way of understanding or experiencing objectivity partially in terms of subjectivity with the reparative result of healing the Kantian divide that separates the inherently unknowable domain of noumena, or things in themselves, from the sequestered world of phenomena, or things as we experience them. We might ask whether metaphor is precisely that phenomenon of differential relation Jung called an "acausal connecting principle" (CW 8). The suggestion was made by Joseph Cambray (2009) in a study of the links between analytical psychology and quantum mechanics. "[S]ynchronicity," he said, "could be treated as . . . an objective metaphorizing tendency of the world itself" (p. 31).

Further loosening archetype from its Kantian underpinnings, Hillman (1975) emphasized three salient attributes, the archetype's metaphorical modus vivendi, its tendency to impose fixity upon the conscious mind, and its nature as paradox:

> The curious difficulty of explaining just what archetypes are suggests something specific to them. That is, they tend to be metaphors rather than things. We find ourselves less able to say what an archetype is literally and more inclined to describe them in images. We can't seem to touch one or point to one, and rather speak of what they are like. (p. xviii)

Archetype therefore describes a form of experience produced in imagination. "Archetypes throw us into an imaginative style of discourse," Hillman said. "In fact, it is precisely as metaphors that Jung . . . writes of them" (p. xix). With his usual adherence to the Kantian distinction between expressions of the archetype and the thing itself, Jung said, "An archetypal content expresses itself first and foremost in metaphors" (CW 9, pt. 1, par. 267). In a yet more fundamental claim, he applied metaphoricity to analytical psychology as a whole. "Our science," he said, "is a language of metaphor" (CW 6, par. 428). Despite its tendency to be ungraspable, Hillman said, the archetype has the capacity to establish truth:

> Let us then imagine archetypes as the deepest patterns of psychic functioning, the roots of the soul governing the perspectives we have of ourselves and the world. . . . But one thing is absolutely essential to the notion of archetypes: their emotional possessive effect, their bedazzlement of consciousness so that it becomes blind to its own stance. (p. xviii)

Meaning made from, or consequent upon, archetype has the tendency to seize and seize up, to constrict "the plurality and freedom of styles within the structures of myth" (Hillman, 1978b, p. 143), through a conversion of pathos into logos. "The archetype *per se* is ambivalent and paradoxical, embracing both spirit and nature, psyche and matter, consciousness and unconsciousness; in it the yea and nay are mingled. There is neither day nor night, but rather a continual dawning" (Hillman, 1987, p. 12). Hillman's (1978b) shadings of archetype risk a psychology whose dynamism eludes the conceptual fixity of the analytical mind expressed by the terms *psychoanalysis* or *analytical psychology*. The structural ideas of his imaginal genre are "phenomena of complexity in distinction to simple, partial, elementary phenomena" (p. 144).

The use of the term *imaginal* reflects two sources. First, it is a product of the Jungian tenet that images are the raw material of psyche (CW 13, par. 75). Second, *imaginal* stems from the work of Henry Corbin, and refers to what Corbin called a "*mundus imaginalis*," an intermediary (Hermetic) world that comprises, said Hillman (2004a),

> a distinct field of imaginal realities requiring methods and perceptual faculties different from the spiritual world beyond it or the empirical world of usual sense perception and naïve formulation. The mundus imaginalis offers an ontological mode of locating the archetypes of the psyche, as the fundamental structures of the imagination or as fundamentally imaginative phenomena that are transcendent to the world of sense in their *value* if not their appearance. . . . As phenomena they must appear, though this appearance is to the imagination or in the imagination. (p. 15)

Stressing the phenomenality of such a "middle ground," imaginal psychology is "a work in service of restoration of the patient to imaginal realities"

(Hillman, 2004a, p. 15). In what follows, I call the school of psychology propounded by Hillman *imaginal* rather than *archetypal*. Of the terms, *imaginal* better expresses the priority of the specific image over the general category into which it might be classified. In addition, *imaginal* will serve as a de-literalization of "imagination," a faculty of mind that can be idolized by Romanticism just as the understanding is idolized by metaphysics. The term keeps *archetype* in play, reading images as *text*, inherently interpretive, always in the process of formulating, and thus open to continual phenomenological investigation, rather than as fixities that represent an absolute presence extant beyond the domain of representations. Put differently, imaginal representation is not a re-presentation of eternity in experience; it is the cognitive process that, as Hillman (1975) said of soul-making, "turns events into experiences" (p. xvi). That is, it expresses the objective in terms of the subjective. Following Michael Vannoy Adams (2004), I place into question the utility and therapeutic value of a theory of psyche that emphasizes regulative concepts, such as *anima*, *persona*, *shadow*, *self* (or ego, id, superego) over the content-rich images that give rise to such concepts.

The interrogation of the concept (though not its rejection) was a principal strategy employed by Hillman in the development of imaginal psychology and, in my view, is an important part of what constitutes it as a psychology of metaphor. In their influential theory of metaphor and embodiment, George Lakoff and Mark Johnson (1981) said, "The essence of metaphor is understanding and experiencing one kind of thing in terms of another" (p. 5). Hillman (1983a) supplied a gloss on such a definition in a comparison of what he regarded as the allegorical style of Freud and the metaphorical style of Jung—that allegory and metaphor "both start off saying one thing as if it were another" (p. 35). Working from what I regard as a formal engagement with metaphor, analytical psychologists, especially those of the imaginal school, aver that we *experience and understand* the psyche in terms of the metaphors of our dreams, waking imagination, and eventful environment. In addition, they take our ontological condition to be metaphorically structured. In a generalization of metaphor that will unfold in the following pages, I understand our sense of being to emerge from conditions that can only be considered literary. "The metaphorical mode of speech is for Jung the voice of nature itself," Hillman said (1983a, p. 36). "Jung's favorite metaphor for the dream was that it was nature itself speaking" (p. 36). For imaginal psychology, the invention of the human, to borrow a phrase from Harold Bloom (1998), is a dream spun of a midsummer's night, when Apollo is at his apotheosis yet darkened beneath the earth, and, as Shakespeare wrote, the "imagination bodies forth the form of things unknown" (Act V, scene I). An approach to psychology that treats the image as the basic datum of the psyche, and metaphor as the psyche's "mode of logos" (Hillman, 2004a, p. 33), that is, its *language and logic*, is a psychology of metaphor.

To make ambiguity a virtue—an epistemological virtuoso—as do poststructuralism and archetypology, constitutes a hallmark of the participatory worldview of Romanticism, which favors polysemous awareness over rational objectification. "All knowledge, as Romanticism is aware," said Terry Eagleton (1990), "contains a secret irony or incipient contradiction: it must at once master its object and confront it as other, acknowledge in it an autonomy it simultaneously subverts" (p. 74). Proceeding from such a standpoint, this book attempts a critical approach to the fundamentalisms it encounters in the theoretical schools of which it treats. Tom Cheetham (2012), commentator on Corbin's work, cited Paul de Man for a basic Romantic premise. "Romanticism marks the shift from thinking of poetry as a 'craft' (and of the poet as a 'maker') to thinking of it as a provider of consciousness, even a creator of consciousness," de Man said (as cited in Cheetham, p. 262, n. 12).

Modern metaphor theory, which we will explore as the narrative unfolds, extends this Romantic tenet when, contrary to the long-held view of metaphor as "decorative" language, it posits a basic cognitive function. The re-approximation of metaphor to cognition reconciles the Romantic and the rational by maintaining in ambi-valence what has been sundered. As David Miller (2008) said, the classically "Romanticist" view is one of "splitting thinking and poetry, putting them in opposition, like mind and heart" (p. 247). The set of ideas that constitutes the modern, or contemporary, theory of metaphor instead provides what might be called, after Hillman (2004b), "the thought of the heart." It ensconces reason in image. Every image lands in awareness gripping a portmanteau of rationalizations. In the view I advance here, experience is made—constructed or grasped—by metaphoric impulse. "Soul-making," Hillman (1992c) said of his term of art for the apprehension of experience, "can become a self-steering process through aesthetic reflexes" (p. 59). "The psyche," Hillman said (2004b), "is the life of our aesthetic responses" (p. 39).

Hillman is an apt figure in analytical psychology for a study that is both Romantic and theoretical-critical owing to his revisionary stance toward many of the orthodoxies of the first-generation Jungians and an unalloyed skepticism, one might say annoyance, with the notion of Jung as a metaphysician rather than a psychologist. "It is to [Jung] as a metaphysician that so many turn," Hillman (1989b) said, "and I am indeed a deviant from this main line of interest in Jung because I have been avoiding, even working to annul, his metaphysics so as not to lose his psychology" (p. 215). John Beebe (personal communication, 2015) put it succinctly: "Hillman was never a true believer." (At a 2010 symposium on the Red Book held at the Library of Congress, Beebe and Hillman had each delivered presentations stretching Jungian orthodoxies.) Coming onto the scene of an emerging discipline, analytical psychology, that was predominantly Christian and northern European, Hillman, as an American and a Jew, brought an exilic perspective to the problem Jung had identified, of the psyche's estrangement within Enlightenment thought. His provenance from the margins of European culture incited him to attempt the soul's own far-flung perspective. He was able to see through conceptual literalisms to their metaphoric inceptions. As a consequence, depth psychology's application of metaphor to archetype is nowhere more overt than in Hillman's work. Though I will refer in what follows to the contributions of other imaginal psychologists important to the creation of the field, it is primarily with Hillman's efforts that I will be concerned.

In "Twisting and Turning with James Hillman," David Tacey (1998) distinguished "four intellectual incarnations" of a prolific writer whose output over four decades evinced the "twists, turns and reversals" of a pioneering psychological investigator who embraced "subtlety, elusiveness, tricksterism, self-contradiction" (p. 216). Tacey views Hillman's early work, produced in the 1960s, as classical Jungian analysis. The studies of this period include Hillman's (1992a) dissertation, *Emotion*, and his challenge to dominant psychotherapeutic attitudes about suicide, *Suicide and the Soul* (Hillman, 1997b). Though classical in approach, Tacey (1998) said, the work also displays an impulse to "go beyond" (p. 216). Indeed, it introduces into psychotherapy the notion that psychological perspectives may be had more or less without recourse to the interpretations of the ego. "The concern of an analyst," Hillman (1997b) wrote, "is to maintain his connection with the inside and not to lose his root metaphor," soul (p. 43).

Beginning with *The Myth of Analysis*, first published in 1972, and including his apologia, *Re-Visioning Psychology* in 1975, and *Healing Fiction* in 1983, Hillman worked in an avowedly post-Jungian vein. "This movement," Tacey (1998) said of the turn toward critique, "operated partly within the context of the contemporary American university, and involved the re-visioning of Jungian thought to fit in with the tastes and fashions of postmodern intellectual tradition" (p. 216). It is with the contribution to archetypal thought of such tastes and fashions that we will be most concerned. Following upon his postmodern inflection, Tacey said, Hillman entered a third identifiable stage involving eco-psychological discourse. The work of this stage took place in a Neoplatonic vein. It concerned psyche not solely as a phenomenon of the subject, but as *anima mundi*, the soul of the world. Key works include *Anima* (Hillman, 1985) and *The Thought of the Heart and the Soul of the World* (Hillman, 1992c). A fourth stage, Tacey said, is marked by works intended for a general audience such as *We've Had a Hundred Years of Psychotherapy—and the World's Getting Worse* (Hillman & Ventura, 1992), a conversation with Michael Ventura that first appeared in the *L.A. Weekly*, and *The Soul's Code* (Hillman, 1996), a best seller, which brought Hillman to the attention of a wider reading public seeking the insights of the human potential movement—which, it must be said, he routinely subjected to scrutiny for hints of facile cures, egoic aggrandizement, and retreat from the world.

This book, as noted, concerns itself with the second of Tacey's (1998) stages, the re-visioning of Jungian thought, in which Hillman's work has its most emphatic relationship with poststructural themes. By demarcating the exploration in this way, I do not intend to claim Hillman for poststructuralism. Similarly, when we encounter deconstruction in the text, it will not be to make a reductive claim about the work of Jacques Derrida, but to stay with Derrida as much as I am capable at the tipping point between philosophy and poetry. I do not wish to force complex and multifaceted figures into a single pose. One can imagine Hillman's amplification of Jungian thought as a many-armed deva, Romantic, Neoplatonist, phenomenological, transpersonal, poststructural, ecological. "Each person has some talent," Hillman said. "It's rare to have more than one. Mine is ideation. . . . I am a generator, elaborator, and scathing critic of ideas" (Hillman & Ventura, 1992, p. 145). *Eidos*, he said, "means both something seen like a form and a way of seeing like an eye, a perspective" (p. 145). To stick with the perspectival critique he favored, the contradictions and ambiguities he accommodated, as he explored the *poietics* of psyche, one must accept each ideational elaboration as a provisional purchase never quite attaining the whole. As Tacey noted, Hillman was a writer of overtly mercurial strategies whose ability to cross interdisciplinary thresholds places him in a number of theoretical schools. I focus on the "second" Hillman because my interest is to tease out the complexities of metaphor as it manifests in two unorthodox companions, archetypal psychology and poststructuralism.

PART I

Metaphor in philosophy

1

A HISTORY WITHOUT ORIGINS

A history of metaphor is, in a sense, an ecology of metaphor. Metaphor's growth as a field of study became possible only in the middle of the last century with the appearance of conditions sufficient to establish a habitat. In the several chapters of this part, I present the preparation of the ground for metaphor in philosophy as the result of a reciprocal husbandry. As philosophy became aware of metaphor's influence, so too did metaphor awaken to its own philosophical qualities. The epistemic urges of philosophy and metaphor found themselves co-creatively intertwined. Their congruence followed a prolonged period of latency in which metaphor lay unacknowledged within, just beneath, philosophy proper. In post-structural discourse, *the proper* is a term of art meaning the literal, as in the French *le sens propre*, "the literal meaning." Indeed, the claim of philosophical discourse to a native propriety is in part what determined its literalism and concomitant weeding out of figurative or nonliteral language.

Metaphor's emergence as a topic worthy of philosophical attention was dependent upon the cultivation of and philosophical contention with the idea of irreducible ambiguity. An engagement with doubt has been native to philosophy at least since Socrates' incessant questioning of the Athenians. An ambiguous figure himself, Socrates was a consummate ironist. He interrogated belief in order to instill belief. Seeking to challenge the assertion of the Sophists that knowledge was unattainable outside of individual experience, he proffered the idea that a general knowledge might be arrived at after all, but only if it was approached from an admission of ignorance. He propounded a methodology more than a set of convictions. However, as the character "Socrates" blended into that of Plato, his creator, or one might say, literary executor, a set of convictions definitively emerged. Based in the metaphysical reality of Ideas, Platonism could assure seekers of wisdom that they would be rewarded with transcendent knowledge of the Good, the True, and the Beautiful. Ambiguity in philosophy thus became overgrown with presumptions of truth until, in the eighteenth century, Kant made not-knowing a respectable component of epistemology. As irreducible conditions of possibility emerged into philosophy, so too did metaphor, a claim we will unpack in the subsequent chapter. With Kant, and even Nietzsche, who threw himself onto the suffering creature, metaphor's appearance in philosophy was merely episodic. Not until poststructuralism was the ground significantly disturbed.

Poststructuralism turned over foundationalist truth claims (those asserting themselves as necessary rather than as pragmatically satisfactory). Aerating them, it loosened the densities of philosophical propriety, propagating a field of inquiry that might produce not another purchase upon eternity, but truths no less mortal than the questions that inspire them. It is in this regard that metaphysics releases itself into *metaphorics*. As distinguished here, a metaphorics legitimates fictions, props open the texts of philosophy to reveal their literary propensity. It suggests that an artistic logic is the abiding prelude to a conceptual logic.

My purpose in proposing the term metaphorics is to take up Hillman's (1989b) call "to grapple constructively, positively, with metaphysics" (p. 216). At a conference in 1983 devoted to discussions of his creative endeavor alongside those of Jung and Alfred North Whitehead, Hillman (1989b) addressed the issue of metaphysical literalism, saying, "In my work so far I have shunned metaphysics. I have kept mainly within the critical tradition" (p. 214). Conceding "the paranoid restlessness of the soul to be metaphysically satisfied by ultimates of meaning" (p. 216), Hillman explored the inevitability of "the terrible need for metaphysics" and how it is met in imaginal psychology (p. 215). "Our practice turns ever on its own metaphysics with its own deconstructionist tropic shiftings," he said (p. 219). Invoking "encounters with the psychopompos" as a "way of knowledge" (p. 228), he posed the rhetorical question, "Beyond the verbs that carry us across—to doubt, to ask, to repeat, to twist, to echo—are there any nouns and adjectives on the farther shore?" (p. 220). Unsurprisingly, there are. These he characterized as "aesthetic images" given to the "sensate imagination" (p. 227). Each image toward which we are drawn ceaselessly against the current is another myth, another metaphor, the fundaments of a *poietic* universe, which—to invoke Whitehead contra objectivism—are the "processes and realities" of the cosmos (p. 220). "Cosmology cannot help but be mythical," Hillman said. "Its language will bespeak this mythicality regardless of the very demythologizing purpose of its metaphysical intention" (p. 229). A metaphysical declaration is a declaration of and by a myth. Why, then, not a metaphysics whose farther shore is "quite literally a mythical region, even literarily a mythical region of *poiesis*, making images" (p. 220)? Why not a metaphysics that is overtly a metaphorics?

Fielding a metaphorics entails sticking with the *poietic* propensities in imaginal psychology, which is fostered in the transfer from the literal to the literary. "Cosmologies," Hillman (1989b) said, "are built *in* language and not merely *of* language" (p. 229). Worldviews are word views, purchases upon reality afforded by language. "Words are little mythical beings" (p. 230), Hillman said, and the metaphysics of an imaginal psychology is an "unpredictable diction" (p. 230).

The engagement with metaphor by Hillman and other "imaginologists" (Adams, 2008a) unsettles the literal and transcendental claims of metaphysical systems. As Patricia Berry (2008) put it in her essay on Demeter, "the concrete natural world, unlike the mystical denial of it, is the very way and expression of soul" (p. 26). Like Demeter in search of what has been lost to the depths, imaginal psychology wanders the earth, the vale of soul-making, its phenomenological progress de-literalizing the absolute to let rhetoric flower.

From its earliest philosophical formulations, metaphor has been regarded defensively. Like *res extensa*, it has been split off from reason, and like the carnal in Christian morality, it has been warned against, condescended to, at best admired for superfluous loveliness. As decorative speech, it has been denied the capacity to engender knowledge. Metaphor is vexing because it requires of philosophy that it justify itself. It questions conceptual origins, intervening between the concept and its claim to primordiality. The logic of metaphor grapples with *ontotheology*, a term first employed by Kant (1996) to indicate a rationalism that "believes it can know the existence of an [original being] through mere concepts, without the help of any experience whatsoever" (A632). The term was adopted and redefined by Heidegger to describe the conflation within metaphysics of the question of being, ontology, with the question of a supreme being, theology. In contradistinction to ontotheological speculations concerning the grounds of Being that may or may not pertain beyond the actualities of existence, metaphors appear *in medias res*. The middle of things, as Heidegger (1962) in particular insisted, is where we always already find ourselves. Our embeddedness in a life-world situates us amidst both cultural and natural contingencies, a circumstance Heidegger called the *facticity* of our being (p. 174). Hans Jonas (2001), the scholar of Gnosticism and a prewar student of Heidegger's, said of Heideggerian phenomenology that it was a turn toward "the phenomena of existence, i.e., the individual enmeshed in the *concerns* of life, being more than an *ego cogitans*, being engaged in the business of living and dependent on the 'facticity' of his being which he had not chosen himself" (p. xv).

As Heidegger (1962) saw it, the basic circumstance of the human is as *Dasein*, "being there" or "being here," a situated quality, or *thrownness* into a pregiven world. Working out this state of entanglement in his philosophy, Heidegger intended to make metaphysics capable of a sense of Being more commodius than the *ego cogitans* or thinking thing postulated in the Cartesian tradition. Hillman (1983a) said that for the psychology that draws on Heidegger, *Dasein* denotes "psychic existence" (p. 94), the soul's essential want—its desire and lack, a Sartrean notion of nothingness against which existence has its constitutive state. Nothingness, as Vernon Gras (1973) put it, "yearns for the condition of a thing-in-itself" (p. 9). For Sartre, of course, the yearning is in vain yet also the inspiration of human freedom. For Heidegger, however, the appeal to transcendence had not to do with the inaccessible in-itself, but with the importunate accessibility of *Dasein*'s mortality, its relationship to death, the awareness of which is its defining characteristic. *Dasein*'s temporal circumstance was distinguished by Heidegger not as a chronology, but as an engagement with the question of Being, what to make (*poietically*) of our life in time. Dasein is a temporal disclosure, a *clearing* by which a world becomes manifest. The finitude of this world is not solely composed of the thinking human, but of all forms of being within its horizon. He expressed the idea in part with the terms *present-at-hand* and *ready-to-hand*, pointing, in the former case, to the objects of the world as they might be perceived in objective insularity, and, in the latter, in environmental relationality. By metaphorizing human being in terms of existential relation, Heidegger redressed the theoretical need for predication of the ontological on the theological—the essentialist in-itself despaired of by Sartre.

Not an existential psychologist, Hillman (1978c) was nevertheless a psychologist of the existential. A central theme was "the transformation of psyche into life" (p. 3). He reminds us that in the tale by Apuleius, Psyche is mortal (p. 53), and (quoting Aileen Ward's biography of Keats) "had to submit to a world of circumstances" (p. 55n). It is the investigation into the phenomenology of being-in-the-world that links the work of Heidegger and Hillman. Neither is trying to appeal from the encounter with circumstance to another order. According to Roberts Avens (2003),

> The path they [Heidegger and Hillman] have chosen to thread literally leads nowhere. It is as if they were trying, in the wake of Hui Neng, one of the early patriarchs of Zen Buddhism, "to awaken the mind without fixing it upon anything." One might call it a deflating enterprise peeling the hundred integuments of the onion and finding that there is nothing special at its center. . . . As a result, the most prominent feature these two men have in common is a certain style of thinking or a style of consciousness rather than certain views about the world aiming at overall coherence. (p. 2)

One imagines that Avens's term *deflating* is a description that Hillman, the deflater of analysis, may have well appreciated. The deflationary aim, said Avens, "is to destruct the very impulse to imprison reality in a system of concepts which frame it out and circumscribe it" (p. 2). Critical insight into the ontotheological residues within metaphysics coincides in poststructural thought with a reconsideration of the opposition concept/metaphor, and, as Avens said, characterizes the style of both Hillman and Heidegger as one that destabilizes absolutes. Hillman (1978b) assigned a central role to the process of *seeing through*, construing it as seeing deeply, penetrating the literalization of the facts and memories that structure our ego-identifications, so as to see them as archetypal fantasies, "primary patterns," or lived myths "established in the imaginal world," the province of symbols and poetic imagination to which they can be "led back, reverted, returned" (p. 50) so as to open the polysemic possibilities of existence. "Hillman's strategy," said Avens, "consists in 'seeing through,' which is the counterpart of Heidegger's method of destruction or deconstruction of Western metaphysics aiming at a new, and at the same time more original, experience of Being" (2003, p. 6).

The novelty premised of seeing through is no ultimate formation, but a constant accommodation of ambiguity. *Facticity* spans an abyss of contingent meaning that becomes foreclosed by conceptualization. Metaphor maintains the modicum of undecideability, eschewing Cartesian first principles. A metaphorics is not a discourse of absolutisms, but of situated paradigms, each of which is to a greater or lesser degree therapeutic. On the ideological scale of absolutism to relativism, it tends toward the relative, particularly in William James's (1975) formulation, as a "pluralistic monism" (p. 14). "The world is indubitably one if you look at it in one way," James said, "but as indubitably is it many, if you look at it in another" (p. 14). The theory of paradigms, or rejection of absolutes, ascribed to in this book, takes reality, in Hillman's (1978b) expression, to be "partly observed and partly conjectured" (p. 225). Truth is not entirely given nor entirely constructed; it is an interplay. As Hillman also put it, "Seeing is believing, but believing is seeing" (p. 221). Foundational principles, including that of the discontinuous paradigm, and their inherent relativity, are, to borrow from Edward Casey (1976), "co-essential" (p. 38). This capacious, inherently roomy view is given expression by Richard Tarnas (2006) in his discussion of two contrasting strains of historicism, a rise toward reason and a falling away from the sacred:

> One is reminded here of Niels Bohr's axiom in quantum physics, "The opposite of a profound truth may well be another profound truth," or Oscar Wilde's "A truth in art is that whose contradictory is also true." What is difficult, of course, is to see both images, both truths, simultaneously: to suppress nothing, to remain open to the paradox, to maintain the tension of opposites. Wisdom, like compassion, often seems to require of us that we hold multiple realities in our consciousness at once. (p. 14)

Stephen Pepper (1970) identified the varieties of philosophical speculation as "world hypotheses," a term metaphysically uncharacteristic for its provisional nature. Each of philosophy's overarching, globalizing theses, Pepper said, is based on distinctive suppositions or root metaphors. Again, Hillman (1975): "We see what our idea lets us see" (p. 126). In this perspectival sense, metaphor marks a semantic bifurcation point amidst the always-already at which something new and provisionally decisive is inscribed into experience. Metaphoric ambi-valence is irreducible, singularly ungraspable. It renders the as-if unto perception as from a lacuna, "opening" as possibility and as gap. At the crossroads of the subject, it piles philosopher's stones, marking the leap between the synapses that extrudes signifier and signified, image and concept, from the dark matter of the cognitive fire. In Avens's "more original" experience of "Being," relative and absolute entail one another as kin and shadow.

But, you say, wherefore is metaphorics not an ontotheology? Hermes is a god. Does not the trickster figure figure doubly as the lack to be despaired of, the *deus absconditus* who has absconded with God, *and* the "psychic existence" of being "there" or (was he) "here"? Indeed, nestled unobtrusively among the ready-to-hand examples that Heidegger (1962) supplies for "items of equipment whose specific character as equipment consists in *showing* or *indicating*," one finds an entry for "boundary-stones" (p. 108). Metaphorics, then, requires of us that we reverse ourselves and aver that while factical being arises in metaphor's plastic nature, it culminates after all in first principles or contra-metaphorical fixities: the world *as* it *is*.

Hillman (2000b) said, "[N]ature is itself a metaphor" (p. 14), by which he meant not to question the reality of nature but to suggest that the nature of reality is metaphorical. How to classify this oddity of *physis*? The question has compelled thought at least since Aristotle, who bequeathed a definition in the *Poetics* based in the taxonomic imperative he impressed into history. "Metaphor," Aristotle (2005) said, "is the application of an alien name by transference either from genus to species, or from species to genus, or from species to species, or by analogy, that is, proportion" (§1457). This formula will be at issue in the coming discussion, but for now, suffice it to say that, *pace* Aristotle, metaphoric definition appears to be susceptible of variety.

The metaphors for metaphor are countless. David Leary (1990) catalogued a few of them:

> Metaphor has been likened to a filter, a fusion, a lens, a pretense, a screen, a tension, a displacement, a stereoscopic image, a form of linguistic play, a false identity, a semantic fiction, a contextual shift, a translation of meaning, a twinned vision, and an incongruous perspective. (p. 4)

I add to this list later in this part, and bring a fresh sense to it in Part II based on contributions from imaginal psychology. Metaphor as a literary trope is defined customarily as "simile with the preposition 'like' left out" (Pepper, 1973, p. 197). In the most ordinary sense, metaphor is description by imitation or comparison. It establishes a resemblance—but, significantly, not an *identity*—that links interpretational events. As Leary put it,

> [J]ust as we turn to a dictionary for the definition of unknown words in terms of more familiar words, so we look to phenomena of other sorts, whether natural or artificial, for analogs of things, qualities, and events—including aspects of our own experience and activity—that we wish to comprehend. And conversely, we often look to our own experience and activity for analogs of other natural and artificial phenomena. (1990, p. 2)

We can say that Aristotle's definition is itself metaphorical because he describes a linguistic phenomenon, the relation of words, in terms of a spatial phenomenon, *metapherein*, a transposition or carrying beyond, that is, a substitution or alteration of place.

Stephen Pepper (1973) used the Apollonian language of metaphysics to describe the effect of transposition when he called metaphor "the use of one part of experience to illuminate another" (p. 197). Significantly, the illumination that transpires when categories searchingly encounter one another depends upon what Paul Ricoeur (1975) described as metaphor's "deviation," a glancing action (meaning both to deviate and to see), "in which the meaning of a word departs from its lexically codified usage" (p. 4). Departure establishes the mode of the metaphoric play with its turning between identity and difference, attraction and repulsion. Elaborating upon this signal distinction, Pepper said, "The paradox of a metaphor is that it seems to affirm an identity while also half denying it" (p. 197). When Thales asserted that in primeval form all things are water, he was "affirming an identity and yet acknowledging that it is not obvious, and that what is more obvious is the difference" (p. 197).

The modern view of metaphor is based in its generalization from rhetoric to cognitive process. Thus, Leary (1990) maintained that metaphor is not solely "a distinctive use of language," but "more fundamentally a form of *thought*, having basic epistemological functions" (p. 1). Hillman (1975) reinforced this judgment when he said, "Metaphors are more than ways of speaking, they are ways of perceiving, feeling, and existing" (p. 156). Leary attributed the gradual emergence of "the view that metaphor characterizes human thought and language in a truly fundamental way" to a lineage of "empiricists and pragmatists . . . idealists and intellectual anarchists," among whom he includes Hume, Kant, Bentham, Peirce, Nietzsche, Cassirer, and Hans Vaihinger (Leary, 1990, p. 3).

The cognitive turn in metaphor theory follows upon the insight of such theorists that in every event the application of metaphor is the application of a different metaphor to an existing metaphorical understanding, bringing about not merely a rhetorical alteration, but a change of fundamentals. In a discussion of Nietzsche's perspectivalism, Alexander Nehamas (1985) made the point; Picasso, he said,

> created something in the very act of depicting it. . . . And to the natural question whether the laws of motion did not exist before Galileo and Newton formulated and quantified them, Nietzsche's answer would be that of course they did—just in the way that all the surfaces of material objects were there to be painted before Picasso showed us for the first time how it could be done. (p. 61)

One way to understand the application of metaphor as the unconcealing of the world is with reference to Wittgenstein's (1958) notion of *seeing as*, by which he meant the "noticing" or the "dawning of an aspect" (pp. 193–195). Wittgenstein, said Laurence Goldstein (1999), conceived *seeing as* to be a meaning-making function (p. 110). A more radical notion of unconcealing can be found in Rorty's (1999) theory of language, drawn in part from Wittgenstein, in which propositions are understood not as conforming more or less well to preexisting realities (as in a linguistic analysis of truth claims), but as tools of greater or lesser use in helping us do what we need to do. "Once we found out what could be done with a Galilean vocabulary," Rorty said, "nobody was much interested in doing the things which used to be done . . . with an Aristotelian vocabulary" (p. 19). In Rorty's view, some vocabularies are just "better tools for dealing with the world for one or another purpose" (p. 21).

Another formulation of the idea that fundamentals are *metapherein*, or carried over one to another, is the biological concept of *codetermination.* An evolutionary theory, codetermination indicates the intricate ways in which organisms and environments are mutually influential. Its central tenet, said Francisco Varela, Evan Thompson, and Eleanor Rosch (2000), is that it is the structural relationships in a given ecology that bring forth its constituents. The world is not "pre-given," that is, an object that might be viewed from a variety of perspectives. Rather, "what constitutes the world of a given organism is enacted by that organism's history of structural coupling" with its environment (p. 202). The appreciation of metaphor as a change of fundamentals was available, though not elaborated, at the start of theorizing. "It is from metaphor," said Aristotle (2005) in the *Rhetoric*, "that we can best get hold of something fresh" (§1410). Yet philosophy, alarmed at metaphor's heterodoxy, sequestered it, a circumstance from which it emerged only with the poststructural recognition of the vital nature of difference.

From Plato on, philosophy has known itself as much by what it claimed not to be—an expression of the imagination—as by what it was—a methodology of reason. Roger Scruton (1996) said the virtue of abstract philosophical questions of the sort propounded by Socrates "is in freeing us from self-interested illusions; they set us at a distance from the world of emotion, and enable us to see it for a moment as though we ourselves were not involved" (p. 13). The objectivist tendency was called by Owen Barfield (1973) the "anti-poetic, or purely rational" (p. 94) faculty of mind. In a spatial allusion that bears upon a depth psychological consideration of metaphor, Barfield marked a contrast between what he called "the ascending rational principle and the descending poetic principle" (p. 94). For Hillman, depth is a natural concomitant of a poetic basis of mind, which is therefore the starting point of a depth psychology. Freud, Hillman (1983a) said, "placed mind on a poetic basis" (p. 11) when he formulated the Oedipus complex, establishing psychological first principles in myth. The poetic basis, said Thomas Moore (1989), takes "every fragment of life and every dream as myth and poetry" (p. 15), and presupposes "the metaphorical ear" (p. 2) of the artist. In *Re-Visioning Psychology*, Hillman (1975) broke ground for an imaginal psychology thusly:

> I am suggesting both a poetic basis of mind and a psychology that starts neither in the physiology of the brain, the structure of language, the organization of society, nor the analysis of behavior, but in the process of imagination. (p. xvii)

Later, when he came to enrich the imaginal premise with a theory of "healing fiction," Hillman said, "I am suggesting the poetic basis of therapy, of biography, of our very lives" (1983a, p. 21). To de-literalize the constructs of reason with those of the imagination, Hillman (1975) said, is to plumb "depth without measure" (p. xvii), Barfield's principle of poetic descent. Here let us add another iteration of the trickster archetype to those cross-cultural forms already listed: Hermes Trismegistus (the "Thrice-Greatest"), apocryphal magus of the Gnostic tradition, whose advent reflects what Frances Yates (1964) saw as a turn from Platonic reason to a sense of felt intuition in the Hellenistic religious imagination.

It is as just such an intuitive element that Hermes was manifest at the inception of imaginal psychology. In the winter of 1969–1970 a group of analysts from the Jung Institute began to meet informally on the Untere Zäune east of the Limnat in central Zurich to discuss the medieval Hermetic text known as the *Picatrix*, which they had learned of from Yates's work. The conversations, recalled years later by Rafael López-Pedraza (2007), unleashed "an emotional explosion" among the participants. The involvement with the text "unexpectedly touched complexes" (p. 252) in the members of the group, López-Pedraza said. "This reading constituted a revelation to us, as well as a formidable psychological experience, for it opened feelings among the group that participated in it. We said very strong things to each other" (p. 252). A sumptuously imagistic manual of sympathetic magic, the *Picatrix* is concerned with the ritualistic preparation of religious objects. It seems itself to have served as talisman for the quickening of an overtly literary psychology based in what López-Pedraza called "archetypal rhetoric." The distinctive characteristic of the text is its impasto profusion of conventionally unrelated images plied thickly one upon another. The result is a kaleidoscopic effect of fierce and unrestrained signification. It is a singular example of the metaphoric nature of alchemical and Gnostic literature. In its own estimation it serves as "a house of images" (Greer and Warnock, 2010, p. 243), sheltering the unlikeliest of cohabitants, including humors, minerals, celestial bodies, glyphs, numbers, incantations, animals, body parts, seasons, emotional qualities, all in familial conjunction.

The meaningful encounter with the *Picatrix*, whose appearance in the thoroughfares of twentieth-century Zurich surely qualifies as an anachronistic apparition, unsettled the analytic pretenses of Jungian orthodoxy. Seen, as López-Pedraza apparently did, from the point of view of Jung's theory of psychological types, the swell of emotion may have reflected the activation of the third function. "Psychotherapy happens in the third function," López-Pedraza said (2007, p. 247):

> [T]o go from the first and second functions—from where our personality has been conformed in the first part of life—to the opposite, to the third function, and to approach the fourth is very painful and is possible only if emotions appear that break the barrier created by the first and second function. (pp. 255–256)

Seemingly, this jolt from the psychic third rail inspired a reawakened outlook: "This is how what I call the study of the archetypes was born, helping us to read images, as I denominate it," and pushing the group past analytical psychology, which was "stuck in concepts," toward the raw datum of the image (p. 254):

> I think our interest was to conceive a psychology focused essentially in the here and now, where the life of feeling and emotion is. Possibly the experiences [of emotional intensity in the *Picatrix* conversations] were an opening that helped value irrationality, where the soul is the field of emotions. (p. 260)

Wary of defining that inestimable term, *image*, which lent its name to the emergent school of the *Picatrix* group, López-Pedraza nonetheless cited an indispensable constituent, one which harkens to Romanticism's compensatory response to the overweening rationality of the age of analysis. "I really don't know what the image is," López-Pedraza said,

> and I prefer not to discuss it either. I know it is something that contains an emotion and, through that emotion, knowledge, psychic knowledge. But I don't dare define an image, or say what an image is, because I believe this would instantly destroy it. (p. 264)

Cultivated as a spiritual, aesthetic, or therapeutic practice of Romanticism, emotion is that type of knowledge called by Isaiah Berlin (2013) "a matter of understanding the forces which move in your own life" (p. 16). It is, for better or worse, a counterweight to the "calm and smooth rules" of "universal reason" (p. 7). The *reading* of singular images, their contemplation as distinct from their interpretation, is reflective, said López-Pedraza, of a movement away from "the rhetoric of wholeness" (p. 268) toward the recognition that "we are all incomplete" (p. 265). This sentiment can apply to the trajectory from structuralism to poststructuralism, described by Joe Milutis (2013) as the "abandonment of pure semiology in pursuit of a paradoxical science of the singular" (p. 186). The errant quest of the poststructuralist becomes apparent, Milutis said, in "the existential moment of reading," a fair description of the encounter on the Untere Zäune. Recognition of incompleteness casts psychological reality in terms irreducibly individual. It suspends—though it cannot cancel—the formal value and the rational necessity of the sweeping metaphysical category.

Traditionally, the language of metaphysics is concerned with naming eternal verities; it tells of reason in pursuit of the truth of being, and requires an exactitude that binds thought to its object. For Plato (1963), dialectic was the sole method of distinguishing truth with precision. Rhetoric was dialectic's *bête noir*, a discourse unable to distinguish between originary, formal Ideas and the forgeries of our familiar, empirical existence. Plato's complaint, expressed in the *Gorgias* and the *Phaedrus*, is that rhetoric represents all things equally, and thus falsely. In the *Republic*, he accused rhetoricians and poets of being imitators "at three removes from nature" (§597) and "three removes from being" (§599) for their imitative proclivities, which produce copies of the sensible world, in itself a copy of the Real world of the Ideas known to reason.

Images in poetry, art, or rhetoric mimic, and thereby disparage, the truth. Their danger lies in the power to mislead the non-philosopher into taking them as truth, thus poisoning the citizenry with impiety—the very charge brought by the Athenians against Socrates, an irony to which we will return. "Like one who gives a city over into the hands of villains, and destroys the better citizens, so we shall say that the imitative poet likewise implants an evil constitution in the soul of each individual," Plato said (1957, §605). The analogy of city to soul, expressed in this passage, is one of Plato's most sustained metaphors, lending the *Republic* its structure. To discern the nature of the just individual, Socrates imagined how justice might be expressed under different political systems. These he likened to individuals whose souls are in varying states of imbalance. The best, or utopian, community, said G. R. F. Ferrari in *City and Soul in Plato's Republic* (2005), is one in which "reason is the ruler of soul" (p. 62). In the city/soul metaphor, said Ferrari, "Reason stands to the soul as rulers stand to the city" (p. 62). On the basis of this metaphor, Plato exiled the unreasoning poets from the ideal state—though not without allowing for the possibility that they might make a case for "the charms they exercise upon us" and gain their repatriation (1957, §607).

Plato (1957) marked his belated arrival at the scene of the "ancient quarrel between philosophy and poetry" (§607), or what Geoffrey Hartman (1981) called "the conflict of dialectic with rhetoric, of *ratio* with *oratorio*" (p. xv), by relating certain *ad hominem* epithets hurled in the course of the age-old antagonism, including such beauties as "yelping hounds," "master's bitches," "assemblies of fools," and "conquering rabble." What must have been at stake to generate such heat? Socrates provided a clue when he inveighed against the propensity of lyric poetry to excite the passions:

> And with regard to sexual desires, and anger, and all feelings of desire and pain and pleasure in the soul, which we say follow all our actions, you observe that poetic imitation produces all these effects in us. They should be withered, and it waters them and makes them grow. It makes them rule over us, when they ought to be subjects if we are to become better and happier, instead of worse and more miserable. (Plato, 1957, §606)

The performance of poetry, he said, causes "what by nature is best in us" to "relax its watch" and to acquiesce to passions that "by reason" would be "held down" (§606). By juxtaposing the rule of dispassionate reason to that of the passionate imagination, he was warning against the contagion of irrationality. Spread through coarse sympathies as people come to identify with their most unconsidered motivations, irrationality can become a fever. Conflagrations of base irrationality can reduce humanity to a Hobbesian war of all against all, as history never tires of demonstrating. By holding the accepted reality of the imagination to a single, philosophic instance, the Reality of the Forms, Plato preserved for the philosopher a certain lucidity in the face of the imagination's maddening waywardness. In fact, it is this very quality of irresolution that might well explain why the imagination has rarely been satisfactorily theorized. In his phenomenological study of the imagination, Edward Casey (1976) clarifies a range of theories that "are not only diverse; they are also confused, inconsistent, and even self-contradictory" (p. 7). Casey's study provides a hint as to just who, archetypally, might be behind this frustrating state of affairs. The imagination, Casey said, is not only "evanescent" and "ephemeral," it is

> resistant to conceptual specification of a precise sort. Although we normally apprehend an imagined object with remarkable facility, we do so only for an instant, since it tends to elude us in the very next instant: "one glimpse and vanished," says Beckett. (p. 7)

These Hermetic qualities would seem to make imagination an incorrigible candidate for dispassionate philosophical consideration. "In the case of the imagination," Casey said, "we are dealing with an extraordinarily elusive phenomenon, one that easily slips off the tenterhooks of both observation and theory" (p. 7).

For Plato, the philosopher, in salutary contrast to the poet, was detached from the passions, and at peace. "The prudent and quiet character," Socrates said, "is always at one with itself" (Plato, 1957, §604). The admonition delineates the boundaries of philosophic propriety. It reflects a prescription for equanimity, yet one that also risks enervation. The fine line is discerned by Paul Raimond Daniels (2013) in his study of Nietzsche's *Birth of Tragedy*: "Lyric poetry, with its musical metre and communication of the primordial pains of willing and existing, connected with the inner Dionysiac drive . . . [thus] disrupting the Greek from his serene participation in the city" (p. 43). Poetry and rhetoric, then, are the barbarians at philosophy's gates.

Another instructive reading of this central "bipolarity" in the Western cultural tradition occurs in an influential essay by Roman Jakobson (1973) that postulated a binary opposition between metaphor and metonymy. It was Jakobson who introduced Lévi-Strauss to structuralism when both were exiles in New York during the war. Jakobson's essay proposed a theory of aphasia in which he related contrasting types of the disorder to metaphor and metonymy. Associating metaphor with similarity and metonymy with contiguity, Jakobson related each to specific conditions found in aphasic individuals. "Metaphor is alien to the similarity disorder, and metonymy to the contiguity disorder," he said (p. 123). In the years since this groundbreaking work, metaphor has been re-visioned more commodiously. It is no longer regarded merely as a function of similitude, as we will explore more fully in Chapter 4 on the cognitive turn. In a passage on metaphor's association with Romanticism, we can discern not only the presence of poetry at one pole of the metaphor/metonymy opposition, but also the presence of philosophy at the other. "Poetry is focused upon sign and pragmatical prose primarily upon referent," Jakobson said (p. 127). Jakobson's examples of "pragmatical prose" are from literature, not philosophy, and refer to the realist and formalist traditions as a contrast with Romanticism. Yet, philosophy, too, is not-poetry. Philosophical writing goes to great lengths to employ highly distilled language in avoidance of the often densely imagistic and evocative style of metaphoric composition. The hallmark of the philosophic style is referential precision. In service of the precise reference of term to concept, the textual weave of philosophy is exceedingly sheer. Jakobson's insight into these contrasting modes casts the ancient quarrel between poetry and philosophy as an expressive difference so stark as to render each interlocutor aphasic to the other. The difference is also indicated by Roland Barthes's (1972) distinction between the *écrivan*, a literary writer in whose work there persists a surplus of meaning, and the *écrivant*, who, said John Sturrock (1992), "is a transitive writer in that he has a direct object" (p. 65). The former emphasizes the endless play of signifiers, the latter the surety of the signified.

The valuation in the philosophy/poetry hierarchy that incited the images of monstrosity referred to by Plato becomes disrupted in metaphor's transcategorical process of meaning-making. "Monsters," said Sylvester Wojtkowski (2008), are "examples of interstitial concepts, that is, existing between, and in contrast to, ordinary categories" (p. 296). With reference to Michel Foucault's archeology of espistemic orders in the history of Western thought and society, Wojtkowski said, "By conflating cognitive boundaries recognized as the basis of the order of things, images of monsters challenge the moral and cosmological order; this is the reason why monstrous deviations are so terrifying" (p. 296). In an etching from 1797, *The Sleep of Reason Produces Monsters*, Francisco Goya depicts a writer troubled by dreams of grotesqueries as he dozes at his desk. The monstrosity of unreason that plagues the sleeping writer is perhaps that quality of madness valorized by Foucault as the resistance to internalized social constraints that mold the subject to their own slavish purposes. It is also perhaps that same "monstrosity" that occurred as the concluding word of Derrida's (1978b) lecture at the International Colloquium on Critical Languages and the Sciences of Man in which the deconstructive thinking of the interstitial occurs as a "*conception*, *formation*, *gestation*, and *labor*" of a "question . . . as yet unnamable which is proclaiming itself" at the ancient gates of philosophy (p. 293). If so, it is that same "orthographic monstrosity" proclaimed by Saussure (2005, §54), that is, Derrida's *writing*, the *trace* of absence, gap, or uncertainty that denies philosophy its sought-for unity with ontotheological presence, and that is exemplified by metaphor's basic ambi-valence.

Writing's natural slippage, its inability to know fully what it intends, marks the philosophy of metaphor as I am working it out. Reason and metaphor form a dyad in which each implicates, and is unavoidably bound up with, the other, a phenomenon that Karl Kerényi (1976b), writing of Hermes, called "the dissolution of fatal opposites" (p. 7). To preserve its pellucid waters, reason must constrain the cross-currents of metaphor. Yet metaphor rushes on, carving out the landscapes of philosophy. One is left to wonder whether reason itself is not a metaphoric fantasy. Does the sleep of metaphor produce dreams of reason?

Hermes, for all his antithetical influence, is himself a structure susceptible of conceptual calcification. Yet Hermes *as* the structure of undecideability stands in a transcendental relationship to structure. He is both a "condition of possibility and impossibility," a distinction applied by Derrida scholar Rodolph Gasché (1986, p. 317) to the philosophical circumstance of metaphor, which has its personification in Hermes. Nevertheless, the transcendentality or archetypality of Hermes is not a thesis or a propositional truth; Hermes' transcendentality *is* only *as* hypothesis. Gasché used the term *quasi-transcendental* to avoid the connotation with "absolute." Metaphorically construed, the dual elements of the sign, signifier and signified, define the site of undecideability in the construction of a philosophy. They constitute, said Gasché, the "border of the space of organized contamination which they open up," as they operate semantically "at the margin of the distinction between the transcendental and the empirical" (p. 317). By "a certain irreducible erratic contingency," they invoke "the very conceptual difference between subject and object" (p. 317). Philosophy occupies a perch on the border of Gasché's space of "organized contamination," a term he takes from Derrida. It was perhaps the philosophic ego's horror of its own shadow that Derrida (1981) discerned when he remarked, "Metaphoricity is the logic of contamination and the contamination of logic" (p. 149).

Plato's dialogues established logical deduction as the native language of philosophy, but it was Aristotle who produced a taxonomy that categorized forms of poetic discourse as anti-philosophic. In this negative regard, Aristotle (2005) was metaphor's expositor *par excellence*. Though he conceded that "the greatest thing by far is to have a command of metaphor" (*Poetics*, §1459), his definition proved a bulwark against a cognitive theory of metaphor. "It is with this famous definition," said Mark Johnson (1981), "that the troubled life of metaphor begins" (p. 5). Johnson has provided a synopsis of philosophical considerations upon which I will base the following review of the pre-Kantian period in the history of metaphor.

There are three entailments of the Aristotelian definition that cement the perception of metaphor as anti-philosophical, Johnson (1981) said. First, Aristotle circumscribed metaphor's semantic power. By raising the topic of metaphor in a discussion about nouns, he located its action at the level of individual words. The reason metaphoric meaning is hamstrung by this placement becomes clear when we apply a useful definition by Owen Barfield (1973). Employing a seemingly structuralist distinction, Barfield said, "Meaning includes the whole content of a word, or of a group of words arranged in a particular order, other than the actual *sounds* of which they are composed" (p. 41). Aristotle's limitation of meaning to the surface of individual words, pegging them as narrowly referential word-to-object designations, deprives it of the two modes of manifestation identified by Barfield, the "whole content" of words, that is, their allusive qualities, and their "arrangement in a particular order." Barfield's appeal to context likewise draws the interest of modern metaphor theorists, as we will eventually see.

Second, Johnson said of Aristotle's definition, the use of metaphor entails alienation from the truth. Aristotle understands metaphor as an unnatural application. It transfers a word to an "alien" category where it is estranged in its environment. By abetting falsity in this way, metaphor renders itself hopelessly anti-philosophical. In effect, it is an instance of what Gilbert Ryle (1949), in his critique of Cartesian dualism, called a "category mistake" (p. xx). The difficulty metaphor poses for categorical thinking is addressed by Joel Weinsheimer (1991) in an essay on the role of metaphor in Gadamer's hermeneutics. Weinsheimer notes a distinction in the faculty of understanding as variously conceived in epistemology and hermeneutics. Both address the application of terms to objects that was the concern of Aristotle. Normative epistemology organizes experience by engaging the separative tendencies of reflective reason. Knowledge depends upon disentanglement and classification. "We understand something when we determine the schema, law or rule under which it falls," Weinsheimer said (p. 195). In hermeneutics, however, the methodology shifts from monologue to dialogue. It involves a comparison of discourses, or forms of expression, each providing its own terms of art and presuppositions. Understanding proceeds not by the "unilateral" categorization of terms, but by their "reciprocal" application. "[E]ach term is applied to the other. Each modifies and acts on the other so that they interact. Not unilateral action but only this interaction furthers understanding, for it establishes a common ground previously unthought of," Weinsheimer said (p. 196). Interaction is the defining idea of modern metaphor theory, and we will explore it in more detail further on. Here, let us simply note Weinsheimer's assessment that, for Gadamer, interaction, and therefore metaphor, serves "at least implicitly" as the "archetype" of hermeneutical application (p. 196). Whereas for philosophy as epistemology a conflict of discourses ends only in a misapplication of terms, that is, in a misunderstanding, for philosophy in its hermeneutic mode, such Aristotelian misapplication *is* "the event of understanding" (p. 197).

The third move in Aristotle's strategy of outflanking metaphor, according to Johnson, is to constrain metaphor to similarities, the "underlying resemblances which make the transfer possible" (1981, p. 6), whether from genus to species, species to genus, species to species, or by analogy. Therefore, the metaphorical tropism of a word cannot overcome misuse to create new meaning. Aristotle's approach is less anti-metaphorical on its face than in its effect. In Aristotle's view, according to Johnson, metaphors can "render poetic diction both clear and interesting, when properly employed. . . . So there is an appropriate place for deviance from ordinary usage. But the fatal separation—figurative vs. literal—has been made" (p. 6).

The result of what Johnson called Aristotle's "triad of half-truths" is that "there is a good and a proper, as well as a bad, use of metaphor" (1961, p. 6). Johnson cited this critical passage from the *Rhetoric*: "Metaphors, like epithets, must be fitting, which means that they must fairly correspond to the thing signified; failing this, their inappropriateness will be conspicuous" (p. 6). For example, Aristotle (2005) said metaphor must not be ridiculous or theatrical (§1406). "It ought 'to set the scene before our eyes' with a vividness that induces an alteration of perspective that lets us 'get hold of new ideas'" (Johnson, 1981, p. 7). But "whether metaphors are fitting or farfetched," Johnson said, "hinges mainly on the appropriateness of the relevant similarities emphasized" (p. 7). Similarity becomes the necessary and sufficient condition of metaphoric expression in the era of its Aristotelian subordination. "The future of metaphor," Johnson said, "is prefigured in terms of these three basic components, (i) focus on single words that are (ii) deviations from literal language, to produce a change of meaning that is (iii) based on similarities between things" (p. 6). How metaphor works is assumed by philosophy to be a function of similarity until the influence of semiotics. In the intervening generations, metaphor was more or less ignored by philosophy. It subsisted at the margins of the philosophic enterprise. Thus, similarity held as the basic metaphorical function not because it withstood scrutiny, but because it escaped the eye of philosophy altogether.

The rhetoricians and theologians of Hellenism and the Middle Ages, Johnson said, "Show a certain Aristotelian respect for metaphor, but neither focuses any special attention on it" (1981, p. 8). Indeed, the consideration of metaphor by Latin thinkers, notably Cicero (106–143 BCE) and Quintilian (c. 35–c. 100), had the effect of further diminishing its importance for philosophy. Whereas Aristotle established metaphor as the genus within which other figurative tropes—analogy, simile—were the species, the Latin thinkers reverse the order. For them, metaphor is merely a shortened form of simile, a comparison that expresses itself with greater economy, but less forthrightness, abandoning simile's reliance upon "like" or "as." In Cicero's formulation "a metaphor is a brief similitude contracted into a single word" (as cited in Johnson, 1981, p. 8). This terse rendition excises any faculty for the elaboration of meaning. Cicero followed Aristotle's practice of damning with praise. "There is no mode of embellishment more effective as regards single words, nor any that throws a greater luster upon language," he said (as cited in Johnson, 1981, p. 9). The great danger of error is nevertheless inveighed against in Cicero's admonition against misuse, as summarized by Johnson: "There are numerous ways metaphor can fail or mislead: it may be too lowly, exalted, or crude for the subject; it may be farfetched (where dissimilarity overcomes resemblances), or it may be overused" (p. 9). The traces are thereby tightened.

A contrasting theme with particular force that issued from the medieval period was the ecclesiastical compunction against metaphor. "Just as one must be suspicious of immoral pagan art," Johnson said, "so one must take care not to be led astray by pagan eloquence" (1981, p. 9). The ecclesiastical appropriation finds expression in the work of the Venerable Bede (c. 673–735). Though Bede carried forward the classical conception of metaphor as stylistic, not inventive, it was not his intent to argue that its every use was a potential perjury. His primary concern was to demonstrate that figurative language has a rightful place only in Scripture, not in logic. "Teachers of secular eloquence in any age," Bede said, "have not been able to furnish us with any of these figures and tropes which did not first appear in Holy Writ" (as cited in Johnson, 1981, p. 9). Bede's entry into the conversation:

> establishes a pattern of ecclesiastical warnings that will contribute to the decline of metaphor for many centuries to come: rhetoric is distinguished from logic and then reduced to a manual of style. Thus metaphor, treated traditionally under rhetoric, becomes a stylistic device divorced from serious philosophical argument. (p. 9)

Like Bede, Thomas Aquinas (1224–1274) asserted that necessity of metaphorical expression extends only to Scripture. His contention in the *Summa Theologiae* is that "it is sometimes useful to 'hide truths' in metaphors for the 'exercise of thoughtful minds and as a defense against the ridicule of the unbelievers'" (as cited in Johnson, 1981, p. 10). The nature of the ecclesiastical "devaluation" of metaphor, Johnson said, served to narrow it to eloquence and to maintain silence on its other *poietic* faculties. The ecclesiastics considered "only style, dropping any discussion of invention, disposition, and memory" (p. 9).

Frances Yates (1966), however, suggested that medieval theologians acknowledged metaphor and memory were in fact intricately bound up together. A scholastic embrace of metaphor would demonstrate the common, if surreptitious, co-occurrence of contrasting epistemologies in the work of many thinkers, as seen, for example, in the alchemical interests of Isaac Newton or in Plato's simultaneous rejection of and reliance upon poetic constructions. In her explorations of Hermeticism, Yates discussed the practice by Aquinas of an "art of memory." Taught to him by Albertus Magnus, it trained the mind to retain vast catalogues of information though symbolic association. Aquinas called the mental library a "*thesaurus inscrutabilis*" (Yates, 1966, p. 171). For Albertus Magnus it was a "*metaphorica*" with the power to "move the soul" (as cited in Yates, 1966, p. 65). We will further explore metaphor and memory when we come to Nietzsche. At present it is enough to say that metaphor emerged from the medieval theological prism as a device whose scriptural or memorial use might lend itself to the careful handling of powerful spiritual truths, but whose inexactitudes cloud the eye of reason. "The same underlying conception remains," Johnson said. "Metaphor is a *deviant* use of a *word* to point up *similarities*" (1981, p. 11).

Neither did metaphor fare any better at the hands of empiricists and rationalists, whose accounts, Johnson said, are dominated by "mistrust, rather than appreciation" (1981, p. 11). Johnson noted the approach to metaphor by four shapers of the modern age, the empiricists Thomas Hobbes, John Locke, and John Stuart Mill, and the central figure of idealism, G. W. F. Hegel. Each drew the misgivings of the classical-medieval-ecclesiastical tradition into Enlightenment thought, preserving the preeminence of literal language for the scientific project. The circumscription of metaphor was used by Hobbes (1588–1679) to legislate an inside and an outside of Enlightenment philosophical discourse. In *Leviathan*, Hobbes (1968) rejected "the use of metaphors, tropes, and other rhetorical figures, instead of words proper" (p. 114). Like Aristotle, Hobbes assigned metaphor to rhetoric, holding that it impedes knowledge because it employs words to mean other "than that they are ordained for" (p. 102). To reason by dint of metaphor, he said, would amount to "wandering amongst innumerable absurdities" (p. 117). He appeared to regard the use of metaphors as a kind of heresy. They "openly profess deceit," he said; "to admit them into council or reasoning, were manifest folly" (p. 137).

It was no small matter for Hobbes to restrain figurative language in this particular way. In the view of Kirk Pillow (2003), metaphor's free associative tendency so undermines the exercise of determinate judgment critical to reason that it is looked upon as a case of madness (p. 233), the very monstrosity observed by Wojtkowski and Goya. It is worth recalling in this regard Michel Foucault's (1965) argument that madness is constructed by the perhaps equally mad imperatives of an ordered society. By excising imagistic thinking from reason's "council," Hobbes renews the Platonic decree against lyric "fools" and "rabble."

Locke (1632–1704), too, regarded metaphor as a danger to rationality. In the *Essay Concerning Human Understanding*, Locke (1959) placed his comments on metaphor in a chapter called "On the Abuse of Words":

> If we would speak of things as they are, we must allow that all the art of rhetoric . . . all the artificial and figurative application of words eloquence hath invented are for nothing else but to insinuate wrong ideas, move the passions, and thereby mislead the judgment, and so indeed are perfect cheats . . . and where truth and knowledge are concerned, cannot but be thought a great fault. (p. 146)

Mill (1806–1873) as well dismissed metaphor from *reason*able company. He maintained that it has no relationship to the derivation of logical proofs, but he allowed that it might serve the reasoning process in a subordinate capacity. "A metaphor," Mill said, "is not to be considered an argument, but as an assertion that an argument exists; that a parity subsists between the case from which the metaphor is drawn and that to which it is applied" (as cited in Johnson, 1981, p. 13). A picaresque expression of the same point was offered by Max Black in a seminal essay, which we will come to in a subsequent chapter, that altered the course of metaphor theory. As an epigraph, Black presented Sir Walter Raleigh's *bon mot*, "Metaphors are no arguments, my pretty maiden" (as cited in Black, 1962, p. 25).

Hegel (1770–1831) has a more complicated relationship to metaphor. Though the role in his system of the determinative Concept foreclosed the possibility that metaphor, with its freely associative *modus vivendi*, might attain epistemological status, Pillow (2003) noted that in the *Aesthetics* Hegel assigned significance to metaphor as an intermediate level in the *Aufhebung*. It "expresses a certain boldness of the imagination," Hegel said (as cited in Pillow, 2003, p. 209). But he characterized it as "subjective caprice" and "piquant impulse" (as cited in Pillow, 2003, p. 208), assessments that indicate its incommensurability with "rational unity made literal in the world" (p. 268). Metaphors, Pillow said, "will gain their true and determinate meaning by their elevation into [Hegel's] system" (p. 268). Significantly for our eventual discussion of Nietzsche, Hegel referred to metaphor as "the purely *bacchanalian* delight of fancy" (as cited in Pillow, 2003, p. 208; emphasis added). The comment anticipated Nietzsche's theme of metaphor's Dionysian flux and the association proposed by Hillman (1978c) of Dionysus with the psyche's imaginal function.

It is worth noting that Hegel's (1998) two most well-known aphorisms are examples of complex metaphors: "The night in which all cows are black" (p. 52), a tart dismissal of Schelling's metaphysics for its supposed failure to demonstrate a distinctively evolutionary outcome, and "Only when dusk starts to fall does the owl of Minerva spread its wings and fly" (p. 327), an image of the self-realization attained by the Absolute at the natural culmination of philosophy. Practically no word in these proclamations has a literal meaning, and none can be secured within the confines of the statements themselves. Each syntactic arrangement must point for understanding to external context. That is, neither of the statements take the philosophically valorized form of a self-present logic.

With regard to the latter aphorism in particular, a question arises. If a metaphorical sentence passes as the quintessential expression of the apotheosis of determinate, conceptual thought, does such thought paradoxically attain ultimacy only in metaphor? Were a satisfactory case to be made that the *telos* of the Concept lies, psychologically speaking, in its metaphorical "shadow," such an argument would provide an application to metaphysics of Jung's concept of *enantiodromia*, the turn of libidinal energy toward its opposite, and a probable example of how metaphysics can be thought of as a product of metaphorics. "The higher its charge mounts," said Jung, speaking of the repression of psychic contents, "the more the repressive attitude acquires a fanatical character and the nearer it comes to conversion into its opposite, i.e., an enantiodromia" (CW 8, par. 425).

According to Max Black (1981), complex metaphors such as "the night in which all cows are black," which point outside themselves for literal meaning, are not precisely metaphorical, but better described as riddles, allegories, or proverbs (p. 65). Black did not raise the possibility that they may be viewed as mythemes or "mini myths," the Vichian designation of metaphor that influenced Hillman. If Hegel's metaphors were to be considered as mini myths, it would distinguish him as a mythmaker and place his work in a literary tradition as well as a philosophical one. The designation would correspond to the suggestion put forward by Richard Rorty (1997) that philosophy can be considered a genre or style of writing. It would provide an example of how metaphorics, the logic of metaphor, produces metaphysics. Hegel would join Plato (at the least) among philosophers (writers) who perhaps disingenuously sequestered *logos* from *mythos*, but whose work entailed striking examples of mythmaking. Taken in terms of the psychological and imaginal significance that myth holds for the creation of cultural identity, such an argument is but a modest addition to the poststructural re-visioning of metaphysics as the logocentric and ethnocentric mythmaking tradition of the West.

The final thinker in the prefigural line of thought for whom we will account is Jean-Jacques Rousseau (1712–1778). In the survey of metaphysics with which Derrida (1997) demonstrates the futility of originary absolutes, "Rousseau" is the very signature of a nostalgia for the literalism of origins. Yet a seeming ambivalence in his work about the use and nature of metaphor hints at a contrary theory. As Paul de Man pointed out, Rousseau made ostensibly incompatible statements on figuration. In the *Second Discourse*, Rousseau appeared to endorse the classical theory that names attach to things when he said that "the first nouns could only have been proper nouns" (as cited in de Man, 1973, p. 487). In his *Essay on the Origin of Language*, however, Rousseau asserted that "man's first language had to be figurative" (as cited in de Man, 1973, p. 487). From the first statement, one could assume that Rousseau, in de Man's words, "separates the literal from the metaphorical forms of language and privileges the former over the latter" (p. 486). Yet such an assumption would find its refutation in the second statement, leaving one to conclude that, on this point at least, Rousseau's opus fails to cohere.

De Man (1973) undertook a reading in which he detected "the presence of some degree of conceptuality (or metaphor) from the start, within the very act of naming" (p. 488). In ascribing a name, de Man said, "one freezes hypothesis, or fiction, into fact" (p. 490). The name is a metaphor, a "mere possibility," that in the denomination process asserts itself as certain (p. 490). Further, denomination has a double nature. It arises spontaneously, from the "passion" of the mind by which hypotheses are generated, and then is fitted to a circumstance such that excess or aberrance becomes masked. In this interpretation, Rousseau appears to be anticipating the modern theory in which the concept is the reified product of a metaphoric impulse: "What Rousseau calls 'truth,' designates neither the adequation of language to reality, nor the essence of things shining through the opacity of words, but rather the suspicion that human specificity may be rooted in linguistic deceit" (de Man, 1973, p. 495). In this view, Rousseau avoids essentialism to serve as a forerunner of a theory in which metaphor's ambiguity is seen as an inventive, fictive undertow beneath categorical propriety. He would be an exception to the Aristotelian tradition that paradoxically understands language "by means of causal categories that are themselves dependent on the genetic [taxonomic, multiplicative] power of the origin for which they are supposed to account" (p. 481).

De Man's Rousseau is avant-garde. Philosophy's condescension to metaphor at the onset of modern thought is more generally seen as a continuation of the Aristotelian view that a name has its proper object, and that figurative language dangerously weakens the bond of truth between the word and its referent. Johnson (1981) termed this view the "literal-truth paradigm" (p. 12), and assigned it three elements:

> The human conceptual system is essentially literal—literal language ("words proper") is the only adequate vehicle for (a) expressing one's meaning precisely, and (b) making truth claims, which together make possible correct reasoning by the philosopher.
>
> Metaphor is a deviant use of words in other than their proper senses, which accounts for its tendency to confuse and to deceive.
>
> The meaning and truth claims of a metaphor (if there are any) are just those of its literal paraphrase. (p. 12)

The stream of thought holding that "metaphors are words used in other than their proper senses, [that] they are liable to seduce and mislead us by their eloquent charms" (Johnson, 1981, p. 13) carried from classicism into modernity. Only in the Romantic sensibility, in which philosophy and poetry began to recognize in one another compensatory epistemological inclinations, did an alternative understanding arise. Johnson wrote:

> Romantic artists and poets tended to see metaphor as a fundamental creative activity or principle of language that transcends our everyday literal understanding. Worship of poetic genius was based on its alleged ability to transcend ordinary rational categories to achieve a profound intuitive insight into nature and life. Metaphor was thereby associated with art and religion and dissociated from "sterile" scientific understanding. (p. 14)

Thus for Rousseau, the earliest of the Romantics, "all language grows by a process of meaning transfer, i.e., by figuration" (Johnson, 1981, p. 15). Rousseau's celebration of the purity and transparency present at the origin of all things led him to exalt metaphor as the form of language closest to truth. "As man's first motives for speaking were of the passions, his first expressions were tropes," Rousseau said; "Figurative language was the first to be born. . . . At first, only poetry was spoken; there was no hint of reasoning until much later" (as cited in Johnson, 1981, p. 15).

It was not until the middle of the last century that philosophers, linguists, and literary theorists became sufficiently galvanized by metaphor's cognitive possibilities to constitute it as a distinct discipline in the humanities. The expounders upon metaphor's epistemological capacity argue that it outfits consciousness with the very tools by which consciousness constructs a world. The pioneers of this cognitive turn were the British literary critic I. A. Richards and the British-American analytical philosopher Max Black. Richards was a theorist of the New Criticism, which emerged in the 1930s and 1940s, and is viewed poststructurally as insufficiently attentive to its own textuality, that is, to the unavoidable interpretive interventions it makes into the canonical works that it reads and then writes about. The New Critics were keen to establish the autonomy of the literary text. They discerned a firm boundary between literary language and literal language, and reserved for "literature" fundamental metaphorical notions of paradox, ambiguity, or tension. The vain attempt of the New Critics to defend a poetic empyrean has not prevented Richards's theory of metaphor from becoming latterly important to the emergence of the cognitive view. Black was an analytical philosopher and scholar of Wittgenstein who made the single most important contribution to what we might, in a Confucian vein, call the rectification of the names, correcting what Johnson (1981) called the "baleful influence" brought down upon the appreciation of figurative expression by logical positivism, a cul de sac in analytical philosophy's linguistic turn, to the verifiability of meaning (p. 16). The logical positivist school takes its place in the long line of accounts that devalued metaphor as incompatible with reason. Black's contravention insisted upon metaphor's semantic power. Richards, writing before Black, though not in philosophy, likewise argued for the meaning-making function. Their views were harbingers of metaphor's vital season.

In its Platonic exile, metaphor experienced a thriving diaspora in linguistics, literary theory, rhetoric, and, notably, in the "sibylline leaves" of Romanticism, which provided a countercultural tug to the aerodynamics of rationality. "With Romanticism," said Richard Tarnas (1991), "the modern eye was turned ever more inward to discern the shadows of existence" (p. 368). Among such existential shadows, said Helena Shulman Lorenz (2004), are specters of "behavior and thought" that have been repressed by the collective consciousness. Forms of awareness that were "discontinuous" with the "uniformity and coherence" of the modern worldview were "exiled" from the "normalized routines" of conventional understanding (p. 226). The cultural environment of modernity, Lorenz said, has been "classified according to fixed hierarchies of binary opposites: latitude and longitude, center and periphery, progress and stasis, order and chaos" (p. 226). Binary opposition has been a feature of thought since Anaximander, in the sixth century BCE, posited the world as an interaction of primary qualities, hot and cold, wet and dry, though it is perhaps the culture of the extractive economy, a withdrawal from the chthonic ebb and flow and its intertidal ambiguities, that has made a fetish of it. Littoral regions become subsumed into literal regions. Among the subversive currents deconstructive of an objectivist purchase is the metaphoric imagination. Richards and Black tacked against the prevailing winds to posit a reconsideration of metaphor in philosophy that has now grown to considerable proportions. In her volume on metaphor and metonymy, the philosopher Susan Handelman (1982) warned of an inherent danger in the metamorphosis of the gods. "We are at present witnessing the coronation of a new philosophical idol," she said. "Metaphor has become the new metaphysics" (p. 35).

The awakening to metaphor that began with Richards and Black is coincident with a general phenomenological turn in philosophy that brackets the presuppositions of rationalism and empiricism to clear the field for the description of phenomena of mind that make knowledge possible. The impact on metaphor of this sea change begins, of course, with Kant and reaches high tide with Nietzsche. Kant introduced "analogy" as a structure of mind that serves in his architechtonic as the keystone between the pure and practical reason. Nietzsche advanced the argument that all thought is an aesthetic product of the instincts, or "drives," a way of saying that all thought is metaphorical. The work of both thinkers erected the scaffolding for the twentieth century's reconstruction of metaphor, which set two theories into contention. The first of these, the comparison theory, exhibits the argument from literalism that held from Aristotle into the Enlightenment and the modern era. The second, the interaction theory, argues from a poetic basis of mind and is the seed of contemporary theorizing. We will examine the theories later in the section. First, we will turn to the contribution made by Kant to metaphor's swerve into philosophical consciousness.

2

KANT

Kirk Pillow (2001) said of Immanuel Kant (1724–1804) that he "is one of the few modern philosophers for whom metaphors are philosophically honorable" (p. 193). On this ground, an exploration of Kant's contribution becomes essential to a history of metaphor. I propose to use Pillow's work, as well as that of A. T. Nuyen and, in somewhat greater detail, Clive Cazeaux to indicate that the slumberings of metaphor within philosophy were first disturbed by Kant's transcendental deduction. Both Pillow and Cazeaux approach the topic of Kant and metaphor with an exposition of the third *Critique*, in which analogy surfaces as a significant element in Kant's epistemology. I begin with Cazeaux, whose philosophical spade work uncovers a richly layered metaphoricity in the *Critique*. I then turn to Pillow and Nuyen for a comparison of Kant's concept of the aesthetic idea with the interaction theory of metaphor.

Although Kant is, of course, the principal architect of modern philosophy, the excavations presented here reveal a fracturing simultaneous with a founding, a necessarily interpretive substructure or metaphoric a priori upon which or against which philosophy enacts the drama of pure reason. "We may not forget," Hillman (1975) said, "that philosophical thinking must speak in terms of purity. Its abstract asceticism is part of the puritan dignity of the philosophical style itself" (p. 131). Citing Jung, he said, "most disciplines try 'to forget their archetypal explanatory principles, that is, the psychic premises that are the *sine qua non* of the cognitive process'" (p. 131). Avoiding the fallacy of psychologism (everything reduces to psychic principles), we can understand Jung's invocation of archetype to indicate the metaphorical, or interpretive, mode in the activity of philosophy. We will see how Jungian archetype, in its derivation from Kant, might be further de-literalized in the view of a third scholar, Stephanie De Voogd, whose work we will examine at the end of the chapter.

Kant's revolutionary contribution, his prolegomena to any future metaphysics, as he titled a summary of his ideas, was the argument that any assertion about the nature of reality, any metaphysics, must be founded upon a theory of knowledge that takes into account how it is possible for the mind to know what it claims to know. Metaphysics must not only acknowledge the primacy of epistemology, but any valid epistemology must account for the cognitive structures that make knowledge possible. The influence of Kant's theory of mind on the worldview of modernity was monumental. In the face of controversies about the nature of the objective world that set empiricist against rationalist, Kant ratified the defining claims of the scientific enterprise to regularity and predictability by reconceiving certain features of experience, presumed to be entirely objective, as instead a priori, inhering in cognition in advance of sensory perception. Our means of grasping the world, Kant (1977) said, presupposes a "form of sensibility which in me as a subject precedes all the actual impressions through which I am affected by objects" (p. 282). Such precedential sensibility was of two types: faculties of perception, which Kant called the forms of the intuition (time and space), and universal concepts, which he called the categories of the understanding (significantly including causality, which Hume had demonstrated cannot be objectively found). That features of the world might be given by the mind in advance of any sensory data elevated cognition to a determining role in the construction of reality. Yet in Kant's view it also entailed the differentiation of a *phenomenal* domain, of which we can make scientifically warranted observations because its universal and necessary features are intrinsic to our cognition, from an unknowable *noumenal* domain, the world as it might exist *transcendentally*, in itself apart from our cognitive sensibility. The error of rationalism and empiricism, Kant said, was the attempt to establish the objectivity of noumenal factors, such as time, space, and causality. These cannot be known in a general way, he said, but only as they appear in conjunction with data presented to our senses.

The central challenge confronting Kant was to explain how two domains as distinct as sensible phenomena and immaterial noumena might interact at the crossroads of the subject to produce experience. The problem was not new. Plato was left with the same dilemma, how to account for the relationship between the ideal originals of substances and virtues, and their imperfect reflection in material appearances or human actions. Plato and Kant shared a motive and a solution. W. K. C. Guthrie (1950) pointed out that for Plato the postulate of immutable Ideas was necessary in a seemingly transitory world to establish "the whole possibility of scientific knowledge" (p. 88), which requires "fixed truths" for its object (p. 128). To establish the connection between the metaphysical and the physical, Guthrie said, Plato took "recourse to metaphor" (p. 90). The Idea was a "model" or a "pattern," and the appearance its "interpretation"; their relationship was a "sharing" or a "participation" (p. 90).

Kant, too, invoked metaphor to reconcile incongruent domains. The question, here put by Cazeaux (2007), was, "how do (supersensible) pure, transcendental concepts projected in advance of experience accommodate (sensible) empirical intuitions" (p. 35). The solution, which appears in the *Critique of Judgment* (1790), the culminating work of the transcendental philosophy, was a layered use of analogy. Cazeaux's assertions were that "metaphor is a condition of the possibility of judgment," Kant's integrative faculty, and that, as such, "Kant's philosophy cannot be rendered systematic" without its underlying "series of metaphors and analogies" (p. 36). I intend to follow the steps Cazeaux took to establish Kant's metaphorical imperative, the implication of which is that the metaphysics sustaining modernity was established upon a foundation of metaphor.

Kant (1987) did not use the word metaphor in the *Critique of Judgment.* He spoke instead of analogy, which, in the taxonomy of tropes from Aristotle, appears as a category of metaphor, and indeed as metaphor's paradigmatic case. In the *Poetics*, as noted, Aristotle classified analogy as a species of metaphor. In the *Rhetoric*, he enhanced analogy's status, naming it as metaphor *par excellence*. "Analogy is vital to Kant's architectonic," Cazeaux (2007) said,

> because, as a creator of relationships, it allows him to explain how the key terms in his system interact with one another. The main gulf which has to be bridged is between the sensible and the supersensible. The supersensible in this context refers to human reason and, in particular, its capacity for going beyond what is given in immediate (sensible) experience. (p. 33)

Cazeaux characterized the structure of the third *Critique* as a "nested series of analogies" (p. 42). He identified four analogical relationships that inform the *Critique*. The first three enable Kant to establish the transcendental principle that provides the rule of judgment. A fourth analogy provides for its operation.

Judgment is Kant's term for our capacity to relate abstract concepts and specific content. In the *Critique of Pure Reason* it appears as the built-in logic of our cognitive capacity, but in the other *Critiques*, which concern intuitions of an indeterminate type, such as freedom or beauty, rather than determinate intuitions that structure our experience of the natural world, it must operate *analogically* to find relationships that establish the schematic link between the rational concept and its empirical content. To establish the rule of judgment in the third *Critique*, Cazeaux said, Kant first looked to the governing ideas that he formulated in the first two *Critiques* to support the conclusion that a similar law-giving idea might also pertain in the rule of judgment. This led him to the analogy that the sought-after principle, like the earlier two, must be of an order of understanding that pertains in advance of experience, in other words, one that is transcendental. Third, he drew an analogical relationship to the rule of practical reason established in the second *Critique*. Like the relationship of reason to perceived moral imperatives and to freedom of action, the sought-after principle must be discerned empirically. Once he exercised these analogies to arrive at the rule of judgment, he then took the climactic step of looking to analogical thought for the operation of judgment. The analogies to pure and practical reason enabled Kant to establish judgment as the mediating term in his system. The task now is to follow Cazeaux in examining the analogies in turn.

Kant's project of uniting the sensible and the supersensible, Cazeaux (2007) said, also involved "reconciling two concepts of the supersensible: the supersensible substrate of all appearances in accordance with the laws of nature, and the supersensible substrate of our freedom to act in accordance with the moral law in ways which are not determined by nature" (p. 36). Kant had to account for the relationship of pure to practical reason. The joinder of the supersensibles was necessary to the formation of a coherent system because they entail no more overlap than either of them have with the sensible domains they govern. "The concept of freedom," Kant (1987) said,

> determines nothing with regard to our theoretical cognition of nature, just as the concept of nature determines nothing with regard to the practical laws of freedom; and to this extent it is not possible to throw a bridge from one domain to the other. (p. 36)

Cazeaux attributed these gaps to the spatial metaphor, traditional to philosophy, with which regions of being are thought:

> Accounts of sensibility lead to discussions of supersensibility because of the terms in which these debates are set in the history of philosophy and, in particular, the spatial or "realm" metaphors which are used to mark philosophy's central distinctions, for example, the material and the ideal, the sensible and the intelligible, the immediate and the transcendent. (p. 36)

In other words, the literalisms native to philosophizing suffer from the want of a crossing over by which they might participate in what Hillman (1980) called a "composite of differences" or "metaphorical field" (p. xx).

Kant's initial analogy, Cazeaux (2007) said, was to the supersensible substrates posited in the first two *Critiques* as "the source of the conditions of possibility which allow sensibility to come into being" (p. 36). Having postulated separate a priori governors for both pure and practical reason, Kant (1987) concluded that

> we have cause to suppose by analogy that [judgment] too may contain a priori, if not a legislation of its own, then at least a principle of its own, perhaps merely a subjective one, by which to search for laws. Even though such a principle would lack a realm of objects as its own domain, it might still have some territory; and this territory might be of such a character that none but this very principle might hold it. (p. 16)

The introduction of analogy took a specific form whose significance Cazeaux (2007) emphasized as follows:

> An important metaphorical theme is introduced here, namely, the absence of a domain. . . . Metaphor (of which analogy is a form) is introduced

> precisely because it is the disrespecter of domains, the cognitive principle which, lacking a domain of its own, operates by *rupturing* the conceptual landscape and placing two formerly incongruent semantic fields side by side. (p. 37; emphasis added)

I accentuate the word *rupture* to indicate that it hearkens to Derrida's use of the same term, noted in the Introduction, to describe the emergence into philosophy of its deconstructive propensity. The term serves as a thread in our text locating the monstrosity of, as Wojtkowski put it, the "interstitial" imperatives metaphor and deconstruction within the labyrinth of metaphysics.

Kant (1987) analogized from the rule of the understanding, presented in the first *Critique* as the legislator of nature, and from the rule of reason, presented in the second *Critique* as the legislator of freedom, to a similar governance of the conditions of judgment. With regard to judgment, however, he claimed no sphere of influence, only the possibility that there may be such a sphere *like* that in the other *Critiques*: "Once again we have thought perceived in spatial terms, although in this instance it is the *applicability* of a concept which is represented spatially. . . . [A]ccording to Kant, the principle he seeks does not have its own domain" (Cazeaux, 2007, p. 37). In this way, Kant made a distinction between concepts and their method of creation. Though he used the spatial metaphor to establish the operation of judgment, he took a decisive step away from the absolutism of the concept-in-itself to observe the conception of conceptuality. The rule of judgment does not in itself, that is, necessarily and universally, constitute a spatial realm; rather it is understood, or applied in thought, by reference (analogy) to the spatial terms, "domain," "realm," "territory,"[1] giving it the quality of a *pseudo-domain.*

Kant (1987) laid bare the process that underlay the selection of concepts to which he attributed sufficient necessity and universality to qualify as categories of the understanding. By leaving visible the metaphorical scaffolding of the rule of judgment, he provided not another transcendental principle, but an indication of how such principles might be determined. Frederick Copleston (1964) drew attention to this point when he noted that the rule of judgment:

> is not an a priori principle in precisely the same sense that the principles considered in the *Transcendental Analytic* are a priori. That is to say, it is not a necessary condition for there being objects of experience at all. Rather is it a necessary *heuristic* principle which guides us in our study of the objects of experience. (p. 144)

Hans Vaihinger (2009), whose philosophy of *as-if* Hillman (1975) identified as an influence on his thinking about metaphor, went even further. Vaihinger asserted that not only the rule of judgment, but all Kantian principles (and philosophies in general) are constructed heuristically. What allows, or perhaps requires, the rule of judgment to be exemplary rather than constitutive is that it pertains not to rationality, but to affect. Karl Jaspers (1962), whose phenomenology of mind was influenced by Kant, wrote of the power of judgment that, "its predicate is not a concept, but a feeling of pleasure or pain . . . [its] universal validity is therefore fundamentally different from that of a logical judgment" (p. 78). It is noteworthy for an argument that takes metaphor's emergence in philosophy to be an intrusion by a poetics of mind into rationality that Kant employed analogy specifically when he came to consider the rule of judgment, whose intrinsic concern is with individual sensibility. As we saw, metaphor's exile had in part to do with Plato's determination that it is based in *pathos* and therefore incompatible with *ratio*. Kant, too, confronted this problem when he distinguished judgment in aesthetic terms, yet he solved it not with a refutation of figurative language, but by its affirmation and application.

Following upon his first argument from analogy, the suggestion of a supersensible substrate of judgment, Kant employed a second analogy, nested, as Cazeaux (2007) said, within the first. On the basis that the substrates of pure and practical reason each involve a regulatory function, pure understanding and practical reason respectively, Kant set about to identify the legislative principle at work in the transcendental *pseudo-domain* applicable to judgment that we might, after Gasché, refer to as *quasi-transcendental.* The steps in his argument begin with the division of the agency of judgment into two types, aesthetic and teleological. Indeed, the *Critique* is a book of two halves, each devoted to an exposition of one of the types of judgment, and to the mutual problem they present to deduction: the question of how to think their a priori. "Both forms of judgment, Kant avows, go beyond [the epistemic structure of the] intuition by invoking concepts which cannot be explained *in terms of their application to intuition*" (Cazeaux, 2007, p. 37). The types of judgment appear to make an unwarranted categorical leap from apprehensions in the domain of the subjective and the sensible to conclusions in the domain of the universal and the supersensible. Kant's definitions, paraphrased by Cazeaux (2007), set forth the problem. Aesthetic judgments

> are a description of a personal feeling in response to an object [that] nevertheless extend beyond this subjectivity to make a claim about the object's beauty or aesthetic merits which arguably should hold for everyone. In other words, they claim a level of universality normally attributed to conceptual determination. (p. 38)

Teleological judgments are those asserting that

> complex or living systems, such as plants, animals, people, can best be explained in terms of ends or aims or purposes. Whereas a causal account explains behavior as an aggregate of mechanical events, one leading "blindly" to another, a teleological explanation projects an end in advance of experience which allows various elements to be seen to be working together as an organic whole in pursuit of the end. Thus, in a teleological judgment, there is the assumption of a concept which allows us to perceive unity in a situation for which there is no basis in the mere causal structure of events as observed through intuition. (p. 38)

In both cases, Cazeaux said, an antinomy pertains between the particular and the general:

> [It is] the conflict between, on the one hand, a judgment (whether aesthetic or teleological) seeming to be about what is personal . . . and, on the other, the same judgment also seeming to employ a concept (universal agreement in aesthetics, and organic unity in teleology) for which there is no empirical warrant. (p. 38)

Kant (1987) resolved the antinomy via the ramification of the rule of judgment into two modalities, the determinative and the reflective, the latter of which consists in a straightforward assertion of analogical agency.

The determinative modality operates by the association of objects and experiences with the qualities of which they partake, categorizing them. The reflective modality operates in cases where universal principles are not apparent. Reflective judgments, Cazeaux (2007) said, "are attached to experiences where no determining concept is available or where an available concept is inadequate to the experience" (p. 38). Kant discerned aesthetic and teleological judgments as reflective, removing the difficulty that, despite the theoretical need for one, there is no empirically warrantable concept to universalize such forms of judgment. In the absence of a clear candidate for conceptual supersensibility, Kant allowed that one might be drafted analogically from sensibility. Cazeaux said,

> [S]ince judgment, by Kant's own lights, always requires a concept, what reflective judgment does in these circumstances, he argues, is not categorize its object but *produce a concept* [emphasis added] which reflects its own capacity to form a judgment, to get a purchase on the phenomenon before it which is posing this challenge to categorization. (pp. 38–39)

Kant's (1987) schematic requirement that judgment must involve "the ability to think the particular as contained under the universal" (p. 18) demands of reflective judgment an overtly fictive process to assert a supersensible concept appropriate to judgment. "The concept that is produced is 'nature's subjective purposiveness,' the concept that nature appears *as if* [emphasis added] it were designed for our awareness" (Cazeaux, 2007, p. 39). Reflective judgment, Kant (1987) said, posits an a priori principle that

> what to human insight is contingent in the particular (empirical) natural laws does nevertheless contain a law-governed unity, unfathomable but still conceivable by us, in the combination of what is diverse in them to [form] an experience that is intrinsically [*an sich*] possible. (p. 23)

Subjective purposiveness, then, is the regulator for the classification of contingent experience. To restate, Kant's formulation of purposiveness as a projection from the phenomenal realm onto the noumenal realm resolves the antinomy raised by the formation of judgments that, Cazeaux (2007) said, concern either individual aesthetic sensibilities or "material events produced in accordance with 'blindly' mechanical laws," and require the application of a concept, whether "universal agreement in aesthetics" or "organic unity in teleology," that appears to have "no empirical warrant" (p. 38). "Purposiveness," Cazeaux said,

> represents not the presence of a particular order in nature (this would mean the concept of purposiveness was being exercised determinatively) but the possibility of order in nature, not the determination but the determinability of nature. . . . Claiming aesthetic and teleological judgments as reflective therefore removes their respective antinomies, since their universal character is shown to follow not from the determinative application of a concept . . . but instead from reflection on the purposiveness of nature for our judgment. (p. 39)

In this way, subjectivity is seen not to conflict with generalization, the requirement to think the particular under the universal. By reflecting on *what must be* were its perception to be valid, subjectivity produces the deductively unwarrantable, but cognitively necessary, concept of purposiveness to satisfy the need of perception for universality and necessity.

Reflective judgment *analogically* fashions the rational necessity for contingencies to cohere. "The analogy at the heart of the concept of nature's subjective purposiveness," Cazeaux (2007) said, is "the possibility that the mind can intersect with a *determinable* nature" (p. 39). To obtain its validity as the regulator of judgment, subjective purposiveness requires that the open-endedness of empirical contingency be understood *as if* it were compassed by a structuring, transcendental circumstance. Kant was, in a sense, circling back to his starting point, the rescue of metaphysics from Humean skepticism, and doing it via metaphor.

Significantly for our eventual consideration of metaphor in imaginal psychology, the path Kant forged between the insular domains leads him from a pivotal analogy directly to archetype. The passage in the third *Critique* that Cazeaux (2007) said amounts to "the most forthright" (p. 39) account of the analogy establishing subjective purposiveness is Kant's (1987) claim that

> the purposiveness that we must presuppose even for cognizing the inner possibility of many natural things is quite unthinkable to us and is beyond our grasp unless we think of it, and of the world as such, as a product of an intelligent cause (a God). (p. 282)

We here arrive at the inevitable logocentric singularity. The analogical context, however, enables us to construe *intelligent cause* without reference to a vanishing point outside the play of signifiers. Indeed, it suggests that intelligent cause is the play of signifiers.

Kant referred to this cause, in the terms he reserved for the structures of pure reason, as the *intuitive understanding*, and also as an *intellectus archetypus* (p. 292). As a consequence, the archetype, or a priori concept of metaphoricity, might be understood as the *modus vivendi* that conciliates the double oppositions necessary to Kant's analytic: noumena and phenomena, and pure and practical reason. The domains become adequated, as Cazeaux demonstrated, through the function of the analogical "as-if." Kant's critical method, which looks beyond truth claims to the conditions of their possibility, contains, in the instance of the *intellectus archetypus*, a suggestion of metaphysical supposition *as* metaphorical process. Were we to surpass Kant's transcendental boundary, in the company of a certain guide of souls, we would expect in that undiscovered country to encounter the archetype-in-itself. Would not this spectral figure *be* the as-if?

Once he nominated subjective purposiveness as legislator in the rule of judgment, Kant (1987) prepared to employ its mediating function in the relations of understanding (nature) and reason (freedom). Linking the supersensibles with one another was a step toward linking the supersensible with the sensible to form a coherent epistemology. To join the supersensibles, Kant had to establish the conditions of possibility that would allow an "understanding other than our own," that is, the intuitive understanding of the pure reason, or what we now know as the *intellectus archetypus*, to serve as enabler of subjective purposiveness, an understanding that *is* our own. For this, he employed the third nested analogy.

The *intellectus archetypus*, Cazeaux (2007) said, "is the origin of its own reality" (p. 40). It allows for "no distinction between the possible and the actual" since "all objects cognized by it simply exist" (p. 40). In contrast, the form of comprehension on the phenomenal side of the transcendental divide is, in Kant's terminology, an *intellectus ectypus*, that which gains a purchase on the world by surveying its perceptions, working discursively from contingency to necessity. Therein lies the antimony. To establish subjective purposiveness, the discursive understanding must identify with a form of immediate, intuitive cognition that is contrary to its very nature as contingency. "How," Cazeaux (2007) asked,

> is it possible to have a concept of the purposive determinability of nature which does not involve a contradiction between, on the one hand, the contingency with which discursive understanding works up from the parts to the wholes and, on the other, the necessity with which the parts follow from the wholes characteristic of intuitive understanding? (pp. 40–41)

Kant resolved the contradiction between the contingency native to the discursive understanding (*intellectus ectypus*) and the necessity inherent in the intuitive understanding (*intellectus archetypus*) by analogy to practical reason.

Only practical reason, Kant (1987) said, can cognize the causality that allows contingencies to seem purposive. Purpose

> could not have arisen according to mere natural laws, laws we can cognize by understanding alone as applied to objects of sense, but requires that even empirical cognition of this form [purposiveness] in terms of its cause and effect presupposes concepts of reason. (p. 248)

The conceptual presupposition, or transcendental regulator, is that of the practical reason, which supplies the contingencies of free will with the adhesion of cause and effect. Because its relationship to contingency is akin to the same relationship had by practical reason, the rule of judgment must be seen to function according to the type of purposiveness that regulates practical reason. "The very contingency [of the rule of judgment] is a basis for regarding the product [of its reflection] *as if* it had come about through a causality that only [practical] reason can have" (p. 248; original emphasis). Subjective purposiveness thus establishes its regulation of judgment by way of analogy to the rule of practical reason.

Aesthetic and teleological judgments can thus assert universality because they presuppose the form of purposiveness in which contingencies are exigent. Cazeaux (2007) said,

> The concept of practical reason can supply this sense of contingency because of the distinction it admits between moral necessity and causal necessity. The objective necessity of a moral, duty-bound action is of a quite different kind from the necessity that the act would have if it were an event with its basis in nature. (p. 41)

The analogy from the rule of practical reason to the rule of judgment that provides subjective purposiveness with its regulative agency suggests the further deduction that the border between practical and pure reason may similarly be replete with analogy. Kant's "as if," the marker of metaphorical deduction, demonstrates, Cazeaux said, "How discursive understanding [whether of practical reason or of subjective purposiveness] can borrow a notion of determinability from the concept of an intuitive understanding" (p. 41). The as-if serves to affiliate the disparate transcendental domains by analogical reference of one to the other, in the process coaxing new subjective possibilities into awareness.

From the perspective of analytical psychology, which posits the studies of the alchemists as a metaphor for individuation, what we could call the subjective purposiveness of the psyche, the analogies that bootstrap contingency to purpose qualify as an *opus contra naturum*. Similarly to the sense of universality attained by reflective (aesthetic and teleological) judgment in its analogy to the universal and necessary a priori of pure and practical reason, individuation amounts to a differential relation in which distinctiveness is grasped as situated participation in, or *as*, the *manifold*. (Both Kant and Jung use the latter term. For Kant, it refers to sensibility that is unified a priori in the categories of the understanding. For Jung, it refers to the sensibility that is unified in the categories of the imagination, the archetypes.) Reflective judgment works against "nature" by employing reason's determinate presuppositions for determinable ends. Patricia Berry (2008) is helpful here. The determinate "nature" against which psychological purpose is engaged (note the paradox of an oppositional *engagement*) is not the prima materia of "the animal, the body, the dark, the sensual, the feminine" (p. 156). It is "nature" as a naturalistic reduction, "an archetypal mode that would justify things in terms of their being 'only natural', nothing-but, bread-and-butter, down-to-earth, factual, practical" (p. 154). Such a mode is unaware of its "metaphorical value" (p. 157). By framing contingency in terms of purposiveness, and thereby transposing subjectivities into objectivities, reflective judgment introduces metaphorical value into determinate experience. It admits of a regulatory, or archetypal, mode, subjective purposiveness, aware of its metaphoricity. Reflective judgment is in this sense an *a-propriation*, that is, a de-literalization; it deflects the *proper*, the determinate, by *re*flecting it in terms appropriate to its own (*propre*) idiosyncratic stance. Reflection, the opus of the speculative tradition, becomes aware that its claim as a mirror of nature amounts not to a re-presentation of any absolute, but instead to an absolution or abreaction, a cathartic presentation, or making-present, of psychological inclinations. Hillman (1985) put the schema of analogical referral among domains in depth psychological terms when he said of the phenomenology of the anima that it tends to be given in compensatory and speculative, or mirror-image, tandems or pairings: "[A]nima is the reflective partner; she it is who provides the moment of reflection in the midst of what is naturally given" (p. 23).

We have now seen how three of Cazeaux's nested analogies allowed Kant to account for the reconciliation of the supersensibles. "The mediating condition produced by judgment," Cazeaux (2007) said,

> is the concept of nature's subjective purposiveness. The concept allows us to think of the two supersensibles 'occupying the same space', so to speak, because it represents the idea of the supersensible substrate of nature in terms of, that is, by analogy with, the supersensible substrate of freedom and its contingent effects in the physical world. . . . Mediation between the two supersensibles is conveyed by thinking of the causality of nature being used as a tool by the causality of freedom. (p. 42)

In this sweeping analogical operation, Kant forged commonality between the supersensibles to enable the empirical exhibition of intuitive understanding. By concerning the third *Critique* with "the problem of conceptualization" (Friedrich, 1977, p. xxxix), Kant erected his architectonic at the crossroads of Hume's *is–ought* conundrum, the "gap of nature and freedom" (p. xxxviii). The mutual reference of the supersensible of nature and the supersensible of freedom, their consanguinity in the crucible of metaphor, supplies a basis by which Kant could then cause the noumenal and phenomenal domains to be grasped in terms of one another. Through the determinability of reflective judgment, contingent truths (phenomena) could be thought in terms of necessary and universal, or a priori truths (noumena), and so supplied with purposiveness. The rule of judgment is thus established by analogy to the possibility of an a priori condition, formulated as the concept of subjective purposiveness, and understood to operate, Cazeaux (2007) said, by "the contingency that is appropriate for our discursive power of judgment," in other words, the contingency that enables the particular to be understood analogously to the universal (p. 42). Having achieved by analogy the condition of the possibility of universal judgment, Kant then took the centrality of metaphor a step beyond its identification as the structuring factor in the analytic to a remarkable assertion of "the necessarily analogical nature of judgment" (p. 44), the fourth and final nested analogy.

What reflective judgment reflects *upon*, Cazeaux (2007) said, is our capacity to "apply concepts to intuitions, and to entertain the possibility that alternative concept-intuition mappings are available" (p. 45). This reflective process is intrinsically metaphorical. Like metaphor, its epistemological power lies in its capacity to transfer "a concept from one object to another" (p. 45). It is the metaphorical transfer inherent in reflective judgment that enables us to cognize our capacity for generalized judgment in terms of the a priori concepts that structure our understanding of the natural world and our capacity to exercise freedom of action:

> Analogy becomes not only the "opening of possibilities" which allows the two supersensibles to be combined in a coherent schema, but also the form of thinking which lets us see freedom intersecting with nature, lets us explore how objects or states of affairs *ought* to be conceptualized. (p. 45)

Kant's heuristic depiction of the legislative capacity of reflective judgment, Cazeaux (2007) said, demonstrates how, like metaphor, it holds disparate domains in the same space:

> Because the subject has this possibility [of judgment] within him, while outside [of him] there is also the possibility that nature will [purposively] harmonize with [the judgment], judgment finds itself referred to something that is both in the subject himself and outside him, something that is neither nature nor freedom and yet is linked with the basis of freedom, the supersensible, in which the theoretical and practical power are in an unknown manner combined and joined into a unity. (p. 229)

The metaphorical mode of antithetical relationality native to reflective judgment links "subject and object, or freedom and nature . . . without entirely collapsing the distinction between [them]" (p. 46). This is the same interactive quality that characterizes the metaphorical *pseudo-domain* encountered earlier in which interactive empirical and theoretical domains "are never wholly combined to produce a new domain but always remain in a complex or tensile state" (p. 46). Purposiveness, as a concept produced by reflective judgment, is not only created by analogy, but "represents or embodies the performance of analogical thought itself" (p. 45). Put another way, analogy is "the procedure by which the concept of purposiveness operates in Kant's system" (p. 45).

With his conclusion that purposiveness, the pivotal term in the inquiry, functions as an analogical transaction, Cazeaux's (2007) spade work has attained a level of depth at which the layered concepts in the critical project give way to sheer liminality:

> In order for there to be determinability between our faculties and the world there must be, in between them, an analogical middle-ground of possible presentations which is not itself a domain where theoretical or practical legislation takes place. This is what purposiveness, exhibited as the meeting of two causalities, represents. (p. 45)

The fulcrum of Kant's critique lies at this transactional level of thought:

> It is, I suggest, the density of analogy which on the one hand allows Kant to claim unity for his system by apparently collapsing the distinction between the inside and the outside of the subject ("something that is both in the subject himself and outside him, something that is neither nature nor freedom"), yet which on the other hand allows Kant to keep the subject-object distinction in place by maintaining the notion of an "external" object for judgment ("judgment finds itself referred to something . . . [supersensible] in which the theoretical and practical are in an unknown manner combined and joined as a unity"). (Cazeaux, 2007, p. 46)

Cazeaux's study suggests that Kant was able to accommodate the paradoxes of his system by imbricating it with the paradoxical ana-logic of metaphor. Discerning the metaphoric nature of Kant's keystone, subjective purposiveness, Cazeaux awakens us to the weight (or wait) sustained by metaphor in philosophy.

To extract from Kant's work an anticipation of the modern, interaction theory of metaphor, I now turn to Kirk Pillow and A. T. Nuyen. Interaction will concern us in more detail when we consider its founding thinker, Max Black, in Chapter 4 on the cognitive turn. For our immediate purposes, it is sufficient to employ Pillow's definition, although with a variance. Of the argument from interaction, Pillow (2001) said, "Metaphors establish original affinities between features of the world, rather than discovering pregiven ones" (p. 197). By "pregiven," I take Pillow to refer to the view of the pre-interaction, or *comparison*, theory of metaphor that words correspond in a determinate way to their referents. The allowance by the interaction theory of a generative impulse marks a departure from the school that prevailed from Aristotle on, taking metaphor at the level of substantives as a comparison of the features of one thing to those of another. I want to doubt an indication that "pregiven" may refer to the Romantic tenet that latent features woven into the fabric of the implicate order might be unconcealed by the co-creative subject. I do not believe that the interaction theory entails a rejection of discoverable meaning. In my reading, interaction is consistent with the view that meaning is discovered as well constructed. An argument might be made for either position alongside the view of metaphor as a cognitive disposition that calls forth worldviews.

Interaction is of consequence because it demonstrates that metaphors do more than draw attention to established aspects of comparative subjects; rather, the "comparisons" are juxtapositions generating new knowledge and new realities by forging nonobvious relationships. The theory unconceals metaphor's cognitive aspect, hidden for millennia by philosophy. By demonstrating that metaphor is not merely a decorative—and misleading—form of language, but a cognitive process that creates meaning, interaction makes a case for metaphor's philosophic agency contra the view that it obscures the truth. Perhaps more radically, by staking an epistemological claim for metaphor, interaction integrates philosophy's split-off poetic dimension.

A central tenet is the idea of metaphor's inexhaustibility. Interaction makes no anterior presumption of a final point of semantic convergence. The interaction that takes place in the play of signifiers is seen to be open-ended, a process in which a coevolution of domains produces continual semantic novelty in that it "applies terms beyond their accepted domains" (Pillow, 2001, p. 193). It transfers a domain of meaning occupied by an object or event to that of another object or event, producing a reorientation that expands the semantic boundaries of both domains. Using Black's classic example, "People are wolves," Pillow (2001) notes that what gets transferred between "people" and "wolves" amounts to more than apparent similarities. The *transference* invokes "a set of connotations" or an "implication-complex" (p. 197) that, once activated, alters our understanding of both relata. "The process is 'interactive'," Pillow explained,

> because the primary subject influences what connotations of the secondary subject seem relevant, those connotations in turn spark a new consideration of the primary subject, and our understanding of even the secondary subject is transformed through the invented isomorphism. Assuming we find some truth in the metaphor "people are wolves" (we may well not), our perspective on both people and wolves is transformed in the process. (p. 197)

In another explanatory remark that can be read in our context to further the connotation to psychoanalytic transference, Pillow said: "By this [interactive] means, metaphor promotes the reorganization of our patterns of discrimination extending terms into new territory by forming novel links between previously unrelated phenomena" (p. 197).

A similarly undetermined view of the meaning-making function is also expressed by Jung. Regarding the carrying capacity of the archetypes, he said,

> the discriminating intellect naturally keeps on trying to establish their singleness of meaning and thus misses the essential point: for what we can above all establish as the one thing consistent with their nature is their *manifold meaning*, their almost limitless wealth of reference, which makes any unilateral formulation impossible. (CW 9, I, par. 80)

Immediately following this remark is another that is also allusive of metaphoric interaction. "Besides this," that is, the manifold meaning of the archetypes, "they are in principle paradoxical, just as for the alchemists the spirit was conceived as 'senex et iuvenis simul'—an old man and a youth at once" (CW 9, I, par. 80). We will revisit this configuration in Part II when we query whether Hillman's formula *senex et puer* is emblematic of an imaginal metaphorics.

Pillow (2001) discerned presentiments of the interaction theory in the aesthetic idea described in the third *Critique*. Not surprisingly, given what we know from Cazeaux (2007) about the structuring role played by metaphor in the *Critique*, the aesthetic idea provides Kant with a means to link rational concepts to lived experience. We must therefore first inquire into the topic of the rational concept to effectively broach that of the aesthetic idea. Though Pillow explains that the exhibition of the rational concept is not Kant's sole application of the aesthetic idea—it is also "the expressed content of works of art" (2001, p. 202)—for purposes of this overview, I will treat only its application to the rational concept. The rational concept is among three types, with the pure concept (the forms of the intuition and the categories) and the empirical concept, proposed by Kant as regulators of experience. The three types of the concept, and their expressions, are given explanatory treatment by Nuyen (1989) in his essay "The Kantian Theory of Metaphor." The project of distinguishing among the concepts that occupies Kant in the *Critique of Judgment*, Nuyen said, is one that seeks to delineate rational concepts from empirical concepts. At an earlier stage of the critical project, Kant made a demarcation between rational concepts and pure concepts. Both are at issue in the *Critique of Pure Reason*, the former in the transcendental dialectic, the latter in the transcendental analytic. As we know, the task was to distinguish the means by which the conceptual domain makes contact with the empirical domain, the joinder of supersensibles to the sensible. The schema of the critical philosophy, Nuyen said, requires the adhesion provided by a factor Kant thought of as "real" meaning, or "significance" (p. 96). Absent this criterion, the concept in itself fails as a universal condition of experience; instead "we only have a mere word with no more than a 'logical' meaning" (p. 96). Concepts then lack empirical necessity, as with Hume's causation, and we fall back into the error of all prior metaphysics.

There will be more to say about how pure and empirical concepts obtain significance below, but briefly, Kant (1987) distinguished the real meaning of pure and empirical concepts as, in a sense, ready-made. On the one side, the categories of the understanding have inherent significance for the sensible realm because of their formal quality. On the other side, the real meaning of empirical concepts is equally self-evident because they are experiential to begin with. But rational concepts, what Nuyen (1989) followed Kant in calling "ideas of reason," and their distinction from empirical concepts, give cause for greater difficulty. This is so, Nuyen said, because ideas of reason—"freedom," "immortality," or "God" are Kant's most prevalent examples—"could be empirical under some circumstances, but rational under others" (p. 96). As Nuyen said,

> If [the rational concept] "justice" is regarded as derivable from various just acts in the way envisaged by Aristotle, then the concept is empirical. If, on the other hand, it is regarded as an ideal form in Plato's sense, of which various just acts are imperfect instantiations, then it is a rational concept. (p. 96)

Kant (1996) said that the "Ideas [of reason] contain a certain completeness to which no possible empirical cognition is adequate" (A568/B596). Therefore, if such ideas are to be susceptible of experience, that is, if they are to express real meaning, it is necessary for them to couple with forms of empirical presentation.

Rational concepts are susceptible of two types of presentation that enable the empirical realization of the logical object: symbols and aesthetic ideas. As noted, it is the aesthetic idea that Pillow (2001) perceived as a forerunner to metaphor on the interaction theory. In his view, the presentation of the rational concept in symbolic form can be assimilated to the earlier, Aristotelian theory. Beginning with the aesthetic idea, let us examine how each of these metaphoric operations create the significance or real meaning that connects noumenal and phenomenal realms. Kant (1987) set forth his system of aesthetic ideas in Section 49 of the third *Critique*. The "proper function" of an aesthetic idea, he said, "is to quicken the mind by opening up for it a view into an immense realm of kindred presentations" (p. 183). Such expansiveness conjures the host of meaning marshaled by metaphor on the interaction theory. "Kant characterizes the aesthetic idea more specifically as a presentation of the imagination that spurs an open-ended reflection on the meaning of some given concept," Pillow said (2001, p. 199).

Kant's (1987) term for the imaginative presentations of a concept is *aesthetic attribute* (p. 314). The attributes, taken collectively, yield the idea. Attributes provide the empirical "exhibition" (Kant's term) of "an object whose concept is a rational idea and hence cannot be exhibited adequately" (p. 314), Pillow said. By the presentation of an object as the sensible correlate of a rational concept, attributes are able to manifest an otherwise non-empirical idea. The "exhibition" to sensibility of a rational idea requires such an articulation as the attributes provide because rational ideas "lie beyond the bounds of experience" (Kant, 1987, p. 314). In further pursuit of the archetype-as-metaphor theory it becomes relevant here to note that Pillow's explication of Kant adds nuance to the Kantian etiology of the Jungian archetype.[2] A chain of inference emerges linking the aesthetic idea to metaphor and both to archetype and its carnal imperative. The exhibitionism of the rational idea, its necessity of objectification, evinces a relation between the aesthetic idea and the archetypal image, both phenomenal presentations of an inaccessible noumenal domain. Further, the Kantian metaphorics that Pillow brings out enables us to understand the phenomenology of the archetype as an aesthetic production of the poetic basis of mind. It allows us to see metaphor-in-the-world. Using terms coined by Hillman (1983a) to render the worldly quality of soul, or anima, we might describe this form of *poietics* as the "animalized" or "animated" nature of archetype (p. 72).

Kant's examples of aesthetic attributes are the eagle and the peacock. These animal images endow a terse conceptuality with articulation, enlivening it, giving it flight:

> Thus Jupiter's eagle with the lightening in its claws is an attribute of the mighty king of heaven, and the peacock is an attribute of heaven's stately queen. [Through] these attributes, unlike [through] logical attributes, [we] do not present the content of our concepts of the sublimity and majesty of creation, but present something different, something that prompts the imagination to spread over a multitude of kindred presentations that arouse more thought than can be expressed in a concept determined by words. These aesthetic attributes yield an aesthetic idea, which serves the mentioned rational idea as a substitute for a logical exhibition. (Kant, 1987, p. 183)

Like metaphors on the interaction view, Pillow (2001) said, the aesthetic idea is "fulfilled" by the multiplicity of connotations initiated by the maker of the image and the interaction with these connotations by those who experience it (p. 200). The "open-ended unfolding of connotations," Pillow said, enables the likening of the aesthetic idea to the view of metaphor as an interactive phenomenon (p. 201). Further, similar to the aesthetic attribute, metaphors produced by the interaction of diverse semantic domains enable the expression of latent or even uncreated realities, effectively bringing them into conscious existence. It is principally this latter effect, the formation of new paradigms, that distinguishes metaphor on the interaction theory—in Pillow's lexicon, *strong* metaphor—from the ages-old Aristotelian form, the comparison of preexisting attributes, which Pillow called *weak* metaphor for the reason that it deals in known quantities and stops short of opening unheard of perspectives.

Pillow's (2001) weak form is Kantian analogy, a display of the objective correlate of the rational idea not via aesthetic attributes building to an aesthetic idea, but via symbolic exhibition. In Section 59 of the *Critique*, Kant (1987) distinguished two means by which objects become illustrative of concepts: schematic and symbolic exhibition. The difference, Kant said, is that "schemata contain direct, and symbols indirect, exhibitions of the concept" (p. 227). The Kantian "schemata" are immediate associations of categories of the understanding to objects. Again, the pure a priori concept is understood to be given to awareness complete with its objects in schematized form. Schematic association, Pillow said, constitutes "an intuition that literally embodies the content of the concept" (2001, p. 194). Paul Ricoeur (1978), drawing out the illustrative agency of "image" in the operation of the imagination, said schematic association is possible in part because of the properties of "seeing" and "picturing" by which the imagination "generates rapprochement" across "logical distance" (p. 150). The schematic mode, as in the case of practical reason, is not always pertinent to cognition. Because experience is not consequential with the rational idea, Pillow said, its significance, the "real" meaning necessary for the schema, is therefore borrowed from "analogically expressive intuitions," that is, symbols (2001, p. 195).

The explication of symbolic exhibition requires that we distinguish two meanings of *symbol*, its indication in analytical psychology of libidinal force, or as Hillman (1978b) put it, of "an emotional atmosphere" (p. 139), and its Kantian use to mean depiction by analogy. The function of analogy, Pillow follows Kant in explaining, is such that three given terms, *A*, *B*, and *C*, infer an unknown fourth term, *D*, in the ratio *A*:*B*::*C*:*D*. In a quantitative analysis, the fourth term is determinate. Three known quantities produce a definitive fourth. But in a qualitative analysis, such as the a posteriori search for objects of practical reason, only the rule underlying the operation is determinate. The fourth term is determinable; it must be sought in experience. "Instead of providing an intuition that literally embodies the content of the concept, symbolic exhibition appeals to an incongruent entity whose concept shares analogical features with the original," Pillow said (2001, p. 194). The practical reason rifles through intuitions in search of an empirical association that will confer significance, or "real" meaning, upon the rational idea. Kant's famous examples are the analogies of despotism to a hand mill and of constitutional monarchy (under which he lived) to an organic process:

> Symbolic exhibition uses an analogy . . . in which judgment performs a double function: it applies the concept to the object of a sensible intuition; and then it applies the mere rule by which it reflects on that intuition to an entirely different object, of which the former object is only the symbol. Thus a monarchy ruled according to its own constitutional laws would be presented as an animate body, but a monarchy ruled by an individual absolute will would be presented as a mere machine (such as a hand mill); but in either case the presentation is only symbolic. (Kant, 1987, p. 227)

Kantian symbols, "analogically expressive intuitions" (Pillow, 2001, p. 195), in this way become the connective tissue through which vital exchange takes place between the noumenal and the phenomenal.

Having availed ourselves of Pillow's insights into two types of Kantian metaphor, aesthetic ideas and analogical symbols, let us turn to his thoughts on Kantian imagination. Although the imagination provides the defining quality of the transcendental subject, the a priori synthesis of the forms of the intuition with the categories of the understanding absent which there can be no apperception of sensible objects, Kant (1996) was equivocal about its status. In the first edition of the *Critique of Pure Reason*, he conceived of the synthetic operation that enables sensible representations presented by the forms of the intuition to find recognition under the categories of the understanding as a function of the imagination.

In the second edition, however, he conflated the imagination with the understanding, remarking that they were two names for the same function (B162n). Henry Allison (1983) ascribed the alteration to "Kant's concern to avoid the criticisms that were raised against the first edition . . . because of its apparently psychological and phenomenalistic thrust" (p. 163).

Pillow (2001) considered each of Kant's uses of *imagination* to refer to cognition, but in differing senses. The revised imagination of the second edition, seen as an aspect of the understanding, Pillow regarded as cognitive in the strict sense of a rational function of mind. But the term as used in the first edition, he suggested, can refer to cognition in a broader sense that encompasses knowledge derived on an aesthetic basis, one that is affective and not strictly analytical. The revised use describes the operation referred to above, the synthesis that unites the intuitively structured presentations of sensibility with their conceptual categories. Kant (1996) called this synthesis an operation of the *productive* imagination (as distinguished from the *reproductive* imagination, which has to do with memory). "The principle of the necessary unity of the imagination's pure (productive) synthesis prior to apperception is the basis for the possibility of all cognition, especially of experience," he said (A118). But in the original sense, Pillow said, imagination "plays with its productive powers independently of conceptual determination" (2001, p. 204). Exceeding its role as a function of the understanding, the synthesis makes possible the antecedent affinity of the manifold within which rational cognition exercises its discriminatory capacities. "Only if imagination provides an affinity-limned whole to conceptual thinking," Pillow explained, "can elements of that whole be ordered in the manner specific to subsumption under concepts" (p. 204). In this broader construal, imagination is both precedential to analytical cognition, and, in an emphasis of Pillow's word choice, it is liminal. Not only does it constitute a threshold condition for analytical cognition, but, functioning independently of the rule-bearing understanding, it also "explores the indeterminate affinity of the manifold" (p. 204). Like metaphor on the interaction theory; it is *acategorically* creative. Were we to conceive of thought as a field of exertion drawing philosophy and poetry into the möbiuslike relation described by their intersection in the Western tradition, we might see such a synthetic process as a product of the liminal imagination. We could regard the liminal imagination in the manner of reflective judgment, also conceived as a function of autonomy, to be free-associative or amplicative. Susan Rowland (2006), writing on Jung's theory of the numinous, said of liminality that it is "a quality denoting disputed regions between consciousness and the unconscious, the conceivable and the unknowable, the 'inside' psyche and the 'exterior' cosmos, of the distinction between form and matter" (p. 98). The quality of inter-regional, or inter-modal passage among discrete domains of mentation is also invoked by Pillow in his description of the aesthetic imagination, in which he employs a key term of the metaphorics advanced in this study. The aesthetic imagination "celebrates the inter-connectedness of all presentations," Pillow said, "and in metaphorical expression realizes this affinity in instances of *uncanny* relation" (2001, p. 204; emphasis added).

Here again we can take the uncanny as a metaphorical dynamism that forges relation among incommensurable faculties of mind and the perceptions they synthesize. For philosophical consciousness, as I argued, such a factor may appear "monstrous." A poststructural awareness may regard it less menacingly as a "rupture," or a bifurcation in the logocentric ecology that furthers efflorescence. The role of the aesthetic imagination in the constitution of an integrated subject, and its kinship with metaphor, provides a philosophical counterpart to the application of the terms *imagination* and *metaphor* in imaginal psychology. There, as we will see in Part II, the *mundus imaginalis*—a *tertium quid* that is neither (and both) phenomenal and noumenal—functions as metaphorical *pseudo-domain*.

In the history of metaphor, Kant's third *Critique* represents an axial shift. As Pillow demonstrated, it contains vestiges of Aristotelian sensibility while it also anticipates a philosophical theory conducive to the richness of metaphor's epistemological—or as Rorty (1979) suggestively put it, post-epistemological, or hermeneutic—potential. Pillow's formulation of Kant's schema, in which the "imagination discloses the affinity of the manifold to be the aesthetic condition of all conceptual cognition" (2001, p. 204), indicates the basic *poietic* circumstance. An overtly aesthetic theory of cognition would have to await the arrival of Nietzsche, but it can claim a forerunner in the counter-philosophical strain of Kant's thought. Just when Kant, the avatar of the *Aufklärung*, arrived at the pivotal moment to set in place the keystone of his analytic—the supporting element at the intersection of the sensible and the supersensible—he turned to Romanticism. For the Romantics, Richard Rorty (1999) noted, "imagination, rather than reason is the central human faculty" (p. 7).[3] Advancing the interaction theory, Black (1962) gave credit for its inception to Richards, whose ideas on metaphor derived from the Romantic poets. "Coleridge and Wordsworth in particular," as Pillow (2011) said, "borrowed their idea of an artistically ingenious, productive imagination from Kant's aesthetic theory" (p. 206). Nuyen (1989) as well endorsed the chain of inference. "It is the Kantian theory," he said, "that gives epistemic legitimacy to the visions of poets and artists, long relegated to the fringes of knowledge" (p. 108).

Before we leave Kant, we must consider one other analysis of his work pertinent to metaphor and imaginal psychology. It was undertaken by Stephanie De Voogd (1977), who invoked Goethe to make the point that Jung's avowed adherence to Kant's theory of knowledge was contrary to Jung's own discoveries. Goethe was no detractor. In a conversation with Schopenhauer cited by Patricia Kitcher (1996), he "compared reading a page of Kant to the feeling he had when entering a brightly lit room" (p. xxvii). Despite the overwhelm of clarity, De Voogd quoted Goethe as saying of the *Critique of Pure Reason*, "What is omitted here is the imagination" (1977, p. 179). As we have seen, this is not strictly true. More specifically, what De Voogd discerned in Goethe's remark was that the imagination is absent from Kant's schema in a nonliteral sense.

For Kant, De Voogd (1977) explained, the defining question was whether anything could be said about the transcendental realm. Kant, she said, did not argue that noumenal entities do not exist, but that they are not cognizable by the senses, which, for him, served as the starting point of experience. But once we take note of imaginative experience, De Voogd said, "We can no longer regard the [sensate] world as the starting point of human experience. Instead, we must now regard that experience as always embedded in an imaginal context" (p. 179). With reference to the problematizing of the literal in *Re-Visioning Psychology*, De Voogd concluded that rather than a question of noumena versus phenomena, "the real issue was one of literalism versus de-literalization" (p. 180).

The revolution in Kant's thinking, De Voogd (1977) said, lay in his reclassification of noumena from objects of knowledge to objects of belief. Kant established the existence of things-in-themselves as analogues to experience, the conditions that must pertain to render experience as it is. But he did not similarly insist upon the analogical nature of the noumenal realm. Kant "opposed the positing of *literal* transcendent worlds *literally* peopled by *literal* transcendent entities" (De Voogd, 1977, p. 180). In other words, "he changed their status from 'transcendentally real' to 'as-if real': he deliteralized them" (p. 180). Yet by positing the noumenal as absolute, Kant deliteralized it "in a literal way" (p. 180). Jung's adherence to the validity of the Kantian epistemology holds a line against claims that he was more mystic and metaphysician than medical doctor and scientific investigator. Nevertheless, said De Voogd, Jung "dissolved" the Kantian distinction between "bread-and-butter" phenomena (recall Berry's use of the same descriptor for a naturalism devoid of metaphorical value) and "other-worldly" noumena by formulating experience as a *metaphorical* embrace of both the tangible and the imaginal.

"Imagination," De Voogd (1977) quoted Goethe as saying, "is the fourth faculty in addition to the sense, the Understanding and Reason" (p. 179). (Is this perhaps an argument, echoing Jung's in another context, for the assumption of a fourth, and compensating, element into the dry trinity of philosophical thought?) To sound an early note on a theme that we will have occasion to revisit in Part II, the literalism of the transcendental is precisely where human shipwreck lies. Kant (1996) put it this way:

> This land [of the pure understanding] is an island, and enclosed in unalterable boundaries by nature itself. It is the land of truth (a charming name), surrounded by a broad and stormy ocean, the true seat of illusion, where many a fog bank and rapidly melting iceberg pretend to be new lands and, ceaselessly deceiving with empty hopes the voyager looking around for new discoveries, entwine him in adventures from which he can never escape and yet also never bring to an end. (p. 303)

Islands of truth, emerging as they do on the horizon, undoubtedly exert their charms, appearing to literal, philosophical "man" as surety against illusion, yet they are accreted of metaphor, this-worldly function struggling to be born of imagination. In his preface to the essays of Gaston Bachelard, Northrop Frye (1964) said the "constructing power" of the imagination is in "the figures of simile and metaphor . . . so adhesive that they spread all over the universe. The pursuit of one mythical complex tends to absorb all other myths into it" (p. vi).

The danger of metaphor, as we are shortly to be warned in our encounter with Nietzsche, is that its status as a "constructing power" becomes forgotten in favor of the hypostatization of any single myth that then "absorbs" all others. A poetics of mind keeps the imaginal faculty, in which metaphor operates, in the foreground of awareness, maintaining the labile quality of mythic structuring. The absence of the imaginal as a coeval and concurrent function of mind alongside the rational creates conditions for the possibility of foundational fantasies in the sense of structural absolutes. Only the imaginal "angle of perception" (Frye, 1964, p. v) discerns the empirical reality of images, archetypes, or conditions of possibility that would otherwise be thought noumenal objects marvelously immune from the de-con-structive (paradoxical) play of signifiers. "Far from marveling at the object," said Bachelard (1964), "objective thought must treat it ironically" (p. 1), that is, it must see through it. A phenomenologist who Hillman (1999) called a "philosopher of imagination" (p. 184), Bachelard made the definitive case for an integrated philosophy, which might serve to synopsize our investigation of Kantian metaphor. "The axes of poetry and of science are opposed to one another from the outset," he said. "All that philosophy can hope to accomplish is to make poetry and science complementary, to unite them as two well-defined opposites" (Bachelard, 1964, p. 2).

Complementarity, to repurpose from quantum mechanics, is a matter of the participation of the observing subject. In a certain sense that can be called Kantian, the human is an interpretive structure. Due to our nature as perspective we cannot know the world as it might exist in an uninterpreted state. But such a world exists for Kant, and though we are unable to know it, it "knows" us, that is, it constitutes us as a form of knowing, as an epistemology. We are "known" by the world. In his conclusion to *The Critique of Practical Reason* Kant asserts the significance of "the starry heavens above me and the moral law within me" (1996, 5:161.33–6). For Kant, said Niall Lucy (2005),

> the regulated movements of the stars above correspond to the immanent regulation of human consciousness, which enable subjects to give to themselves laws which are at the same time universal. Such giving or willing involves not only rational thought but also the imagination. One has to imagine (in a "disinterested" fashion) what a universal law would look like, while at the same time willing that law into existence. The way to do this is to make a decision "as if" there were a universal ground for making it and as if the outcome were directly accessible to the mind. (p. 67)

The re-visioning of the immanence/transcendence opposition in terms of the as-if obviates the notion of the in-itself, exchanging an interpretive for the noumenal factor that the transcendental subject despairs of knowing. The swapping out of a pristine in-itself for an interpretive one goes to the point that our epistemologies become our ontologies. It moves us past or post- the epistemological foundation of metaphysics insisted on by Kant into a hermeneutic mode of speculation. We can, in this mode, cognize a de-literalized Kantian divide, still taking as the condition of our possibility the im*pass*ability to any anomalous singularity. Though we cannot help but retain our prophetic being-toward such a singularity, we can re-cognize the essentialist in-itself world in terms of the efflo*rescence* of the as-if world. The world we know will then serve as the same world that "knows," or formulates, us, a world of successive, discontinuous paradigms, archetypes, or vocabularies.

Notes

1 Cazeaux distinguished among Kant's uses of these several terms, but his level of specificity is not necessary for this overview.
2 Though Jung attributed the term "archetype" to Neoplatonic and Patristic writers, including Philo Judaeus, Irenaeus, and Dionysus the Aeropagite (CW 9, I, par. 5), archetypal structure in Jung is Kantian.
3 As Edward Casey (1976) helpfully points out, both rationalists and Romantics subscribe to a hierarchical notion of mental states in which either reason or imagination "is given the place of honor" as sole self-generating faculty (p. 178). As an alternative to such "overestimation," Casey reasonably proposes an acceptance of "the mind's multiplex structure" over any "vertical view" (p. 178).

3
NIETZSCHE

The environment for metaphor began to shift in earnest with the work of Friedrich Nietzsche (1844–1900). In Nietzsche's psychological re-visioning of philosophy, metaphor was liberated from its exile at the metaphysical boundary. It was, so to speak, unbound. This chapter examines Nietzsche's influence largely as it is portrayed by Sarah Kofman (1993), whose *Nietzsche and Metaphor* offers a post-structural account of the catalytic work of metaphor in Nietzsche's construal of subjectivity. Whereas the Kantian subject knows a world as circumscribed by its own conditions of possibility, the Nietzschean subject finds itself wholly and irrevocably across the transcendental Rubicon. In this domain where sheer will-to-power threatens dissociation, a brutal betrayal of integrity is warded off by the march of ideas, those fulsome images of the world through which the blind, and blinding, will finds representation. The distinction that sets apart the subjectivities can be understood in part as that between positivism and philosophical pessimism, or the tragic sense.

As a modern philosophical orientation, positivism is based in the work of Auguste Comte (1798–1857), for whom the only knowledge worthy of a claim to validity was that which is scientifically derived. Empirical observation of physical objects, to the specific exclusion of imagination, was for Comte the basis of the scientific goals of explanation and prediction. Furthermore, societal evolution advances in three distinct stages, theological, metaphysical, and scientific. The value judgment in Comte's developmental schema is that scientific knowledge will ultimately cure all civilizational ills—the philosophical optimism that came under question concurrently with the structuralist turn. The source of positivism, however, is not Comte, or even Kant, by whom he was influenced, but Socrates. The entire rationalist enterprise inaugurated by the Socratic-Platonic admonition that knowledge is virtue placed before the eyes of the West a beatific vision of the perfectability of man.

Whether conceived in Plato's terms, as religious form, or in Aristotle's, as scientific logic, reason triumphant would deliver us from ourselves. The positivist view finds a compensatory perspective in Nietzsche, who, said Paul Raimond Daniels (2013), "posited creativity rather than reason as the essence of the subject, which led him to propose that metaphor is more 'truthful' than truth" (p. 6).

Nietzsche's metaphorical outlook, asserted at the start of his work, in *The Birth of Tragedy*, had an impetus in the myth of Silenus, the satyr and teacher of Dionysus, who, when pressed by King Midas to reveal man's purpose, replies that for such an "ephemeral wretch" as humankind, the best thing is "not to have been born, not to *be*" (Nietzsche, 1967a, p. 29). Nietzsche's view that in the evident absence of ultimate truth, one might, paradoxically, draw constructive potential from the tragic sense of life had its influence in the work of Arthur Schopenhauer (1788–1860). For Schopenhauer, the pessimism so starkly expressed in the Silenus myth was an understandable consequence of the inexorable churning of the world as will, a blindly groping force of supreme indifference to the human condition. In its purposelessness, the will describes a scathing trajectory, carving out a world of representations, whether of nature or human artifice, like landscapes in the wake of a glacier. A Kantian thing-in-itself, the world as will was unknowable, but it could be discerned from its principal representations, subjectivity and objectivity, in that volition, so often contrary to expressed intention, appears to arise from elsewhere. The world as representation, structured by the world as will, makes for an illusory empiricism, or to add accent to a term of Hillman's, a fictive one. In Schopenhauer's sense, the world as representation is *maya*, the Vedantic term for the illusory quality of the material world, ever the dream of an eternally respiring Brahman. Schopenhauer despaired for such a world, though he found respite in aesthetic contemplation, which might, however temporarily and partially, suspend the will. Nietzsche, however, embraced the fictive quality and expanded it to encompass not only representation, but a desessentialized will as well. He rejected metaphysical abstractions on the order of the thing-in-itself, maintaining that representations, fictions, and perspectives were actualities beyond which it was unnecessary to posit another form of truth. Drawing on Greek tragedy, he promulgated a philosophy in which will and representation were understood to be physical forces characterized as Dionysus and Apollo in metaphoric interaction.

Nietzsche's naturalistic move, said Sarah Kofman (1993), was to identify the "rational animal" as "a product of the metaphorical activity which is common to all living things" (p. 25). His evaluation of ultimacy as unremitting, Heraclitean flux rather than pacific, Parmenidean constancy marks an emphasis on empirical being in its psychological indeterminacy. Nietzsche "never speaks of 'Being'," Kofman said, "or even of 'being,' but of 'Nature' or 'life,' the 'World' or 'Experience,' 'phenomena' or 'appearance'; he substitutes for the concept of ontology that of 'psychology' . . . being for Nietzsche is an interpreted being" (pp. 120–121). Indeed, Nietzsche's philosophy emerges as a product of typology. Kofman said,

> The demystification of metaphysics by Nietzsche consisted in showing that truth was but a fiction necessary to certain living things and their conditions of existence, that the question concerning truth had to be not ontological but axiological or genealogical . . . Nietzsche's question is not: "What is the essence of the Truth?," but "What does the will which wants the Truth want?" for the will to truth is in turn but a symbol and a symptom. (p. 124)

Nietzsche's method was to philosophize with a "hammer," by which he meant not a cudgel, but a tuning fork, producing a depth of reverberation in the genealogical, or categorical, fissures of the metaphysical edifice to unsettle its foundational absolutes.

The psychological inquiry is intrinsic to the engagement with metaphor. The philosophy of the concept, Nietzsche said, amounts to "the complete silencing of the personality" (as cited in Kofman, 1993, p. 23). To get at the psychological basis of metaphysics, he substituted a conceptual reading with a metaphorical one, revealing the figurative process at the basis of conceptual thinking. He lamented that with the triumph of Socratic and Aristotelian epistemologies, as Kofman (1993) put it, "consciousness prevails over the unconscious" (p. 19). He favored what he saw as the aesthetic logic of pre-Socratic "superabundance" over that of the single-pointed logic of Aristotelian non-contradiction; in other words, beauty over truth. In a sense, his work became a prolonged elaboration of the proposition put forward by Heraclitus (so central to Jungian psychoanalysis) that "everything forever has its opposite along with it" (as cited in Kofman, 1993, p. 20).

Nietzsche posited an Apollonian order that makes human existence possible and bearable, and a Dionysian sensorium on the other side of the conceptual veil. Let us explore the relationship of the Dionysian faculty to metaphor and imaginal psychology. The myths say that Dionysus entered the daylight world through the thighs of his father, Zeus. But his birth was attended by tragic circumstances, which required that he be delivered again, this time into darkness. The events were these: His mother, Semele, was a mortal who Zeus had taken as a lover. So ardent was Zeus' passion for her that he promised to give her anything she desired. Zeus' wife, Hera, learned of his promise, and hatched a plot for revenge. She knew that no mortal could survive the unalloyed presence of a god, and so she whispered to Semele that if Zeus loved her, he would forsake his usual disguises and appear to her in his manifest glory. Semele appealed to Zeus to prove his love in just this way. Hearing her plea, he was grief stricken, for even gods are bound by their word, indeed are reduced in a singular tradition to *the* word. Zeus was compelled to do as he had promised and could only watch helplessly as Semele was incinerated in the deathly brightness.

Hermes, observing from the threshold, intervened to save the unborn demigod. He lifted Dionysus from his dead mother's womb and sewed him into Zeus' thigh where he was carried to term. Hera, not one to be thwarted, vowed to destroy the infant. She summoned the Titans, entreating them to tear Dionysus to pieces. They lured Dionysus to his destruction with toys, noisemakers, and a mirror.

But neither would Zeus accept defeat. He recovered the child's heart and mixed it into a potion of pomegranate seeds intended for Persephone, the queen of Hades. Persephone became pregnant by the draught, and so, in the everlasting night of the underworld, Dionysus was born again.

The myth is structured by a dichotomy whose elaboration is a central theme of imaginal psychology. As we have seen, the binary opposition is the foundation of philosophical problems. In this case, the horned dilemma is that of spirit and soul, the former represented by the imagery of ascent most notable in the Christian story, and the latter by descent into more chthonic realms. Hillman's (1978b) discussion of the significance of Dionysus for an imaginal psychology, in *The Myth of Analysis*, brings into relief three depth psychological ideas presaged by Nietzsche: (a) a theory of metaphor as an elemental force, akin to myth, that places figuration at the root of psyche, (b) a generalization of Dionysian ambi-valence or multivalence into a polytheistic psychology, and (c) a formulation in specifically Dionysian terms of the border as a paradoxical phenomenon that entails both separation and connection. I examine each of these features in turn before settling into a consideration of Kofman's Nietzsche.

Making the case for myth as the prima materia of psychology, Hillman (1978c) refuted a scholarly disdain for "amateur" (read "Romantic") uses of the terms *Dionysian* and *Apollonian* to characterize styles of comprehension. What is at stake for psychology, he said, is not a scholarly fantasy of what may or may not qualify as legitimately Greek, but the mythological modes of the psyche as they play out in modern lives freighted with madness and suffering. "We are not talking of the Greeks or their religion. . . . We are talking of the psyche of contemporaries, of ourselves, and of the Dionysian possibilities for therapeutic psychology," Hillman said. "After all, Dionysus was *the* God of madness, even the mad God" (p. 266). The distinction, basic to imaginal psychology, is between an analytical fixation and an imaginal openness to archetypal expressions in lived experience. To reduce the phenomena of myth or archetype to analytic concepts risks obscuring or even obliterating psychological value. "When we speak of a mythical image like Dionysus," Hillman said, "We are not bringing something in, an import from classical scholarship and the history of religion, an extraneous referent as example or metaphor" (p. 267). To work psychologically is not to import myth and metaphor, treating them as epiphenomenal, but to encounter in them the very matter of psyche.

Hillman's propitiation of Dionysus for an imaginal psychotherapy did not come without its caveat, and here we have the second of his Nietzschean tropes, regarding polyvalence. A central understanding of imaginal psychology is "that consciousness moves like Hermes, the guide of souls, through a multiplicity of perspectives and ways of being" (1978b, p. 265). Hillman said of Dionysus, "To evoke him alone would be to commit the error of Nietzsche, who took one God and laid all at his feet, thus perpetuating, despite his intention, the tradition he tried to leave" (p. 266). And further,

> The perspectivalism of archetypal psychology requires a deepening of subjectivity beyond mere Nietzschean perspectives or existential stances. Perspectives are forms of vision, rhetoric, values, epistemology, and lived styles that perdure independently of empirical individuality. For archetypal psychology, pluralism and multiplicity and relativism are not enough: these are merely philosophical generalities. (Hillman, 1983a, p. 46)

For Hillman's polytheistic approach, a single god will not do. In poststructural terms, Nietzsche took only the first of two deconstructive steps by inverting the hierarchy Christ/Dionysus. He valorized the previously marginalized term, but remained trapped within the binary opposition. In order to escape the construct, Nietzsche needed to take the crucial second step of generalizing its terms so that an expanded meaning would expose the value structure dictated by the original hierarchy. To stop short of the second move makes not for a deconstruction or a re-visioning, "only an enantiodromia" (Hillman, 1978c, p. 6). The value structure, though reversed, retains its grip. Invoking the Dionysian lure that for Nietzsche became a fatal attraction, Hillman (1978c) said, "The mythical is the speculum of the psychological" (p. 267). Seeing through the specular image, one encounters the tain, a quicksilver backing, by which reflection might be understood "to move like Hermes through a multiplicity of perspectives."

Making much the same point for archetypal theory that Gilles Deleuze (2006) made for poststructuralist theory in *Nietzsche and Philosophy*,[1] Hillman (1983a) said the question depth psychology must ask "of an event is not *why* or *how*, but rather *what* specifically is being presented and ultimately *who*, which divine figure, is speaking in this style of consciousness, this form of presentation" (p. 47). Invoking William James, he asserted the necessity in a pluralistic universe for a polytheistic psychology. All of this is not to delimit the carrying capacity of Dionysus for imaginal psychology, but to comprehend the basic ecstasis of his dismembered circumstance. "A psychology adequate to [Dionysus'] archetypal view of psychic structure," Hillman (1978c) said, "must reflect this multiplicity of centers and affirm a psychological polytheism" (pp. 265–266). Following upon this comment is something of a credo for imaginal psychology:

> In order to give full value to the differentiated manyness of both the archetypal world of divine figures, daimones, and mythic creatures, as well as to the phenomenal world of our experiences, where psychological actuality is vastly complicated and manifold, we shall focus intensively upon the plurality of the self, upon the many Gods and the many existential modes of their effects. We shall leave to one side theological fantasies of wholeness, oneness, and other abstract images of a goal called self. The abandonment of psychological monotheism is radical indeed. It not only collapses the rule of the old ego; it is a reflection in the psyche that in a certain sense god is dead—but not the gods. (p. 265)

We can detect in this passage the twin styles—Dioscuri—of imaginal psychology: its phenomenological grounding and its polytheistic inspiration.

A third feature of Hillman's approach to Dionysus that adumbrates the role of metaphor is the attention to the Dionysian archetype as a "borderline" phenomenon. "Wherever Dionysus appears," Hillman (1978c) said, "the 'border' also is manifested. He rules the borderlands of our psychic geography" (p. 275). Here we encounter similarities between Dionysus and Hermes as personifications of trickster phenomena. "Dionysian ecstasy," said Karl Kerényi (1956), "had the same function as the trickster myth: it abolished the boundaries" (p. 188). With reference to Dionysian androgyny, Kerényi added, "not least the boundaries of sex" (p. 188). The distinction between Dionysus and Hermes, he said, is that although Hermes disregards boundaries, unlike Dionysus, "he is not a spirit of disorder" (p. 189). Indeed, as I suggest in later chapters, an imaginal theory of metaphor might establish Hermes as the very adjudicator of metaphoric order. Hillman (1978c) elaborated the Dionysian phenomenon of the border by teasing out the binary opposites, instances of the figure's ambi-valence: "Dionysus presents us with borderline phenomena," he said, "so that we cannot tell whether he is mad or sane, wild or somber, sexual or psychic, male or female, conscious or unconscious" (p. 275). Hillman re-visions the border in ambi-valent style as the site not solely of a limit condition, but of joinder, seeking to give the concept "border" the compensatory fullness of the binary opposition. "In Dionysus, borders join that which we usually believe to be separated by borders," Hillman said. "The philosopher is also a lover; Socrates is a drinking Silenus; the riotous Dionysus has but one wife, Ariadne" (p. 275).

Hillman's move to problematize the semantics of the border for depth psychology is similarly taken on behalf of poststructuralism by Derrida (1982) in his essay "Tympan," which opens *Margins of Philosophy*, the volume that also contains his most sustained treatment of metaphor, "White Mythology." The facets of Derrida's approach are too multifarious to explore fully here, but in part they are reflected by the title. "Tympanum" is both the name for the diaphragm in the inner ear that transmits sound to the cerebral cortex (Derrida was making a larger point about the priority assigned by the philosophical tradition to speech over writing as the source of meaning) and also the apparatus in manual printing presses that allows for the accurate measurement of the margin. And, of course, one of the three small bones of the inner ear involved with the relay of tympanic vibrations is the "hammer," Nietzsche's tuning fork. Thus, Derrida: "[T]o philosophize with a hammer. Zarathustra begins by asking himself if he will have to puncture them, batter their ears with the sound of cymbals or tympani, the instruments, always, of some Dionysianism" (p. xii). His cymbolic reference is to the noisemakers with which the Titans lured the infant Dionysus to his de(con)struction. *Tympan* serves as a metaphor of undecideability. Its ambivalent instrumentality establishes it as a biologic psychopompos of sorts, obviating the very boundary it establishes by enabling a portage between outer and inner. Metaphor, as a semantic tympan, sounds out the depths of meaning even unto contrapuntal reaches. It carries beyond metaphysical certainty to the underlying morphological image or "aesthetic signature" (Hillman, 1983a, p. 24) from which certainties derive.

Consistent with the epistemological centrality he assigned to metaphor, Hillman (1983b) lent trenchant voice to the poststructural suspicion of absolutes and ultimate meanings. He said, "Now let's leave meaning, and the search for meaning, and the meaning of life" (p. 58). This departure marks a break with the metaphysical trope that archetype in-itself is transcendental to image. The idea was fashioned as slogan in *stick to the image*, the methodological "golden rule" (Hillman, 2004a, p. 21) of imaginal psychology, coined by Rafael López-Pedraza (2003), who said in his evocation of Hermes, "I merely want to keep to the image side [of analytic psychology], and only mention in passing any possible conflict with the conceptual side" (p. 152).

It is doubtless a Hermetic feint to "mention in passing," and the comment expresses imaginal psychology's reorientation away from absolutes. A *poietics* of meaning that keeps to the "image side" resists reference beyond the differential play of images to any version of a "conceptual side." It avoids the placement by phenomenology (Husserl) and semiology (Saussure) of an ideality of meaning beyond the differential relation, in other words, the classic metaphysical gesture. The suspension of the concept *archetype* from the differential field of meaning-making by an orthodox archetypology is remediated by a poststructural return to contingency. Dan Sperber (1992) likened Lévi-Strauss's work on totemism to an inquiry into "the contingent co-occurrence of sundry manifestations" (p. 30). The approach, Sperber said, "opens up a choice of perspectives" (p. 31):

> Since any object has an indefinite number of features, it can enter into an indefinite number of associations with an indefinite number of other objects. A given culture may highlight some of these features and associations, while the others remain merely potential. (p. 29)

Employing the standard linguistic term *code* to designate the system (*langue*) out of which individual expressions become available (*parole*), Sperber draws out the structural consequence: "The underlying code relates signifiers to other signifiers; there *are* no signifieds. Everything is meaningful, nothing is meant" (p. 28). The lexical code contains more than might be dreamt of in anyone's philosophy. The fullness of metaphoric style, said John Sturrock (1992) with reference to Roland Barthes, favors "the means—which is language—over the end, or the meaning" (p. 65). Imaginal expressivity, in which the archetype is repatriated into the differential field from its exile into conceptual absolutism, may in this sense harbor Hillman's own answer to Job, who interrogates the absolute seeking to know where wisdom—meaning—shall be found.

It is against the backdrop of Dionysian multiplicity that I turn to Sarah Kofman's (1993) *Nietzsche and Metaphor*. I draw upon Kofman for two themes symptomatic of a metaphorics, the effacement of the *proper* and the forgetting of metaphor. To explore the relationship of metaphor to the Dionysian *amor fati* of worldly becoming, I will frame the discussion in terms of a principal conceptual metaphor[2] of Nietzsche's,

Life Is Art, which I believe expresses his significance for the shift from epistemology to hermeneutics occasioned by poststructuralism. The turn to hermeneutics is evident in imaginal psychology's determination to stick with the image. Though it is a phenomenological notion, sticking with the image is hermeneutic in the sense that any image in question is always already an interpretation.

For Nietzsche (1967b), to live authentically required acknowledgment of the aesthetic process generating every truth claim. "An anti-metaphysical view of the world—yes," Nietzsche declared, "but an artistic one" (p. 539). In *Nietzsche and Depth Psychology*, Jacob Golomb (1999) wrote,

> The search for authenticity is seen as the wish to reflect one's own indeterminacy by spontaneous choice of one out of the many possible ways of life. Individuals are types of artists who freely shape themselves as works of art. (p. 13)

In a sense, world hypotheses reflect painterly or writerly gestures. Kofman's expositors Penelope Deutscher and Kelly Oliver (1999) said that for the Nietzsche of Kofman's interpretation, metaphysical truths emanate not from "dispassionate rationality," but from the "drives and body of the philosopher" (p. 9). Nietzsche's philosophy of *pothos*, metaphysics as the soulful yearning of the drives for a world made in their image, trades a notion of metaphysical transcendence (spirit) for one of metaphorical immanence (soul).

The application of Life Is Art creates a palimpsest of the Kantian critique of aesthetic judgment, reflecting, in its way, Nietzsche's own drive to overwrite the illuminated texts of reason with darkness, density, and maenadic physicality. Nietzsche (1967a) understood philosophy as a morphology (§23) of the drives, "artistic powers that burst forth from nature itself *without mediation by the human artist*" (§2). The basic metamorphic-metaphoric idea is expressed in the opening lines of the *Metamorphoses*, where Ovid (1994) wrote, "Bodies, I have in mind . . . and how they can change to assume new shapes" (p. 1). The sense perceptions (*aisthētikos*) that coax *zoë*, infinite life (Kerényi, 1976a, p. xxxvi), to its myriad shapes are, in a Nietzschean sense, stylistic, that is, metaphoric. The instincts are irreducible processes of both natural and symbolic selection. "Nietzsche deletes the metaphysical opposition between the soul and the body and establishes between the two an original relationship of symbolic expressivity," said Kofman (1993); "The body and consciousness are two systems of signs which signify each other reciprocally" (p. 26). This form of carrying over is the generative drive common to all instances of creativity. It must be taken, Kofman said, not

> as a transition from one place to another: it must be taken as a metaphor which, in the *Birth of Tragedy*, condenses several meanings: transfiguration, transformation, ecstasy, self-dispossession and metamorphosis (which is possible only if the distinction into well-demarcated genera and species is erased); as well as: transposition of the truth of Being into symbolic languages. (p. 15)

In shamanic fashion, the artistic power invokes poetry and trickery, song and *ecstasis*—what Eliade (1989) said was "to be carried out" of one's commonplace existence (p. 223), a *metapherein*, and what Heidegger (1962) identified as the basis of *Dasein's* temporality, *Ekstase*, its standing out against the backdrop of a mere "sequence of nows" (p. 474) by virtue of what it *poietically* makes of its past, present, and future. Kerényi (1976a) wrote in his study of Dionysus, "It is not possible to draw a dividing line between religious awe and artistic taste" (p. 8). Nietzsche generalized the point to all facets of life, not solely the religious. "There is an artistic power which holds sway within us," Nietzsche said (1979, p. 51). In contradistinction to the rational animal he affirms "the metaphorical animal" (as cited in Kofman, 1993, p. 25).

Such a being is creative in a Kantian sense. The subjective purposiveness stemming from aesthetic, or reflective, judgment is world-making. For Nietzsche, Kofman (1993) said, "Artistic activity gives everything a surface, it creates forms that do not exist in nature, which has neither inside nor outside, neither top nor bottom" (p. 27). The Apollonian surfaces, such as legislative concepts like subjective purposiveness, are given to experience by the Dionysian play of aesthetic, reflective judgment. As a natural function, metaphoric transposition is basic to both soul and world, *anima* and *anima mundi*. The animating propensity is an endeavor of soul-making. As noted, in one attempt upon a definition, Hillman (1975) said soul "refers to that unknown component which makes meaning possible, turns events into experiences" (p. xvi). *Life as art* evokes the Kantian rule of judgment, which produces purpose from contingency. Aesthetic, reflective judgment establishes subjective purposiveness *as if* it were transcendental. Yet as Kant painstakingly, and ironically, demonstrated, there is no outside text, judgment's necessary a priori results from reflection's excursion through the manifold. The reflective mode, Hillman said of soul, "mediates events and makes differences between ourselves and everything that happens" (p. xvi). Metaphoric selection, soul-making, functions by the process of deferral and differentiation to cultivate Apollonian orientation from the *masa confusa* of Dionysian indifference.

In their unfolding, the drives sublimate into moral positions. Here we pick up the first of our two themes from Kofman (1993), the effacement of the *proper*. For Nietzsche, metaphoric selection is based in the will to power. The idea, said Kofman, developed pursuant to two generalizations, the first of which mapped music onto instinctual force and the second, rhetoric onto being. Nietzsche was an accomplished composer, and, for a time at least, a disciple of Richard Wagner. The full title of his inaugural work is *The Birth of Tragedy from the Spirit of Music*. The prevalent theme of the first generalization is that of loss. As Nuno Nabais (2006) pointed out, the musical compositions that accompanied the work of the Greek tragedians have been lost to time, leaving Nietzsche, and us, with "the abyssal silence of the music" (p. xi). With the second generalization, the expansion of metaphor, and thus indeterminacy, from its rhetorical niche to epistemology and, more radically, ontology, we have the effacing, or wearing down, of absolute being, and of metaphysical propriety, to reveal a groundless depth that is discomfiting, tragic, in its contingency. Metaphysics ceases to be first philosophy, the ground of all assumptions in the social sciences; it is indeed still *writ*, but as metaphor and interpretation. For Nietzsche, Kofman said, "[T]he opposition between philosophy and poetry derives from metaphysical thinking; it is based on the fictitious separation of the real and imaginary, on the no less fictitious separation of the 'faculties'" (1993, p. 17). Nietzsche therefore disrupted the binary opposition inaugurated at the start of metaphor's exile that continued into the Kantian analytic. Hillman (1983a) made the same move when he said:

> Case history as factual history, a true account or knowledge about the "succession of events through which anything passes," is a fiction in the sense of a fabrication, a lie. But it is only a lie when it claims literal truth. (p. 12)

As with Kofman's two generalizations, in Hillman's statement we can discern epistemology and ontology conceived as narrative force.

The first generalization attains its final form in Nietzsche's explanation of essence in terms of interpretation. But it starts in his depiction of the experience of listening to music as a metaphoric transference. "To begin with," Nietzsche (1974) said, "a nerve stimulus first transformed in a percept! First metaphor! The percept again copied into a sound! Second metaphor!" (p. 116). Nietzsche saw the chemical firing of neurological impulse, Kofman (1993) said, as the "primordial melody of pleasure and pain," an image-making reverberation, or "strophic text," analogous to the birth pangs of life and meaning and the power of music to move the passions (p. 7). Significantly, for the development of music-as-essence into essence-as-interpretation, the neural tropism has no determinate origin, but is an irreducible mediation, already not primary. The "impression," or "the starting point" that results in conceptualization, Kofman said, "is itself a metaphor, the transposition of a nerve stimulus which varies from one individual to the next, producing individual sensation-images in the symbolic language of the five senses" (p. 35).

Nietzsche did not at first fully distinguish himself from the tradition that seeks the absolute and understands artistic activity to be mimesis. He had yet to generalize art to life. Rhetoric and poetry produced "a substitutive image which the poet really perceives in place of the idea," he said (as cited in Kofman, 1993, p. 8). In music alone of all the arts did he find an association with primordiality. Music, Kofman (1993) said, was "the primitive echo of the world" (p. 8). As the maenadic art, it was "suited to affirm the manifold diversity of life," she said. "It is, in fact, the mother of all the arts, for it breaks up into a thousand metaphors itself; it is a language 'capable of infinite interpretation'" (p. 11). Thus in the initial association of essence with music appears its eventual construal as interpretation.

To "affirm the manifold diversity" the artist and philosopher must cross into *ecstasis*. The "stripping away of individuality" (Kofman, 1993, p. 12) is a self-transposition that enables the artist to sublimate the Dionysian pleroma into the forms of affective experience. Artistic authenticity, Kofman (1993) said, entails loss. It is obtained at the expense of the *proper*, a term indicating the concerns of philosophy from Plato on, the Form or the *eidos*, the pure, the essential, the immediate, the concept, the literal, the determinate, and the patriarchal order, as in one's "proper" name—in effect, any allusion to the Absolute. "The artist," said Kofman,

> becomes a metaphor for the world and, as such, he is a medium which reflects eternal being. All authentic art involves intoxication, and with it the loss of the "proper," as one is transported out of oneself in a way which alone gives the power to symbolize. Expressing oneself metaphorically and undergoing a metamorphosis can thus be assimilated. (p. 12)

As the *topos* of truth from which Nietzsche generalized, music became for him the site of a *rupture* (again, the Derridean term) in metaphysical literalism that admits of unavoidable contingency. It serves as the stage for catharsis, the place of the displacement of truth by interpretation, in other words, of metaphysics by metaphorics.

The musical coda is commented upon as well by Rüdiger Safranski. For Nietzsche, Safranski (2003) said, music seemed an "authentic reality and colossal power," and its de-essentialization left an "echo of farewell" (p. 19). The loss of immediacy to irreducible transposition seemed both final and tragic. Thus, said Safranski, Nietzsche's philosophy "originated in postsirenian melancholy" (p. 19). Metaphysical essences no longer appeared supple and seductive, but hoary and nihilistic. Derrida (1978a) called them "weathered rock-monsters" (p. 43).

The improper—unseemly—reshaping of essence into interpretation, as with Prometheus' working of tears into clay, is less productively understood in terms of a turn toward radical, and self-defeating, relativism than one toward paradox. "[T]he hypothesis of the will to power," Kofman (1993) said, "is also an interpretation, but one which presents itself as such" (p. 94). Authenticity, the moral strength to say "yes" to life despite its tragic sense—the "gay science" or "joyful wisdom"—requires a recognition that truth is *in-itself* enigmatic. For Nietzsche, as Alexander Nehamas (1985) put it, "there can never be a complete theory or interpretation" (p. 64). "Our views, at every time, are simplifications of the world and are dependent on particular values" (p. 72).

The evolution of Nietzsche's root metaphor, Life Is Art, from music-as-essence to essence-as-interpretation, entailed a revaluation of the concept. "[I]n the relationship which he establishes between metaphor and concept," Kofman (1993) said,

> metaphor is no longer referred to the concept, as in the metaphysical tradition inherited from Aristotle, but rather the concept is referred to metaphor. For Aristotle the concept is primary in relation to metaphor, metaphor being defined as carrying one concept over on to another, or as the transition from one logical place to another, from a "proper" place to a figurative one. Aristotle's definition of metaphor could not be retained as such by Nietzsche since it is based on a division of the world into well-defined

> genera and species corresponding to essences, whereas for Nietzsche the essence of things is enigmatic, so genera and species are themselves but human, all-too-human metaphors. (p. 15)

In the revaluation, there is no longer an absolute, or a proper, because there is no longer an essence. All propers are figural, all essences works of art. Propriety, literal truth, is replaced by artistic force. "[T]he 'proper' itself," Kofman said, "has the status of a simple interpretation" (p. 17). Metaphor becomes

> symbolic of the artistic force of interpretation which constitutes the "proper," the concept, as well as the metaphor. This artistic force will then be designated "will to power." But equally the notion of metaphor becomes totally "improper" since it is henceforth no longer referred to a proper but to an interpretation. (p. 17)

The proper becomes revealed as the consequence of a discursive imperative: aesthetic, reflective judgment.

Nietzsche (2006) cogently expressed the generalization of metaphor to ontological perspective in the essay "On Truth and Lies in a Nonmoral Sense," in which he famously opined that truth is a "mobile army of metaphors" (translations vary):

> What then is truth? A moveable host of metaphors, metonymies, and anthropomorphisms: in short, a sum of human relations which have been poetically and rhetorically intensified, transferred, and embellished, and which, after long usage, seem to a people to be fixed, canonical, and binding. Truths are illusions which we have forgotten are illusions; they are metaphors that have become worn out and have been drained of sensuous force, coins which have lost their embossing and are now considered as metal and no longer as coins. (p. 117)

In the movement from music-as-essence to essence-as-interpretation there is no longer a need to postulate a *proper*. The proper becomes effaced in its singularity, worn down, *seen through* like a veil unto the earthly vale of archetypal guises, masks, and effacements. This must be so because what is left after the death of God is the world, a palimpsest of maenadic density:

> Metaphor becomes a text, the product of a unique perspective, an interpretation which posits an affirmative or negative meaning. If Nietzsche substitutes "perspective" for "metaphor," then, it is because the meaning which is posited and transposed in things is no longer referred to an essence of the world, a proper. The "world," the "essence" are themselves texts written by a specific type of will. The idea of an originary music of the world—a sort of original text making human texts into mere metaphors—disappears: every text becomes the correlate of an interpretation which constitutes specific, provisional meaning symptomatic of a certain type of life's mastery over the world and over other types of life. (Kofman, 1993, p. 82)

With metaphor generalized from rhetoric to ontology (not to assume the mantle of ontology, but to see through it), we move from the effacement of the proper to a second theme of Kofman's (1993), the forgetting of metaphor. "What are we to make of this effacement, this forgetting?" (p. 23), she asked. To *make* of forgetting: metaphor's *poiesis*. (We might recall from Frances Yates that Albertus Magnus called the art of memory a *metaphorica*.) Forgetting, as Nietzsche means it, "does not occur at a specific point in time" (p. 25), Kofman said, but is the necessary condition for concept formation at every point in time. It is not in the historical past that metaphor lies forgotten. Rather, metaphor entails forgetting. In Nietzsche's sense, Metaphor is the forgetting that accompanies every moment of cosmogenesis as the instincts will their conceptual expression and Dionysus gives over to Apollo.

The forgetting, Kofman (1993) said, is an "'abyss' opened up by the metaphysicians, who create two antithetical worlds which they claim to be irreducible" (p. 25). Nietzsche's "strategy," she said, "is designed to fill the abyss, to delete the opposition between concept and metaphor" (p. 25). He filled it with the will to power, "an originary *instinctive* activity, an artistic force creating fictions" (p. 25), and metaphor's "ultimate signification" (p. 82). The will to power

> allows man to remake the world in his image so as to master it: an anthropomorphic transposition which, in order to be effective must necessarily be performed self-effacingly. Metaphorical activity is termed instinctive because it is unconscious, and because like all drives it seeks sole mastery of the world. It is not just a drive like any other; it could be called the general form of all drives. (p. 25)

Metaphor, the forgotten artistic activity of the drives, signifies the unconscious abyss from which flows all conscious, conceptual activity—and the world. "[W]e have always already instinctively transposed 'the world' into a set of forms," Kofman said (p. 28).

Nietzsche postulated two aspects of artistic activity "forgotten" in the unconscious, Kofman (1993) said, "the production of images and their selection," the life force imagined aesthetically (p. 30). "Art idealizes the world," she said, "which does not mean to say that it impoverishes it, but that it highlights some of its principal features and makes others disappear" in the process of generalization that leads from specific images, or metaphors, to concepts in which specificity is subsumed (p. 29). The concept

> itself a product of metaphorical activity, plays a privileged role in the forgetting of metaphor, in that it hides the metaphorical character of the process of generalization by founding it on an essential generality: the concept vouches for the "untruth" and "treacherousness" of metaphor. (p. 35)

Of the concept's role in the forgetting of metaphoric provenance, Kofman said, "For this generalization to stabilize itself, the concept 'true' must intervene" (p. 34).

For Zarathustra, Nietzsche's tragic and yes-saying overman, authenticity means to see through the truth to the awe-inspiring and terrifying metaphorical dynamism that produces it. "Authenticity," Hillman (1983a) said, with reference to the theatrical—cathartic—structure of Dionysian logic,

> is the perpetual dismemberment of being and not-being a self, a being that is always in many parts, like a dream with a full cast. We all have identity crises because a single identity is a delusion of the monotheistic mind that would defeat Dionysus at all costs. We all have dispersed consciousness through all our body parts, wandering wombs; we are all hysterics. Authenticity is *in* the illusion, playing it, seeing through it from within as we play it, like an actor who sees through his mask and can only see in this way. (p. 39)

The ancient Dionysian epithet "Lord of Souls," Hillman says, implies also "Lord of psychic insight, the psychological viewpoint which sees all things as masks in order to see through all things. For where masking is essential to a logic, then seeing through is implied" (p. 39). The rational man is not altogether wrong to raise suspicions of metaphor's epistemological claims, failing only to notice that the treachery occurs when metaphor hardens into the concept.

The irony that masking implies seeing is also expressed in Heidegger's term *alethia*, meaning "unforgetting" or "unconcealment." Hillman (1999) likened it to the English *inquiry* and called it "an activity of mind that initiated all Western philosophizing" (p. xxi). In the myth of Er, which concludes the *Republic*, Plato tells the story that as souls are about to be born they arrive at the banks of the river Lethe where they drink from the waters of forgetfulness, losing awareness of their former lives. For Heidegger, *alethia* is the temporal clearing in which *Dasein* stands out in its *facticity*, or involvement with a world. *Alethia* unconceals such a world and the truths that are peculiar to it, causing other truths to be forgotten. It places the recondite and the revelatory on equal footing. In a passage implicating metaphor, Heidegger said, "Entities look as if . . . That is, they have in a certain way been uncovered already, and yet they are still disguised" (p. 265; ellipsis in original).

The mutual participation of the binaries appearing/concealing is a quality of what Heidegger called the as-structure of being. (It is the jettisoning of the as-structure that redounds to the detriment of that literalist, Semele.) As with the forgetting of metaphor, the as-structure, said Rudolph Gasché (1986), "veils and reveals in the same gesture" (p. 301). For *Dasein*, human being as orientation in the world, Gasché said, entities are understood "primarily as things that serve this or that purpose and not as pure things or objects upon which it subsequently bestows determining attributes" (p. 299). The as-structure indicates a relationality or a *with regard to* at the basis of understanding that "makes all understanding of something understanding of *something as something*. A movement of *epiphora* [transfer], the movement constitutive of metaphor, is present in all understanding of the *as what*" (p. 302).

In other words, *Dasein* is not an object in a series of static, kineographic nows, but a locus of world disclosure in which every now contains a trace of the others of its past and future. There is no perfect present. *Dasein* establishes its presence, taking on meaning, in a process that discloses relationality. Being itself, Gasché (1986) said, is always only in its own deferral (p. 301). Its meaning can be uncovered solely *as* the there at which interpretation—veiling and revealing—takes place.

Apart from this lodging in the duplex of the as-structure, the truth of entities remains untenable. "The as-structure of understanding unearthed by Heidegger characterizes understanding and the saying of Being as hinging on a movement of transfer," said Gasché (1986). The understanding's *with regard to* quality indicates that "a certain metaphoricity is constitutive of the very unity of being" (p. 302). The as-structure reveals the basic metaphoric duplicity. "The metaphorical drive . . . in lying, dreaming, myth, art," Kofman (1993) said,

> dares to admit its perspective and recognize the mask as mask, thanks to a superabundance of life which allows it to will illusion. The drive which urges man to make metaphors . . . is indestructible, for it coincides with life itself. But whereas at times life reveals itself for what it is—evaluative, lying, artistic—at others it veils itself because it is not strong enough to go as far as it can. (p. 76)

The as-structure serves in a compensatory capacity to the forgetting of metaphor. Nietzsche (1956) asserted metaphor's de-volatilization, its conceptual *calcinatio*, as an Apollonian necessity. "[I]n order to act," he said in an invocation of the tragic sense, "we require the veil of illusion; such is Hamlet's doctrine" (p. 51).

The basic *poietic* observation of a postsirenian ethos is related by Miguel de Unamuno (1954) in *The Tragic Sense of Life*: "It is not usually our ideas that make us optimists or pessimists, but it is our optimism or our pessimism, of psychological or perhaps pathological origin, as much the one as the other, that makes our ideas" (p. 3). From the imaginal point of view, "our ideas" take on a transpersonal significance. The rhetorical question posed by a psychology of images is whether the human is the source of the poetic figure or whether the poetic figure is the source of the human. Nietzsche (1967a) said, "Both the deed and the doer are fictions" (p. 264). In a formulation of the autonomy of aesthetic power, Harold Bloom (1998) said, "[W]e are never quite certain whether Shakespeare or Hamlet composes more of Shakespeare's and Hamlet's play" (p. 396).

The same idea was expressed by Jung, who said, "It is not Goethe that creates *Faust*, but *Faust* that creates Goethe" (CW 15, par. 159). Hillman (1978c) cites the passage to support a point that "The *oeuvre* shapes the person who is in relation with it" (p. 20). A psychology of images re-visions the tragic sense—Hamlet's doctrine, and Nietzsche's as well—so that our creative fictions, our metaphors, become the source of our possibility. In a remark cited by Hillman (1978c, p. 36) in the context of soul-making, and suggestive of deconstruction's refusal of the closure of philosophy in any ultimate concept or transcendental signified, Jung said, "Creation is as much construction as destruction" (CW 8, par. 245). Jung's remark goes to the nature of the ultimate binary, life/death, which was Hamlet's vexation, and, in Nietzsche's literalization of Dionysus, his as well.

For Nietzsche, it would appear, the forgetting of metaphor is fated, in the hands of the Fates, the *Moirai*, who, Plato (1957) said, measure the lives of men on a spindle that turns upon the knees of Necessity (*Republic*, §617), the "errant cause," whose opposite is Reason (Plato, 1963, *Timaeus*, §47). As the sovereign of the conceptual economy, metaphor legislates forgetting. In Kantian terms, the forgetting of metaphor enables us to put the contingencies of our world into an explanatory schema. For Nietzsche, the necessity of forgetting is nevertheless catastrophic. It makes quotidian existence possible only by blinding us to the life-sustaining, though fearsome, abyss of Dionysian flux. Nietzsche said,

> When in a forceful attempt to fix the eye on the sun, we turn away blinded, we then have dark-colored spots before our eyes, as a healing agent, as it were: inversely, those bright image projections of the Sophoclean [tragic] hero, in short the Apollinian . . . mask, are necessary productions of a look into the innerness and terror of nature, as it were, luminous spots to heal the look wounded by gruesome night. (as cited in Warminski, 1987, p. xxxvi)

In her consideration of this passage in *Nietzsche et la scène philosophique*, as translated by Andrzej Warminski, Kofman (1993) said,

> There is a double blinding, a double bedazzlement according to whether one passes from shadow to light or from light to shadow: it is what the myth of the cave already taught, that other camera obscura. What is new here in relation to Plato and the Greek myths in which the light and the sun are saving agents is that for Nietzsche light and sun do not draw their pharmaceutical power from the Truth and the Good of which they would be the images, but from appearance and illusion, from blinding. (p. xii)

The double blind in Kofman's (1993) passage necessarily conjures the classic study of schizophrenia—a binary opposition—by Gregory Bateson (1972). The schizophrenic individual is seen to be captive of a double bind, making it both necessary and impossible to leave a field of action (e.g., the mother–child relationship) in which sustenance and hostility are inextricably bound together. Richard Tarnas (1991) likened the schizophrenic dilemma to the modern condition in which, he said,

> We have the post-Copernican dilemma of being a peripheral and insignificant inhabitant of a vast cosmos, and the post-Cartesian dilemma of being a conscious, purposeful, and personal subject confronting an unconscious, purposeless, and impersonal universe, with these compounded by the post-Kantian dilemma of there being no possible means by which the human subject can know the universe in its essence. We are evolved from, embedded in, and defined by a reality that is radically alien to our own, and moreover cannot ever be directly contacted in cognition. (p. 420)

Hillman (1987) provided this psychological gloss on the triumphs of epistemology: "Paradoxically, we are least conscious where we are most conscious [or where] we are the least reflexively aware. Close to the light our sight is shortest" (p. 19).

Symbolized by the camera obscura or the retina itself, where images are already always reversed, Nietzsche's inversion of Apollo/Dionysus began a metaphoric re-visioning. It would require the elaboration of metaphor's cognitive capacity to relieve the tension of opposites in which there could be metaphor or concept, but not both. Joel Weinsheimer (1991) expressed the Hermetic nature of the next step when he said of "the as-structure of understanding" (p. 191), placed in the philosophical foreground by Heidegger, that "*as* means here what it always does: both *is* and *is not*" (p. 192). The sudden experience of a third possibility by one seemingly caught between two equally unacceptable, and opposing options, the binary conundrum, was called by Jung the transcendent function (CW 8). It was likened by Helena Schulman Lorenz (2004) to soul-making. A breakthrough that "unites the opposites in a previously unimagined way," she said, will evince "multiplicity, unconscious edges, silenced possibilities, and spontaneous ruptures" (p. 236). Rupture, we recall, is the term Derrida used to describe the emergence into metaphysics of the revaluation that puts absolutes in play. Nietzsche found it impossible to take the middle way, though destabilizing the generalized principle, that is, the authority of the concept, he achieved a proto-Hermetic stance. Rüdiger Safranski (2003) put it thusly: "Although he was unable to escape this ultimately metaphysical reliance on principles, he insisted that the principle not become a point of repose, but rather a locus of trepidation, perhaps even a heart of darkness" (p. 289).

Imaginal psychology seeks its own locus of metaphorical (if not existential) agitation in a "Mediterranean fantasy" (Hillman, 1983b, p. 2), a journey down and south from Alpine heights—although, it must be said of this imaginal locale that it is more an Aegean fantasy, or an Aegean fantasy of the Mediterranean, which has yet more southerly reaches than Greece. It is, however, upon just such an indeterminate sea that Nietzsche's metaphorical man sets sail. "As Ulysses fixed his gaze on the distance," wrote Kafka (1971),

> the Sirens literally vanished before his resolution, and at the very moment when they were nearest to him he knew of them no longer . . . . But they—lovelier than ever—stretched their necks and turned, let their awesome hair flutter free in the wind, and freely stretched their claws on the rocks. They no longer had any desire to allure; all that they wanted was to hold as long as they could the radiance that fell from Ulysses' great eyes. (p. 531)

Neither summoned by the serenade of absolute meaning nor trembling before contingency, Kafka's Ulysses is perhaps aware of himself as an "artist from the beginning" (Kofman, 1993, p. 25). Addendum: Is it noteworthy that as Hillman and Michael Ventura (1992) sat together in an apartment above Sheridan Square in New York City discussing the absence of a culturally reparative aesthetic mode among the variety of "models for thinking about therapy" (medical, behavioral, analytical, etc.), they were repeatedly interrupted by the sound of wailing sirens from the street below? Did their work of "revisioning therapy as an aesthetic activity" (p. 128) intensify the call (in response to an emergency?) of the anaesthetic culture they were placing into critique?

An excursion on deviance

Kofman (1993) identified Nietzsche's inverted metaphysics—his metaphorics—with the Greek Chronos, the Roman Saturn. For the ancients, Saturn was both proclaimer of boundaries and transgressor of them. Wielder of the scythe if not the hammer, he established his rule over the heavens by castrating his father Ouranos, arresting the potency of an old order. Taking the term from *On Truth and Lies in an Extra-Moral Sense*, Kofman said, "the end of the reign of concepts brings with it a veritable Saturnalia" (p. 77), a reference to the January festivals in ancient Rome during which slaves became masters for a day: "[T]he natural and social orders are transgressed, and it then comes to light that they are not necessary but rest on simple conventions and on metaphors" (p. 77).

Jung (1989) reported that in a dream he was ordered to bow before the image of the Most High; unwilling to touch his forehead completely to the floor, he left a millimeter of space (p. 219). The dream reflects the integration of the shadow. Here as well is the saturnalia, reversal and revaluation of conventional hierarchies. In the subtitle of her study of the astrological Saturn, Liz Greene (1976) called him the "old devil." Perhaps in his dream Jung gave the old devil his due. Jung's struggle with the doctrine of *privatio boni*, evil as the privation of good, is well known (Bair, 2003, pp. 545f). His millimeter may symbolize the compensatory quantum of absence that, as one pole of the binary opposition, makes presence possible. As a boundary condition, it marks an already always breach in the self-same unity of eternity from which emerge the artifacts (art and facts) of the world. The millimeter is possibility and gap, the lacuna entailed by the logic of metaphor.

Bringing about its own forgetting, metaphor turns upon itself with seeming indifference. Conceptual memorialization confers an analgesic, making life possible. Perspective, the *poietic* formulation of a world, and *alethia*, the disclosure of *Dasein's* juxtaposition with a world, are the children of Hermes Psychopompos, transporter of consciousness across the meandering boundary between metaphysics and metaphorics. The astrological Mercury, said Robert Hand (1981), signifies the power to "overcome the gap between separate entities" (p. 55). Jung considered Mercurius to be the archetype *par excellence* of the collective unconscious, inexhaustible symbol of the alchemical enterprise and personification of oppositions (CW 14, par. 660). He theorized the collective unconscious as a domain of mind where oppositions are comprehended in their interpenetration or *coincidentia oppositoria*. Its *enantiodromic* contents, he said, are "mutually contaminated" (p. 463).

The theme is invoked by Derrida (1981) in his treatment of Plato's *Phaedrus*. Socrates related that the Egyptian god Thoth, who, like Hermes or Mercury, personifies communication, offers to the king, Thamus, the gift of writing as a cure for forgetfulness. But Thamus rejects the gift, seeing it instead as a poison to memory. The distancing of words from the presence of their creator causes an identity crisis. Will words not lose their meaning if they lie at the interpretive mercy of the world? Derrida said of Thoth, "If he had any identity—but he is precisely the god of nonidentity—he would be that *coincidentia oppositorum* to which we will soon have recourse again" (p. 93). The recourse refers to the binary opposition speech/writing, the deconstruction of which led Derrida (1981) to coin the term *differance*, meaning both to differ and to defer. The distinction between the word difference and the neologism *differance* (in French, *différence* and *différance*), the substitution of a single letter, appears solely in writing and is not vocalized—it indicates a pronounced difference that is, nevertheless, not pronounced. Because the distinction, though apparent solely in written form, pertains as well in speech, the term of art demonstrates that even the spoken word defers absolute identity with the speaker; a modicum, or *trace*, of otherness is present at the presumed beginning of language, already a *coincidentia oppositorum*. In an instance of the inherent deconstruction of the metaphysics of presence, Plato, in the *Phaedrus* (1963, p. 521), said speech was the writing of the soul. Employing Derrida, we can say that psyche is not so much called up by the grace note of the spoken word as is the collective unconscious plumbed by the metaphoric alterities of difference and deferral. "Metaphoricity," Derrida said, in the conclusion also reached by Jung, "is the logic of contamination" (1981, p. 149). It is presence contaminated by absence; Jung's millimeter.

Derrida described *writing* in its *de jure* antecedence to speech as *archi-ecriture*, that is, originary writing. The paradoxical term indicates that employing the language of metaphysics is unavoidable even in critique. Thinking the origin, center, or absolute is necessary to questioning their unaccountable suasion over thought. In a reciprocal application of archetypology and poststructuralism we can understand *archi-ecriture* to mean archetypal writing as personified by Mercurius, Thoth, and Hermes.

The story is told that when Hermes sprang from his mother's womb, he instantly felt hungry and became determined to steal and eat the cattle of his brother, Apollo. He fashioned a pair of shoes that pointed backwards so anyone who suspected his misdeed would trail him in the wrong direction. He skinned the stolen cows and stretched a hide across the hollowed shell of a tortoise. Stringing the shell with sheep gut, he made the first lyre. When Apollo confronted him, at first he denied culpability and then traded the lyre for the missing cows. "Co-emergent with the creation of the lyre," said Noel Cobb (1992), noting the essential deviance, "is the creation of metaphor" (p. 243). Suzi Harvey (2000) expanded upon Cobb's observation. "When Hermes first sees the tortoise," she said, "he calls it a 'friend of the feast,' for he sees through to the hidden music which will be released with the death of the literal thing" (p. 3). The myth presents us not with esoteric Hermeticism, the hidden truth revealed for the properly initiated, but with a personification of originary deviance—and an original lyre or liar (a homonym, or unity, whose defining heterodoxy is discoverable only in *writing* or *archi-ecriture*).

A further insight into the connection of Hermes to metaphor is made by Lewis Hyde (1998) in his *Trickster Makes This World*. Hyde expounded upon the two kinds of chance postulated by an authority of the unpredictable, Jacques Monod:

operational chance and *absolute* chance. In the first type, a chance event "unfolds along a single path" (p. 119). A roll of the dice or a spin of the roulette wheel are examples of single path contingency. "It is only because the causes are too subtle, the chain of events too long, the sequence too fast, and so forth, that the outcome is an apparent accident" (p. 119).

Contingency of the absolute kind, on the other hand, requires the convergence of *two* events (distinguishing it from the singular Absolute of the ontotheological kind, yet demonstrating that even contingency can be inscribed within essentialist terminology). According to Hyde (1998), Aristotle's example of "accident" in the *Physics* is an instance of this kind of chance. In the example, "A farmer, digging in his garden plot, happens upon a treasure that another man buried years ago," said Hyde, "The farmer intended to grow a crop; the other man intended to hide his gold; when these unrelated intentions meet, we have the true accident, the coincidence of unrelated causes" (p. 119). Similarly, said Hyde, when Hermes "happens upon" the tortoise, two intentions or events coincide, and new meaning is born. The infant Hermes, who, as we have seen, will come to serve as the midwife of Dionysian ambivalence, already abets the metaphoric production of meaningful coincidence.

Just as Apollo personifies clear-sighted consciousness, so Hermes, confabulator, trader, liar, thief, represents what is absent from it, the shadowy, irrational domain beyond the River Lethe. "Of course," said Hillman (1979b):

> Lethe played a poetic part in romanticism, but she also has had a significant role in the development of depth psychology, which began with Freud's investigation of the forgotten (in hysteria) and of the slips and holes, the tiny forgetfulnesses of consciousness. (p. 154)

The personification of anima that best corresponds to the gaps and possibilities of the unconscious may be the androgyne and ambivalent Dionysus, god of dismembering and re-membering, for whom Hermes was midwife. Metaphor's originary deviance, forgotten in the Apollonian concept, is memorialized in psyche, where the *metaphorica*, the art of memory, predominates. "We believe Freud," Hillman said, "not only because of the reasoning of his logic or the empirical demonstration of his evidence. We feel conviction because of the metaphorical substructure in the theory, which evokes in our memorial psyche the archetypal realm of the underworld" (p. 23).

What I want to call *lethography*, the forgetting of the libidinal and generative force of originary *writing* (in the sense of Nietzsche's generalization of metaphor to mean interpretation), results in an eventual return of the repressed, an incursion from the margins, the dwelling place of Hermes. The banishment of rhetoric as a danger to conceptual verity becomes a form of recovered memory in the style of Freud's hysterics. They occupied the gendered margins of the era; their will to power manifested in the fictions and fantasies of the consulting room, their life as art. Nietzsche, for whom maenadic truth was a bracing reality (the tragic sense) anticipated Freud as a theorist of the libidinal imperative of the unconscious.

Deutscher and Oliver (1999) said Kofman's Nietzsche rejected the pretense that "philosophy is distanced from sexual economy" (p. 6). Kofman, they said, pointed to the ideation of woman as an indicator of philosophical blind spots (p. 5). In a typical provocation, Nietzsche (2006) wrote, "The truth is a woman" (p. 311). "If woman *is* truth," Derrida (1978a) said, "*she* at least knows that there is no truth" (p. 53). When the Sphinx leapt to her ruin—and left Oedipus to his—might she have taken the riddle with her, leaving behind only deathly answers? "For Nietzsche," said Deutscher and Oliver, "truth originates in an abyss of metaphor" (p. 6). The abyss into which the Sphinx leapt, the *coincidentia oppositorum*, is precisely that domain of metaphoric morphology, "silenced possibilities, spontaneous ruptures," that engulfs, separates, remembers, forgets.

In its exile, metaphor—deviance—contemplates the pattern of its fate. Its ambiguity (from a root meaning "to wander") has yet to resolve; it cannot go home. Indeed, in the sense of a final cause, a *telos*, it has no home save that which it ap*propri*ates. It awaits the command of Apollo to unconceal truth in myriad fictions, upsetting, in the succession of paradigms, one patterning for another. "[T]ruthfulness (and metaphor)," Nietzsche said, "have produced the inclination for truth" (as cited in Kofman, 1993, p. 34). *Truth* is a concept, therefore a metaphor. The metaphoric urges named Artistry and Mnemosyny function as an unconscious process that spans and respans an ontological abyss even before self-awareness sets in, marking conceptuality, and the proper, as belated events.

By emphasizing the occurrence of forgetting at the inception of truth, metaphor's blanching in the blinding moment of concept formation, Nietzsche destabilized a structure of epistemology. Memory, along with perception, is a foundational pillar of knowledge that enables us to understand how we know what we know. If memory relies upon its negation, forgetting, to establish itself as a basis for truth, then we are justified in a philosophical project that transcends conceptual memorialization and takes image as an a priori. Richard Rorty (1979), problematizing foundationalist epistemology, such as the regime of reason seated in, and by proclamation of, the Cartesian *cogito*, said, "It is pictures rather than propositions, metaphors rather than statements, which determine most of our philosophical convictions" (p. 12). In the aftermath of Nietzsche, the philosophical task that remained was to analyze the dreams of the concept, its metaphorical depths, in search of a reality that cannot be had solely by the wisdom of reason.

Notes

1 "And so the question 'which one?' reverberates in and for all things: which forces, which will? This is the tragic question [i.e., the Dionysian question]" (Deleuze, 2006, p. 77).

2 *Conceptual metaphor* is a term of art introduced by George Lakoff and Mark Johnson (1980) to indicate a general category into which are grouped metaphors expressive of a particular concept. For example, the conceptual metaphor Conscious Is Up and its correlate Unconscious Is Down entails the expressions Get *up*, Wake *up*, I'm *up* already, He *rises* early in the morning, He *fell* asleep, He *dropped* off to sleep, He's *under* hypnosis, He *sank* into a coma.

4

THE COGNITIVE TURN

> The integration of the ape cures the "king." (Hillman, 1987, p. 46)
>
> The alluvial plain of metaphysics, flooded with certainty, richly Nile-istic: Thamus sojourns with Thoth, animal presence, baboon-headed *simia dei*, "scribe and teacher." (Hillman, 1987, p. 48)

The Platonic theory of mind in which "figurative or poetic assertions are distinct from true knowledge" finds its compensatory other in the poetic basis of mind, which asserts that "human cognition is fundamentally shaped by various poetic or figurative processes" (Gibbs, 1995, p. 3). The awakening of metaphor and philosophy to their co-creative possibilities evokes the poetic basis, which is also a principal presupposition of imaginal psychology. Hillman (1975) said of *Re-Visioning Psychology*, his imaginist manifesto,

> Here I am working toward a psychology of soul that is based in a psychology of image. Here I am suggesting both a *poetic basis of mind* and a psychology that starts neither in the physiology of the brain, the structure of language, the organization of society, nor the analysis of behavior, but in the processes of imagination. (p. xvii; original emphasis)

In what follows, I want to regard the poetic basis with specific reference to the interpretive importance of "figurative processes." As Dabney Townsend (1995) points out, theories of metaphor appear under two imprints, the "rhetorical and linguistic" and the "mythopoetic" (p. 199). The former begins with Aristotle and leads to the cognitive turn. The latter, whose theorists include Coleridge, Barfield, Cassirer, and Langer, are of less concern, both for reasons of space and because our narrative principally has to do with metaphor's cognitive bona fides.

Yet two explanations are called for. If Hillman "worked toward" a psychology that did not "start" in the structure of language, how might his metaphorics be considered poststructural, a designation implying a start in language? Further, if Derrida opened the possibility of reading philosophy as mythopoesis, why elide the mythopoetic theories?

The answer to the first question is that poststructural theories are *linguistic* not in the strict sense of their involvement with language as another indubitable starting point for methodological construction, but because *language* designates the uncartesian doubt that such a starting point is attainable. This is not to say that starting points are dispensable. On the contrary, they are necessary, but like all philosophical bedrock, they are the product of molten circumstance. The best we can do if we want to be perspectival is to recognize that our sacred ground, whether it be language, reason, imagination, matter, spirit, or soul, is provisional and in continual differential relation with us, and to check our invocation of it against our intentions, interrogating our moralities for their effects. This is to say, then, that imaginal psychology need not unequivocally "start" in language to be poststructural—or for that matter, Hermetic—it need only "work toward a psychology of image" as differential relation. My double contention is that *image* in imaginal psychology adequates to metaphor, and that metaphor and differential relation are personified in the figure of Hermes. Under his aegis, *language* takes part in an archetypal, that is to say *poietic*, structure characterized by difference and deferral. Regarding the second question, it is not sufficient in a deconstructive sense merely to supplant the rational basis of mind with a poetic basis. Reversing the cognitive hierarchy without revaluing its terms simply maintains the rule of presence in a Romantic rather than a rational sense; the purity of *oratorio* replaces the purity of *ratio*. A revaluation requires that "poetic basis" indicate the interpretive trait subordinated in either hierarchy. My point is not to argue for an aggrandizing mythopoetic view of metaphor against a reductive analytical view, but to accentuate the *poietic* quality inherent in either view, to put metaphor in *play*.

Perceptions of metaphor in the lingering era of its repression have been itemized by Zoltán Kövecses (2002), who catalogued five popularly held beliefs that pertain today but are no longer regarded by scholars as adequate to the topic. These beliefs hold that metaphor is:

1. a property of words; it is a linguistic phenomenon;
2. used for some artistic and rhetorical purpose;
3. based on a resemblance between the two entities that are compared and identified;
4. a conscious and deliberate use of words requiring a special talent;
5. a figure of speech that we can do without, used for special effects, and not an inevitable part of everyday human communication, let alone everyday human thought and reasoning. (pp. vii–viii)

Metaphor theory has burgeoned since these properties were first called into question by Richards and Black as early as the 1930s. It now involves scholars from wide-ranging disciplines. It is beyond the scope of this book to navigate the various tributaries spilling from an increasingly robust academic specialty. In this chapter, I will follow the development of the contemporary theory of metaphor, as described by Mark Johnson (1981), from its beginnings in the classical word-to-object approach espoused at the end of the nineteenth century to the contemporary view, which I interpret as a systems theoretical notion. "Systems thinking," said Fritjof Capra (1996), "is 'contextual' thinking" (p. 37). It marks a perceptual shift from objects to processes. "In the systems view," pictured in biology, physics, cognitive science, and gestalt psychology, Capra said, "we realize that the objects themselves are networks of relationships, embedded in larger networks. For the systems thinker the relationships are primary" (p. 37). The relationships among processes in an overall system give rise to "emergent" properties that distinguish levels of complexity. The complexities at one level of organization result from interactions at a lower level whose constituents do not on their own exhibit the properties that emerge from their conjunction. Susan Rowland (2005) made the association of metaphorics to systems thinking in analytical psychology when she said of Jung's style of argumentation that it favors analogy over a "hierarchical logical model" (p. 76). "[A]nalogy," Rowland said, "is more of a web or a network" (p. 76). My intention is to focus on the importance to contemporary metaphor theory of context, which shifts the sense of metaphor from linguistic object to interrelation. I want as well to further the argument that, for imaginal psychology, metaphor is the basic mode of soul. "[P]syche," Hillman said, "exists wholly in relational systems" (Hillman & Ventura, 1992, p. 83). Based on Johnson's survey of modern theorizing, the coming discussion will involve four significant themes, *similarity*, *comparison*, *interaction*, and *metaphor as pragmatics*. It will also be concerned with the influence of Richards and Black, lingering on the open-ended, tensional nature of the interaction theory to which they jointly contributed, and which, in my reading, enables a revaluation of falsity. As we move through developmental stages of the contemporary theory, I will populate a table of terms for further use in Part II.

Johnson (1981) formulated "the problems of metaphor that have been of interest to philosophers, linguists and psychologists" (p. 20) as a set of three questions: what is metaphor, how does it work, and what is its cognitive status? These are inquiries into metaphor's *transposition* from a category of rhetoric to a process of cognition.[1] In the modern view, "Metaphor is not merely a linguistic entity, but rather a process by which we encounter our world," Johnson said (p. 15). Applying Hillman's distinction above regarding a psychology of image, we can say that the cognitive theory of metaphor (figure, image) *started* in language, but *worked toward* the meta-linguistic claim that, as Johnson said, "all experience has an 'as' structure" (p. 43). The progression of metaphor from linguistic species categorized as an improper but decorative use of language toward a rendering in terms of experiential context was akin to the generalization of *linguistics* by structuralism. As Christopher Hauke (2000) notes, structuralism "is a method for analyzing how humans build up and communicate their apperceptions of [the] world, it is not about that world in a physical scientific sense" (p. 194). Inquiry shifted from a concern with absolute reality to an interest in how realities are constructed. Similarly, metaphoric theorizing left behind its concern for the propriety of meaning to explore "knowledge of speaker, speech situation, and world" (Johnson, 1981, p. 24). In both cases, signification—significance—came to be viewed not in the sense of the external referent and its re-presentations, but in the sense of the contingent, discursive gleanings of that *bricoleur*, reflective judgment.

Johnson's (1981) threshold question, a consideration of kind, shortly began to admit of a certain inconclusivity. The inquiries assumed metaphor's deviance from ordinary speech and sought to locate the point of departure. They reflected the observation made by Thomas Kuhn (1996) that "research under a paradigm must be a particularly effective way of inducing paradigm change" (p. 52). An initial strategy was to seek deviance in syntax, but theorists soon discovered that unconventional syntax was "neither a necessary nor sufficient condition of metaphor" (p. 21). Metaphoric statements could be as orderly and well-arranged as any other linguistic construct. The focus shifted to semantic deviance. Pioneers of the semantic approach included Monroe Beardsley, Paul Henle, and Nelson Goodman. They suggested that metaphor required self-contradiction, specifically "logical opposition" (Beardsley, 1981, p. 112), "a clash of literal meanings" (Henle, 1981, p. 92), or a contra-indication of terms (Goodman, 1968, p. 69). But the theorist Ina Loewenberg (1981) found that semantic deviance, too, fails as a necessary and sufficient condition due to the discretionary nature of sentential context. "Any sentence," she said, "can be provided contexts . . . in which it can receive either literal or metaphorical interpretations" (p. 161).

Loewenberg (1981) urged a consideration of contextuality beyond the sentence. For a metaphorical sentence to aid understanding, she said, its context must extend to knowledge of the speaker's frame of reference. Johnson cited examples of sentences that are metaphorical and at the same time literal, such as "Idi Amin is an animal" or "She lives in a glass house." Amin was *Homo sapiens* and also psychopathological (note that the other species of animals are not said to display psychopathic behavior; the metaphor conveys meaning not as a result of any literal comparison involving the word "animal"); similarly, one may live in a dwelling made of glass and propose an argument easily shattered by its hypocrisy. In these examples, the metaphorical and the literal share a polysemous ground. To distinguish them as metaphorical or literal turns out to be less a matter of *parole*, the usage of words, than of *langue*, the conditions of semantic possibility in which speaker and hearer are mutually intertwined. In a sense, metaphor's transformation from fanciful descriptor of objects to creator of meaning required an imaginative opening to the possibility that metaphor is not a linguistic object to be isolated and identified, but a way of understanding and experiencing meaning-making in terms of a dynamism of differential relations.

Contextual broadening can be seen as an integration of the notion of *play* in a deconstructive and performative sense; metaphor's intertextual *performance* is the enaction of the world. The metaphoric *mise en scène* branched from words to sentences to the furniture of the world, not as pale imitation, but as (cathartic) theatre of ideas. Yet theorizing at first stopped short of revaluing the opposition metaphorical/literal. Only as theorists turned from the perception of metaphorical statements as untrue *vis-à-vis* proper speech did the cognitive possibility enter into view. Scholars worked from Loewenberg's assessment that the horizon of metaphorical context surpasses the sentence, but began to question the dichotomy literal/metaphorical she and others had retained. The perceptual shift was akin to an integration of projection. No longer could theory sustain the view that deviant expression was apart *from* the proper; it began to entertain the startling conjecture that deviance might be a part *of* the proper. We can surmise a paradigm shift, said Kuhn (1996), when "the anomalous has become the expected" (p. 53). Max Black was the leading proponent of the emerging view. "Just as there is no infallible test for resolving ambiguity," Black (1977) said, "so there is none to be expected in discriminating the metaphorical from the literal" (p. 450). The foregrounding of ambiguity and the failure of discriminatory capacity would appear to mark Black's thesis as an argument from liminality.

More rule than exception, deviance has perhaps come to qualify as the necessary and sufficient condition of metaphorical creativity. "[I]dentification of an utterance as metaphorical," Johnson (1981) said, "does seem to involve some strain between the normal sense of the utterance and the total speech situation in which it occurs" (p. 23). Aberration, as even Aristotle admitted, produced textual luster. Rather than normalizing metaphor against its classical categorization as misleading, contemporary theory has embraced the contextual imbalance or asymmetry. The false, the deviant, and the misleading, no longer irrelevant to meaning-making, begin to appear as its unavoidable basis.

The expiration of the taxonomical approach entailed a relativistic account of truth and lies. In the breakthrough to metaphor's cognitive status, falsity might now be seen not as improper word/object pairing, but as the incommensurability native to context, that is, as the weave of differential relation. "We apprehend an utterance as metaphorical," Johnson (1981) said, "not because of its literal falsity (though that may be a clue), but, more generally, because of a tension between the literal reading and its context (of which literal falsity is one instance)" (p. 23). The principal entailment here is the modulating of *cognition* from the Kantian faculty of the understanding to the more commodious definition in aesthetics proposed by Pillow (2001). The literal comes to acknowledge its provenance in the contingent operation of reflective judgment, by which, as we have seen, "the imagination freely plays with (reflects on) a series of representations in search of a unifying principle" (Johnson, 1981, p. 39). In a Nietzschean sense, the meaning that emerges from literalism's contextual imperative is a product of the conflictual drives, instincts sorting themselves out in competition and cooperation to find the semantic fit best suited to an instant circumstance. A discursive nature catalyzes paradigms of fact and value as it encounters itself in its various, and variously compatible, aspects. "The semantic resources of the language," said Ted Cohen (1981), "yield novel meaning when they are made to collide, either with one another or with other parts of the speech situation. The utterance forces at our disposal yield novel acts when they are somehow askew" (p. 196).

The irregularity built into the modern definition conjures Hermes. Recall that Lewis Hyde (1998) identified the trickster with Jacques Monod's *absolute* form of chance, an interaction of two incongruent intentions, distinguished by Monod from *operational* chance, the attenuation of a developmental path to an apparently accidental result. The unresolved definitional question, in effect, metaphor's irresolution, is what offers the possibility of a new orientation to the deviance with which it has been associated. Falsity as distinguished from literal speech leaves us with opposing absolutes, yet falsity as intrinsic *privatio boni*, the "old devil," suggests a formal imperfectability in which contingencies of world and language are susceptible to one another's deviations. The metaphoric process turned out to be prone to a type of indeterminability in the face of investigations seeking to reveal objective properties—metaphor as Schrödinger's cat. Theorists had rightly sensed the signal importance of deviance, but they were nevertheless confounded by it. Drawing from Edward Casey (1976), we can see the problem in terms of phenomenology, which strives, said Casey:

> to make more thematic what is otherwise merely implicit and taken for granted in human experience. . . . The phenomenologist's basic attitude is: no matter how something came to be in the first place, what is of crucial concern is the detailed description of the phenomenon as it now appears. (p. 9)

Deviance did not lend itself to causal determination; it was implicit in experience. It could neither be explained nor explained away. The inquiry into how metaphor might be understood against a background of literal truth may have reached its logical, or logico-metaphorical, conclusion in a description of metaphor as it appeared, that is, as truth in deviance, and, heeding Wittgenstein, maintaining silence about the rest.

Though efforts to affix metaphor to a philosophical proposition or truth claim were spiraling—the vertiginous danger of the hermeneutic circle—into widening, and inconclusive, contextual gyres, the second of Johnson's three questions, how do metaphors work, a question of function, proved more amenable to theorizing. Two operational theories emerged from the new school of metaphor studies, the comparison view and the interaction view. The former is a version of the traditional understanding of metaphor as a substitution of one kind of speech (decorative) for another (literal). Johnson (1981) identified the traditional substitution view as a strong subset of the comparison view (p. 24). The terms *comparison* and *interaction* were coined by Black (1981) in his pivotal essay marking the turn to the modern theory. Their significance for the Hermetic view lies partly in the metamorphosis already suggested of deviance and falsity. As interaction succeeds comparison, the "false" undergoes a change in kind, in keeping perhaps with the "redistribution of individuals among natural families" that marks Kuhn's (1993) theory of paradigm shifts in science (p. 540). Just as Copernicus moved the earth, placing it for the first time in the family of planets, and the moon, removing it from that family, so too did contemporary theorists of metaphor redistribute the false, in this case from the category of the corrupt to the category of the natural. In each case, the shift was metaphorical and astronomical.

Johnson (1981) leads us through the succession of theories. Substitution takes the metaphorical form "A is B" and explains it as "nothing but an indirect way of presenting some intended literal meaning 'A is C'" (p. 24). Comparison, on the other hand, broadens "A is B" to mean "A is like B." The insertion of the prepositional form of "like" is not meant to indicate the absence of an implied "like" in the substitution view, which would reduce the metaphor to a simile, but rather to use "like" as a form of notation that indicates the introduction of context. In the standard example "Man is a wolf," the comparison theory understands the likening of "wolf" to "man" as an extension of references beyond the sentence. "Man is a wolf" generates understanding via uncanny association of canid with human, catalyzing "a set of relevant similarities" not overt in the sentence but extant in an extra-sentential imaginal domain or *pseudo-domain* (p. 25). In the substitution theory, indifferent to context, metaphor is objectified and denatured, "a mere stylistic ornament that is reducible to literal statements without loss of cognitive content" (p. 25).

Comparison, on the other hand, admits of a nascent systems approach in which metaphoric relata can be understood less as billiard balls displacing one another on a woven baize than as corollaries of the weave itself. But as the paradigm shift gathered momentum, comparison proved unsatisfactory in two ways. The first is specificity. As Johnson (1981) noted, "Any two objects are similar in some respects, and the comparison view does not explain how we are able to pick out the relevant similarities in each instance" (p. 26). As a category of linguistic function, comparison is not sufficiently subtle, and as an instrument of measurement it is not precise enough, to sift the operative element in metaphor. The second shortfall is one-sidedness. An emphasis on similarity, Johnson said, "ignores the sometimes crucial role of differences and disanalogies" that can "force us imaginatively to restructure our way of comprehending things" (p. 26). Comparison's forgetting of catalytic difference constrained it from a full compass of metaphor's operation. This is so because it regarded metaphoric deviance not as given, but as insurgent, making semantic incursions from the Dionysian border into any self-enclosed Apollonian system of meaning.

In effect, comparison had yet to reflect a loosened, Dionysian, state of awareness. It halted at an epistemological border. In a deconstructive sense, its focus remained on the positivity rather than the interstice; it perceived the word, the logos, as an object rather than as a relation. It was Derrida's insight that the constituting factor in structuralism's system of differential relations was not the presence of the contrasting elements, but the unthematized absence of the space between them. "Spacing," Derrida (1997) said, "is always the unperceived, the nonpresent, and the nonconscious" (p. 68). By reading for latent deconstructive tendencies, Derrida made room in philosophy for the unsettling spectre of its unperceived spaces, "the structurality of structure" (p. 280). By applying the deconstructive trope of spacing to the development of modern metaphor theory, we can reiterate the above citation from Hillman, and understand theorizing as a "working toward" the discernment of image as a network of relations. If it is the case that metaphysics constitutes itself *linguistically*, that is, differentially or metaphorically, which are tantamount to the same thing, then it must as well partake of the conditions of *linguistic* possibility, which are not suspended in the presence of a transcendental signified. This latter, no matter how high, is still perched in a field of infinite play.

Following upon their recognition of comparison's shortcomings, theorists delivered a *coup de grâce*, contending that metaphor can function in the absence of comparison altogether. Whether, like Monroe Beardsley (1981), they sought to reimagine classical theory, or, like John Searle (1981), to maintain it in principle, theorists moved metaphor beyond language and into the world. Beardsley and Searle unchained operational theorizing from literal word-to-object comparison with a shared insight that, as Johnson (1981) put it, "metaphors need not depend on actual properties of existing objects, but rather on relations at the level of meanings or of beliefs about objects" (p. 26). The analytical inquiry into how metaphor works saw itself transposed to ask instead the self-critical question of what world hypothesis metaphor *works toward*. For example, in a consideration of point of view rather than absolute properties, we can understand the metaphor "Idi Amin is an animal" as an invocation of intertwined beliefs, in the form of subsidiary metaphors, at work within the sentence as presuppositions about race and "lower" animals as "beasts" or "brutes" (a condition tacitly, and erroneously, assumed by the metaphor to have been overcome by some other order of human).

As the joint insights of Beardsley and Searle demonstrate, the paradigm shift was furthered by cognitivist thinkers and literalists alike. Searle's (1981) assertion that a metaphor reduces to the literal meaning of its words led him to reject the argument from similarity. "Though similarity often plays a role in the *comprehension* of metaphor," he said, "the metaphorical assertion is not necessarily an *assertion* of similarity" (p. 259). He offered classic examples, such as "Sally is a block of ice," which appear not to operate by means of empirical likeness. It may not be difficult in this simple metaphor to grasp the speaker's intention to convey Sally's "coldness," but Searle's larger point is that for a hearer to grasp the meaning of any metaphor requires knowledge of the speaker's intention, or, put differently, that speaker and hearer partake of common assumptions. Searle referred to such contextually derived intention as "utterance meaning," contrasting it with literal "sentence meaning," discernable within the four corners of the sentence (p. 249). It is not alteration in the meaning of the sentence that makes the metaphor, Searle argued, but the extra-sentential intention. "Our task in constructing a theory of metaphor," he said, "is to try to state the principles which relate literal sentence meaning to metaphorical utterance meaning" (p. 250).

Searle's invocation of intention followed from his view of metaphor as pragmatics, the branch of linguistics concerned with sentences not as statements, but as actions. We will explore the consequences of extending metaphor theory into pragmatics shortly. Though Searle's own intention was to maintain the literal integrity of the sentence, one could take his formulation of the task at hand to indicate that any adequate theory must situate the literal within a metaphorical surround—perhaps depicting it, as in a pointillist portrait, dissimulating into its environment. With each broadening of contextuality, from words to sentences to intentions, theorizing moved further toward a systems view in which the elements of metaphor, whether words, sentences, or intentions, are not objects, but processes interacting within a larger process of interpretive experience.

Another opening to context had been expressed by Beardsley (1981), who set out, he said, "to distinguish what might be called a thing-approach and a word-approach to the problem of analyzing metaphor" (p. 105). In the thing-approach, an "object comparison theory," a term foreign to the literal setting of the sentence, a "modifier," as Beardsley termed it, is understood as imported into the sentential situation for its ability to delight sensibility. Beardsley (1981) used an example from T. S. Eliot's *Four Quartets*: "Frigid purgatorial fires / Of which the flame is roses, and the smoke is briars" (p. 106). To discern the meaning of the metaphor, said Beardsley, the thing-approach asks that we connect the relata "smoke" and "briars" by reference to the properties of briars—thorny plants evidently used to make tobacco pipes (which produce smoke). The thing-approach may be likened to analytical method, a means, Capra (1996) said, of "taking something apart in order to understand it" (p. 30). Yet by placing its focus on the relata, it leaves us with an impoverished sense of their conjoined implications. It lacks for elegance, and, one might say, conjures a universe awaiting a Keplerian paradigm shift. Until Kepler worked out the mathematics of elliptical orbits, the motion of the planets was tethered to the ideal of a perfect circle, requiring the imposition of epicycle upon epicycle in order to avoid the specter of deviation from a faultless state. By shrugging off the absolute, metaphor frees perception from scholastic contortions. Beardsley's word-approach, a "verbal opposition theory," brings into comparison not literal characteristics, but allusive connotations, the briar-like crown of thorns in the Christian story. The difference, later picked up by Searle, is that "the connotations are controlled not only by the properties the object actually has but by those it is widely believed to have—even if the belief is false" (Beardsley, 1981, p. 107). Beardsley said the thing-approach limits semantic possibility by requiring "aptness," the search for a comparison that would make literal sense of metaphorical image. Aptness insists upon the interpolation of extraneous and unnecessary elements to satisfy the logical mind.

The imposed elements insult the integrity of the rhetorical figure. Beardsley (1981) supplied the example of Brutus' sword in Mark Antony's speech: "Mark how the blood of Caesar follow'd it, / As rushing out of doors, to be resolv'd / If Brutus so unkindly knock'd or no." In an interpretation, cited by Beardsley, of the metaphor "rushing out of doors," the critic found the need to interpolate the action of a page opening a door (p. 107). There is no page in the passage, and Beardsley warned that the need for a referent—the objective factor jettisoned by Saussure—as justification for significance violates the datum of the metaphorical image. The phenomenology of the trope is overlooked in favor of analytical or causal suppositions. "The correct question," Beardsley said, is not *what referent*, but "what is *meant* by the words—what properties are attributed to the daggers via the *marginal* [emphasis added] meanings of the metaphorical attribute" (p. 108). What Beardsley in effect suggested was that a theory of metaphor stick to the image, which presents its own intrinsic meaning.

Beardsley's invocation of marginal meanings gets at metaphor's Hermetic quality. Each of the three theories here considered, classical substitution, modern comparison, and poststructural interaction, constitutes a Wittgensteinian language game, a world-creating discourse with its own rules or codes of enaction. Having noted deconstruction's metaphor of textual interaction as a field of play, we might understand language games as a special case of *līlā*, the cosmic game of games described in Hindu texts (see Grof, 1998, for a psychological rendering). In the verbal opposition theory, said Beardsley, "a special feat of language, or verbal play, involving two levels of meaning in the modifier" provides the key to the semantic riddle (1981, p. 106). To reprise an earlier theme, we can say that, in its propriety, the object comparison theory sends Meaning to her abyssal demise while the verbal opposition theory maintains a certain aporetic equipoise that keeps Meaning in play. To wit, Beardsley:

> When a predicate is metaphorically adjoined to a subject, the predicate loses its ordinary extension, because it acquires a new intension—perhaps one that it has in no other context. And this twist of meaning is forced by inherent tensions, or oppositions, within the metaphor itself. (p. 106)

The innovation is here epitomized by the use of "twist" to indicate metaphorical play. The notion of inherent twistedness in the occurrence of predicates, givens, predispositions, and assumptions suggests that language entails a plasticity that reflects the Hermetic game of games to which it gives expression. Deviance becomes the very basis of the Apollonian Good, True, and Beautiful.

Beardsley's theory is based in the interaction view, a reimagining of metaphor that shifts its emphasis from words as building blocks to sentences as living forces inextricably embedded in their physical, cultural, and psychological surround. It posits the economy of metaphor as a double interaction: an exchange of value between two semantic domains—the experience of one thing in terms of another—and between the metaphor's producer and its consumer. "Interactionist theories," said Kirk Pillow (2001),

> emphasize the extent to which metaphors serve to organize experience at fundamental levels. They orient perception, self-understanding, and action, and so the production of new metaphors always poses a challenge to the status quo of participants in a given world. Metaphors shape the network of connotations to which they appeal in their transfers; they can alter that network in remarkable ways when people find a transformation of their world compelling enough to validate and enact. (p. 198)

Thomas Kuhn (1993) captured the interactive quality in a rhetorical question. "Is what we refer to as 'the world'," he wondered, "perhaps a product of a mutual accommodation between experience and language?" (p. 542).

In the interaction view, Johnson (1981) said, "understanding a metaphor is not typically a matter of comparing actual properties of objects; rather, it is based upon what the terms of the metaphor call to mind for us" (p. 28). The conjured associations derive from "commonplaces," or "whatever properties and relations are commonly believed to be true of an object, person, event, etc.," even if they are in fact false (p. 27). Interaction causes:

> one entire *system* of commonplaces (e.g., that of *wolf*) to "filter" or organize our conception of some other *system* (e.g., that of *man*). The "interaction" is a screening of one system of commonplaces by another to generate a new conceptual organization of, a new perspective on, some object. (p. 28)

The paradigm shift (a shift of paradigms in metaphor theory, and more generally, a shift to thinking in terms of paradigm) effected by interaction is due largely to such a systems approach. It refrains from taking semantic "objects" of "comparison" in isolation, preferring instead to recognize them as interrelations among sets of processes. It postulates that one set of conceptual associations might participate in the notional associations of another set, bringing forth new and unheard of complexities. The interaction evinces the behavior of constituent processes as each engages the most well-devised fit with other constituents in its semantic environment—*experiencing and understanding "itself" in terms of the other.* Interaction unsettles essence, shifting the paradigm of metaphor's quiddity from artificial linguistic representation to artifact (art and fact) of nature, and to language and culture as nature *extensa.*

The pivotal theorist of interaction was Max Black, who drew from an insight made by I. A. Richards. "Black's account," Johnson (1981) said, "is basically a development of Richards's cryptic remark that the metaphorical generation of meaning results from the 'interaction between co-present thoughts'" (p. 27). Richards, writing in the 1930s, was rejecting received wisdom. As we have seen, his nineteenth-century forerunners in philosophy and literary theory assumed metaphor to involve a swapping out of words. Richards (1981) thought the age-old assumption meager. The "traditional theory noticed only a few of the modes of metaphor," he said, and mistakenly "reduced it to a verbal matter" (p. 51). If we apply to Richards's own work a litmus test he sought in the work of others, we could say that he described "problems to be taken up, reframed and carried forward" (p. 57). The problems he identified as principal were three: the lack of clear terms of art to describe the relata of a metaphoric expression that work together (by pulling against one another) to produce novelty, the theoretical inattention to *how* words interact to produce metaphor, and the failure of theorists to consider metaphor's provenance in thought. Indeed, for philosophy and its disciplinary offshoots, metaphor was in more than one sense explicitly *not* thought.

Richards was the first to coin terms of art for the two ideas that are conjoined in any metaphor. In this naming enterprise, he followed Samuel Johnson (1709–1784). Keeping with classical theory and its admonishments, Dr. Johnson said, "As to metaphorical expression, that is a great excellence in style, when it is used with propriety, for it gives you two ideas for one" (as cited in Richards, 1981, p. 52). In a dialectics of metaphor, these are the ideas whose involvement produces a third iteration that "carries beyond" either of them into novel meaning. The first, or thematic, idea that is acted upon and becomes the subject of elaboration, the melodic line if you will, Richards (1981) called the *tenor*. The second, or transitive, idea that urges the tenor toward new expressions of its basic nature, he termed the *vehicle*. In the familiar example "Man is a wolf," the tenor is "man" and the vehicle, lending the tenor nuance, is "wolf." The act of naming brought into the foreground the agency of these two ideas, enabling their functional interdependence to be discerned. The "co-presence" of the vehicle and tenor, Richards said, "results in a meaning . . . which is not attainable without their interaction" (p. 55). This systems theoretical notion of co-presence was a radical departure from the declining idea of figurative decoration. "[T]he vehicle is not normally a mere embellishment of a tenor which is otherwise unchanged by it but that vehicle and tenor in co-operation give a meaning of more varied powers than can be ascribed to either," Richards said (p. 55).

Richards (1981) upset the notion that figurative language obscures the nature of "plain meaning," hindering cognition (p. 55). He proposed instead that metaphor serves as a basis of reason's meaning-making capacity. Metaphor is not, he said, "a shifting and displacement of words," but "a borrowing between and intercourse of *thoughts*, a transaction between contexts" (p. 51). Though still partly working from a comparativist perspective, he announced emphatically that "*Thought* is metaphoric, and proceeds by comparison, and the metaphors of language derive therefrom" (p. 51). In an archetypal mode that, following Hillman, we can call *personifying*, Richards asserted:

> Our world is a projected world, shot through with *characters* [emphasis added] leant to it from our own life. . . . The processes of metaphor in language, the exchanges between the meanings of words . . . are superimposed upon a perceived world *which is itself a product of earlier or unwitting metaphor*. (p. 60; emphasis added)

The world as a product of "unwitting" metaphor evokes the recondite or (to use Johnson's term for Richards's remark that generated contemporary theorizing) cryptic nature of the characterological ideas with which we identify. These ideas are our proximate causes. We see through them unto a world of their making, but their proximity (we believe ourselves to be identical with them) leaves us without the distance necessary for discernment. We see through them and are incapable of seeing through them, a metaphoric and Hermetic paradox.

In a further departure from the positivist assumptions of the analogical-metaphorical reduction, in which words were analogues of objects and analogy was itself objectified, Richards (1981) introduced into contextualization the role of what he called "missing parts" (p. 50). With the dissociation of the presumptive integrity of "parts" into interactive processes, meaning becomes a consequence of "the delegated efficacy of signs by which they bring together into new unities the abstracts, or aspects, which are the missing parts of their various contexts" (p. 50).

This nod to the lacunae of meaning-making, whereby absence plays a constructive role, anticipates poststructural critiques of the valorization of self-presence—that is, meaning unclouded by "otherness"—in metaphysics from Plato onward. The classical theory held metaphor to be *supplementary* to the proper designation of word to referent. It could be employed decoratively or, better yet, dispensed with to secure transparency. Acknowledgment of cognition's metaphoric basis restored the ineluctability of an absent or supplementary other not to be foreclosed against. Of philosophy's perennial disregard for writing as a distancing supplement that obscures the immediacy of meaning available in speech, Derrida (1997) said that those concepts philosophy regards as supplementary it concomitantly perceives to be reflecting "a debased, lateralized, repressed, displaced theme, yet exercising a permanent and obsessive pressure from the place where it remains held in check" (p. 270). With the invocation of co-present thoughts, we have an already always reserve of otherness in the metaphorics of presence.

The incipient systems approach of Richards's answer to the second of the questions that Johnson said concerned contemporary theorists, how metaphors work, came to be formalized by Max Black (1981), for whom the metaphoric relata "are often best regarded as 'systems of things' rather than 'things'" (p 78). Systems theory, Capra (1996) said, proposes that the parts of an organism exist not *for* each other, as a mechanistic science would have it, but *by means of* each other "in the sense of producing one another" (p. 22). The basic idea is evinced by Lakoff and Johnson (1980) in the modern theory of how metaphor works, for which Black was the forerunner. As we have seen, they supplied the formula that metaphor amounts to "understanding and experiencing one kind of thing *in terms of* another" (p. 5).

It was Black who provided the provocation for this integral view. His essay "Metaphor" (Black, 1981, originally published in 1955) marked the start of modern theorizing.[2] Whereas traction for a cognitive theory of metaphor eluded Richards, Black could claim greater success. Johnson (1981) cited two principal reasons. Richards's work appeared in the heyday of logical positivism when language seemed on the brink of revealing a science of truth claims. Given the climate of objectivism, Johnson said, "It was not prudent to insist that thought is essentially metaphoric, that metaphors are cognitively irreducible and indispensable, and that any adequate account of meaning and truth must give a central place to metaphor" (p. 19). Then, too, Richards was not a philosopher, but a literary critic. Disciplinary boundaries, and the question of the boundary in philosophy, were not ripe for review. Black, on the other hand, could invoke the authority of the analytical philosopher. Although his agitations from within the discipline "posed an unpopular challenge to certain basic assumptions of mainstream Anglo-American philosophy," Johnson said, he nevertheless "succeeded in getting a few adventuresome souls to take metaphor seriously" (p. 19).

Black's (1981) principal innovation was to radicalize the second of Johnson's questions to ask, "[i]n what sense, if any, is a metaphor 'creative'" (p. 64). He thus ventured the hypothesis, later elaborated by Searle, of metaphor as pragmatics, that is, as a motive force in the creation of a world. He did not adopt Richards's terms, *tenor* and *vehicle*, for the "two ideas" that collide (or conspire) to construct (or unconceal) fresh meaning. He expressed the emergent concept of mutual participation with terms of his own coinage, *focus* and *frame*. The focus corresponds to the principal idea in the metaphorical transfer that serves to hold the attention, and the frame to the secondary idea or structuring unit that imposes new circumstances on the focus so as to semantically influence it. With Black's entry into the field, we have a five-part vocabulary, beginning with Dr. Johnson, with which to distinguish the structure of metaphoric operation (Table 1).

We will add to this table as we proceed, producing by chapter's end a lexicon of metaphoric "interplay." The term is Black's (1981, p. 66), and it cannot, in the current context, avoid hints of the use of *play* by Derrida (1978b). As noted, Derrida used *play* to distinguish the elasticity of the differential relation from the fixity of the absolute. Derrida associated play with *tension*, a defining term of contemporary metaphor theory that indicates the nature of the relation between the two ideas that are met in metaphor. The ideas stand in a binary position to one another that becomes revalued or deconstructed by the tensional alchemy of the metaphoric process. For Derrida, an inherent "tension between play and presence" provides that presence is never entirely, or purely, itself, but is always already contaminated by the absence that provides the condition of its possibility (p. 292). As Niall Lucy (2005) notes, the differential relation basic to structural linguistics accounts for "cat" by the "necessary and signifying absence" of "bat," "fat," "sat," etc. (p. 95). Constituted of presence/absence, every positivity is, in Derrida's formulation, "a signifying and substitutive reference inscribed in a system of differences"; it is the compromised product of an endless interplay (p. 292).

Black (1981) invoked pragmatics to formulate metaphoric interplay as empirically generative, calling it the "sense of 'metaphor' that . . . may be the one most deserving of attention" (p. 67). The theory of pragmatics, proposed by John Austin (1975), distinguishes *performative* speech, doing things with words, from *constative* speech, saying things with them. "To issue a constative utterance," he explained, "is to make a statement. To issue a performative utterance . . . is to make a bet" (p. 6). It all sounds straightforward enough, but as Derrida (2007) noted in his essay *Psyche*, which we will touch upon in Part II, "performatives and constatives are never quite themselves" (p. 16); they engage in a "coimplication" (p. 12). A post-Austinian theory would problematize the distinction, subsuming many putatively constative acts into performative speech based on the self-investiture of authority

TABLE 1 Terms of metaphoric transference I

Originator	*Terms*	
Johnson	Two ideas	
Richards	Tenor	Vehicle
Black	Focus	Frame

by any speaker articulating from a world hypothesis, which is to say all speakers. A re-visioned theory would question the inherent claim of every statement to be a natural or neutral articulation baldly communicating about events, and would regard most speech as world-creating, "producing the event in the very act of recounting it" (Derrida, 2007, p. 12). One way to think about such an expanded view is to consider speech as an incantatory power. The articulation of a world-view has empirical impact, participating in the creation of that which it describes, bringing a world into being through the incantation of *poietic* sentences, as we do, for example, when we say, "The earth is a natural resource," an economic asset, or "The earth is like a living organism." Each sentence conjures a reality.

Austin's theory identified speech acts by their intention. In his lexicon, a *locutionary* act imparts factual information, an *illocutionary* act expresses a belief whose truth is conditional, and a *perlocutionary* act induces an effect. Clarity of intention is an issue. An utterance such as "The door is open" might express a fact about the door, an opinion as to whether the door should be open, or a request that it be closed. Black (1981) imported intentionality into his logic of metaphor when he said,

> There are indefinitely many contexts (including nearly all the interesting ones) where the meaning of a metaphorical expression has to be reconstructed from the speaker's intention (and other clues) because the broad rules of standard usage are too general to supply the information needed. (p. 67)

His larger point is that without a consideration of context, syntactical rules are inadequate to account for the operation of metaphor, which, as he maintained, is in any event not a narrowly syntactic phenomenon. A reimagined understanding was needed in which metaphorical syntax referred not just to sentences or truth claims, but to their enaction. The interaction theory precipitates this reimagining. Black (1981) found the notion that metaphor "presents some comparison" did not do justice to metaphor's creative capacity (p. 73). His interaction theory takes a systems theoretical approach in which a "new context (the 'frame' of the metaphor, in my terminology) imposes extension of meaning upon the focal word" (p. 73). Using terms amenable to a depth psychological theory of metaphor, Black says the focus and frame are "seen through" or "projected upon" one another (p. 75), not re-presenting a pre-given circumstance, but catalyzing emergent properties. The relata are thought together, "a distinctive intellectual operation" (p. 79) that evokes a poetic basis of mind in which cognition is not seen as independent of language.

Metaphor propagates context as focus and frame interpret, and thus reinvent, one another. Inventing, Derrida (2007) said, is an *eventing* that has always already "modified the structure of the context itself" (p. 25). From the intertextual vent, Black (1981) said, emerges a "pattern of implications" that "organizes our view" (p. 75) and produces "shifts in attitude" (p. 76). In a thought experiment, Black imagined that he holds up to the night sky a screen made of "a piece of heavily smoked glass on which certain lines have been left clear" so that the stars "will be seen as organized by the screen's structure" (p. 75). Looking through his glass darkly, Black was brought to reflect on the role of intention in the metaphoric "implication system" (p. 77). "The nature of the [metaphor's] intended application helps determine the character of the system to be applied," he said (p. 77). The intention inheres in both sentential and extra-sentential context, systems of associations that implicate one another. Employing parentheses, Black said the system of mutual implication is "(as though the stars could partly determine the character of the observation screen by which we looked at them)" (p. 77). Mechanistically impossible but archetypally discernable, the parenthetical *as though* nudges interaction away from analytical logic toward Peircean logic, a systems view in which worldviews instantiate worlds. As Christopher Bracken (2007) put it in his explication of Peirce, encountered previously, "the universe . . . 'lives and moves' only in signs" (p. 18), and again, with regard to Walter Benjamin's notion of magical criticism, "living forces are really operative in acts of discourse" (p. 6).

A depth psychological understanding of metaphoric contextuality can be had by reference, perhaps unconventionally, to Derrida. In an essay on Austin (which incited an exchange with Searle, who championed Austin's formulations), Derrida noted that speech act theory excepts from ordinary language use certain utterances Austin (1975) called "kinds of ill" (p. 21), which make performative speech "hollow or void if said by an actor on the stage, or if introduced in a poem, or spoken in a soliloquy" (p. 22). Such usages are not serious, and, what is more, they are "parasitic" on normal usage, which requires "ordinary circumstances" (p. 22). Derrida (1982), however, pointed out that the ordinary speech circumstance eludes definition, and as such, in Austin's words, "the 'pure' statement is a goal, an ideal" rather than an actuality (p. 72). In other words, every statement can be repeated, a quality that marks both its likeness to and difference from its other iterations, and that makes iterability inherent to ordinary speech. Derrida asked, therefore, "[I]s not what Austin excludes as anomalous, exceptional, 'nonserious,' that is, *citation* (on the stage, in a poem, or in a soliloquy) . . . a general iterability . . . without which there would not even be a 'successful' performative?" (p. 325). If all language partakes of a general iterability, it is not possible to assert a basis for speech act theory in the intention of the speaker, or to assume immediacy or purity of intention as a quality of "ordinary" language. Speakers have intentions, and intentions have results, but "intention" is an emergent process, not an object that can be analytically isolated from its relationship to, and contamination by, non-intention. The deconstructive—and depth psychological—inquiry into the subverted intentions of "ordinary" speech led Derrida to the "paradoxical, but inevitable" conclusion that "a successful performative is necessarily an 'impure' performative" (p. 325). Austin's admission that "very commonly the *same* sentence is used on different occasions of utterance in *both* ways, performative and constative" (p. 67) provokes Derrida to a reformulated intentionality: "[T]he category of intention will not disappear," Derrida said, "it will have its place, but from this place it will no longer be able to govern the entire scene and the entire system of utterances" (p. 326). The point has also been made by David Punter (2007) with reference to the metaphor of drawing a line in the sand, which is typically used to express resolution without retreat, but actually indicates the opposite, sand being precisely the wrong medium for permanency. The metaphor, Punter said, "is constantly undermining" its users' "claims to be in control of circumstances" (p. 10). Indeed, metaphor itself is such an undermining. Just as the intention-driven ego is not master in its own house, an intentional discourse (that, as Peirce said, "lives and moves") entails non-intentional and "impure" acts, those conceived amid the contaminations of the unconscious.

The lack that inheres in intentionality results in unacknowledged surplus context, elements of reality that fail to correspond to the world hypothesis at issue. As Derrida (1982) put it, "[T]his essential absence of intentionality for the actuality of the statement, this *structural unconsciousness* if you will, prohibits every saturation of a context" (p. 327; emphasis added). Derrida's "structural unconsciousness" is what Michael Vannoy Adams (1995), bringing Derrida together with Jung, called the "compensatory or deconstructive unconscious" (p. 7). It is the faculty of thought, or in a transpersonal sense, of world, that consists in metaphoric saturation. Unregulated intention escapes the rule of pure reason, giving *play* to the analogously derived faculty of subjective purposiveness. It relativizes the analytic propensity to reify images, the "system of translation" that Hillman (1983b) characterized as "this *means* that," the Freudian and Jungian definitional disposition. "Their move, that they both made," he said, "was to translate the images into crystallized symbolic meanings" (p. 58). The move from analysis, so expressed, also entails a move from classical metaphor in which one word simply stands for another. It is a move to apprehend the surplus value of the image, the uniquely metaphorical significance that cannot be relinquished without a loss of understanding. While analytical theory necessarily objectifies the image, contextualist theory takes the objects of metaphor, sentential and extrasentential, not as things, but as semantic-pragmatic processes.

Where Austin built his analytical theory on the incontrovertibility of grammatical logic, Ted Cohen (1981) proposed that illocutionary force and perlocutionary result inhere also in grammatical oddity, the nature and logic of metaphorical expression:

> [I]f there is a kind of logical relation between illocutions [intentions] and perlocutions [consequences], then a total speech act can exhibit an internal anomaly that is something like the aberration of a metaphorical sentence whose semantics are awry. This suggests that if odd juxtapositions within a sentence can produce novel meaning, then perhaps odd juxtapositions within a speech act can produce novel performances. (p. 187)

Cohen's invocation of "odd juxtapositions" to ground the performativity of metaphorical utterance corresponds to a premise of the poetic theory as stated by Gibbs (1995):

> Metaphor, metonymy, irony and other tropes are not linguistic distortion of literal mental thought but constitute basic schemes by which people conceptualize their experience and the external world. Since every mental construct reflects an adaptation of the mind to the world, the language that expresses these constructs attests to the continuous process of poetic thinking. (p. 1)

The oddity is not, then, a distortion of the literal, but is itself a basic scheme for conceptualizing experience. I have suggested that "working toward a psychology of image" entails a systems theoretical view of psyche as a network of relations. On this same basis, we might say the tropes of the poetic function, regarded as oddities by performative literalism, are the motive forces of the nonintentional aspect of mind, what Jung called the objective (nonegoic) psyche. To invoke again the notion of *play*, the metaphoric speech act would be a performance of soul-making, a construal of objectivity by the objective psyche. Performativity would maintain, with Peirce, that signs realize facts. To further the idea, let us add to our list of descriptors for the principles of metaphoric enaction a second set of terms used by Black for the metaphoric relata (Table 2). As synonyms for focus and frame, Black (1981) referred to the *principal subject* and the *subsidiary subject.*

The subjects, principal and subsidiary, in Black's theory of how metaphors work appear as ideational actors on the stage of the natural world, their *citationality* referring to a world between inverted commas.

If Black was correct in discerning metaphor's semantically creative capacity, how, Johnson (1981) asked, are we to understand the nature of the interaction; how do principal and subsidiary subjects jointly "generate a new conceptual organization" (p. 28)? He considers three possibilities. The first, interesting for the richness it adds to our table of terms, is Beardsley's (1981) notion of "verbal opposition." As we have seen, employing the term *tension*, Beardsley postulates a catalytic exchange, or moment of friction, between the interactive subjects at the point of metaphoric conception. As Johnson (1981) described it,

> The inherent tensions within the metaphor cause the metaphoric predicate to lose its ordinary extension and thereby to obtain a new intension . . . More specifically, a term will have a central meaning (its ordinary designation) and a marginal meaning (its connotation). (p. 28)

Mining Johnson's description of the theory, we can place several new entries in our chart under Beardsley's name (Table 3).

TABLE 2 Terms of metaphoric transference II

Originator	*Terms*	
Johnson	Two ideas	
Richards	Tenor	Vehicle
Black	Focus	Frame
Black	Principal subject	Subsidiary subject

TABLE 3 Terms of metaphoric transference III

Originator	*Terms*	
Johnson	Two ideas	
Richards	Tenor	Vehicle
Black	Focus	Frame
Black	Principal subject	Subsidiary subject
Beardsley	Predicate	(No correlate)
Beardsley	Extension	Intension
Beardsley	Central meaning	Marginal meaning

Beardsley's theory, Johnson (1981) said, extends Black's assertion of creativity by "claiming that metaphor does not simply call upon 'associated commonplaces' but may actualize connotations not yet brought forward in our present conceptual system" (p. 29). The idea of an emergent semantics is a *seeing as*, Wittgenstein's coinage that some theorists (Aldrich, 1958; Hester, 1966) adopted to describe the production of conceptual novelty. Referring to Aldrich's construal, Johnson (1981) said *seeing as* "involves an imaginative activity partially subject to the will and not identical with an act of mere perception" (p. 29). It is best compared, Johnson said, to "aesthetic perception," in which "the artist has a special capacity to embody certain aspects in an artwork . . . [unconcealing] aspects of objects previously unnoticed" (p. 29). The aesthetic comparison harkens to Black's denomination of the *subsidiary* idea as a *frame*. Framing can be likened to an "artistic force creating fictions" (Kofman, 1993, p. 25), or to aesthetic, reflective judgment, "the process of seeking a universal under which to think an unfamiliar particular" (Pillow, 2003, p. 2). An imaginative faculty "*partially* [emphasis added] subject to the will" moves us further towards a *poietic* theory in which metaphor can be understood as a perlocutionary force of the "deconstructive" or metaphoric unconscious, catalyzing semantic potential compensatory to analytic positioning.

A second influential hypothesis of the "how" of metaphoric meaning-making is Marcus Hester's (1996) theory of "gestalt switches" or, as Johnson (1981) described them, "flashes of insight" (p. 30) produced by the interaction of the two terms of the metaphoric equation. The basic idea is given leavening by Lakoff and Johnson (1980), who expand it to designate the interaction of "experiential gestalts," or "actions, events and objects" perceived as "structured meaningful wholes within experience" (p. 30). In metaphoric interaction, the gestalts are reconstituted in terms of one another. The idea is drawn from Black's (1981) claim that metaphoric interaction involves whole "systems of implication" (p. 75).[3] Interaction turns from the idea of metaphorical relata as monads of a sort, self-enclosed yet lacking in fractal significance. Re-visioning, Black saw a world in the grain of sand. To express the dynamism, he used terms also familiar to a dynamic psychology. "We can say that the principal subject is '*seen through*' the metaphorical expression—or, if we prefer, that the principal subject is '*projected upon*' the field of the subsidiary subject," he said (p. 75; emphasis added). For Hillman, of course, seeing through, both "to see in terms of" and "to see with discernment," is a basic quality of metaphoric knowing. Metaphor, Hillman (1975) said, "sees through itself. . . . At one and the same time it said something and sees through what it said" (p. 156). For Black (1981), what is to be seen through is a metaphor's interactive ideas, whose "inter-illumination," he said, unconceals novel conceptual possibilities (p. 73).

The third explanation of the metaphorical interaction that Johnson mentions is Gilbert Ryle's theory of *category mistake*, proposed by Nelson Goodman (1968) and Colin Turbayne (1970), providing insight into why the semantic shift of the metaphor unsettles rational consciousness. Each of these ideas, categorical mistake, tension between center and margin, and hybridized gestalt, indicates that the nature and logic of metaphor is intrinsically deviant. In classical theory, deviance was understood to blur the lines of semantic propriety. In the interaction theory, followed to its logical conclusion, deviance becomes the defining principle, a consequence that serves to ground a Hermetic theory. In the evolution of an idea, the deviance remains; only the orientation to it has changed.

The third, and final, question Johnson (1981) posed to organize "the problems of metaphor" concerned cognitive status. Interaction theory makes a basic claim for metaphor's epistemological value, "that the use of one complex system of implications to select, emphasize, and organize relations in another field of implications is a 'distinctive *intellectual* operation'" (p. 36). It was not the invocation of cognitive status alone that riled the adherents of classicism. Black coupled the cognitive assertion with the further insistence of metaphor as an open-ended creative force. "Black might have gotten by with the claim that no literal paraphrase provides the *insight* of the metaphor," Johnson (1981) said, "for 'insight' might have been spelled out in psychological terms. But he raised an outcry with his remark about 'creating' similarities" (p. 36). Black could have made a limited case, as did Searle, for metaphor's illocutionary status—or, as Martin Warner called it, metaphor's "suggestive" or "hortatory" ability (as cited in Johnson, 1981, p. 36)—without also ascribing to it a formal capacity. But Black not only noticed in metaphor a filtering or *seeing as* function, but also an affective or *seeing that* function: perlocutionary force. Black judged metaphor capable of producing truth claims. His argument for interaction entails a word-meets-world co-relationality capable of overarching the Cartesian chiasm.

The most influential promulgation of the cognitive theory has come from Johnson and George Lakoff. They made a case for the metaphorical structure of our everyday notions of how the world works in *Metaphors We Live By* (Lakoff & Johnson, 1980) and for philosophy's debt to metaphor in *Philosophy in the Flesh* (Lakoff & Johnson, 1999). Johnson (2008) is unreserved about the implications for philosophy of the cognitive theory. "In a very strong sense," he says, "philosophy *is* metaphor" (p. 44). He does not, however, set philosophy apart in its metaphorical provenance from other disciplines, nor does he allow it a privileged perspective on the human condition:

> Philosophy's debt to metaphor is profound and immeasurable. Without metaphor, there would be no philosophy. However, philosophy's debt is no

> greater, nor less, than that of any other significant human intellectual field or discipline. Philosophers must use the same conceptual resources possessed by any human being, and the potential for any philosophy to make sense of a person's life depends directly on the fact that all of us are metaphoric animals. (p. 39)

The latter assertion, familiar from Nietzsche, is the central tenet of the cognitive school. Metaphors, say Lakoff and Johnson, derive from the human experience of embodiment. As terms of art for the relata of metaphoric expression, they use the phrases *source domain* and *target domain.* "The source domains," Johnson (2008) said, "come from our bodily, sensory-motor experience, which becomes the basis for abstract conceptualization and reasoning," the target domains (p. 45). In their lexicon, source domains are *mapped onto* target domains. A key example is the metaphoric mapping that gives us the concept of causation. It was Hume's doubt about the objectivity of causation that awakened Kant from his dogmatic slumber and led him to underwrite the entire subsequent scientific enterprise (the absence of objective cause, then, served as Kant's proximate cause). Science is assumed "to be a superior form of knowledge," said Johnson, "partly because of its ability to give causal explanations of events" (p. 40). Lakoff and Johnson (1999) show that there are at least 20 metaphors for 20 types of causation, leaving us, with Hume, at a loss for the literal.

As an example of the experiential basis of the cognitive theory, let us take what Johnson (2008) identifies as "the first prominent conceptual metaphor" of causation analyzed in cognitive linguistics, Events are Motions in Space, that is, "the understanding of change of state as (metaphorical) motion from one location to another" (p. 40). To understand causation in terms of our bodily experience of motion, we map elements of the source domain, Motion in Space, onto elements of the target domain, Events, producing various metaphors that organize the way we perceive and express causation. For example, says Johnson, the submapping Change of State is Movement gives us expressions such as "The water *went from* hot *to* cold," "The system is *moving toward* homeostasis," and "The pizza is *somewhere between* warm and cold." Another submapping, Causation is Forced Movement, is expressed in "The fire *brought* the soup *to* a boil" or "The candidate's speech *threw* the crowd into a frenzy." This method of analysis has enabled Lakoff and Johnson (1980) to uncover a wide range of metaphors that "govern our everyday functioning" (p. 3). Because, as they say, "we act according to the way we conceive of things," their demonstrations of the metaphoric basis of cognition points like none other to metaphor's empirical consequences (p. 5).

The transpersonal view of metaphor as a force of nature that I am pursuing in this book requires that a grounding of metaphor in the body extend beyond the human to the body of nature writ large. The hint of a generalized embodiment is found in a comment by Richard Rorty, although against his intentions. Rorty, as Johnson (2008) points out, was willing to admit the importance of metaphor to philosophy, but he was also a champion of Donald Davidson's view that metaphorical meaning is reducible to literal meaning. Perhaps as a result of its suppressed role in Rorty's thinking, metaphor winks at us through the lines of Rorty's dismissal of its semantic agency. In a passage cited by Johnson to show Rorty's resistance to the cognitive theory, Rorty (1989) marveled at "Aristotle's metaphorical use of *ouisa*, Saint Paul's metaphorical use of *agapé*, and Newton's metaphorical use of *gravitas*" (p. 17), but he was unwilling to concede that these instances of metaphoric meaning-making are evidence of metaphor's cognitive basis. "More plausibly," he said, "they were the result of some odd episodes in infancy—some obsessional kinks left in these brains by idiosyncratic traumata. It hardly matters how the trick was done" (p. 17). The trick, however, reveals how it was done, drawing back the veil in a speculation by Rorty that the cited metaphors, for all Rorty knew, might have been produced by Aristotle, St. Paul, and Newton as "the results of cosmic rays scrambling the fine structure of some crucial neurons in their respective brains" (p. 17). Entering here on backwards shoes comes our transpersonal extension of metaphor from the psyche to the cosmos. From an archetypal point of view, in which, says Joseph Cambray (2009), "the universe is as permeated with psyche as it is with space, time, and matter" (p. 20), obsessional kinks and odd episodes, in infancy or otherwise, are expressions not of skin-encapsulated idiosyncrasies, but of transhuman synchronicities. They derive from mythopoetic *source domains* whose recombinatory potentials are realized in the *target domains* of our lives. Perhaps we might entertain a submapping of Events are Motions in Space apropos of acausality. It might be expressed by the conceptual metaphor States are Locations in Space, also cited by Johnson, although with reference to Monod's absolute chance, a form not of causality, but of coincidence. Recall the eruption of the synchronic structure into the diachronic philology of linguistics that anchored our first chapter. I suggested that time, Chronos, was relativized by space, Hermes. The fleeting location of the contingent event, its presence/absence, punctuates our perception of positivist progress from an origin and toward a *telos* that our commonplace metaphysics conceive of as outside the text, immune from the play of signifiers or extraneous to the weave of the implicate order. Our states of being, the multifaceted ontological events that we are, reflect not only apparent causality or intention, but a fundamentally unintended Hermetic interference that works at cross purposes to the positivist explanations we give of ourselves. If we admit to unintended consequences, we will find ourselves at a tropical locus. The tropes, or turnings, of the metaphors, metonymies, and ironies—the archetypes—that inscribe us in the cosmological epic can indeed "scramble the fine structure of some crucial neurons," dislodging our literalisms and humanisms to remind us that we are locations in space.

In sum, the truth claims proffered by metaphors reflect an interaction in the metaphoric exchange of "systems of implication." The economy of such an exchange is strikingly different than the dollar-for-dollar swap of the comparison view. There is, in the comparison view, a certain semantic value held in reserve to enable the principal subject to retain its *estimable* priority over the subsidiary subject. The open-endedness of the interaction view, however, provides that each subject take the estimate of the other and circulate its own interpretive value in an exchange without end. If the interaction view provides a fitting answer to what metaphor is, how it works, and why it has cognitive value, the next necessary inquiry, Johnson (1981) suggested, would be "how the alleged gestalt switch is possible or why the insight it provides cannot be literally expressed" (p. 39). The question harkens to Kant's dilemma of binary opposites, to which he applied an argument from analogy. Metaphor, it would seem, is inextricably engaged with the categorical boundary, a horizon that disappears as one moves toward it. Theorizing perhaps waits in vain for the moment when metaphor can be seen to retain an intrinsic consequentiality *without* the assimilation to reason, or as Ted Cohen (1979) put it, without having to meet "this canonical test of respectability" (p. 3).

Before we leave our examination of the modern re-visioning, we must raise again (Lazarus-like) the question of literalism. Contemporary theory has it that the problematics of literal meaning has a democratizing influence that opens the way for marginalized perspectives. Yet David Punter (2007) has pointed out how a correction too far in the direction of an anti-literalist theory can suppress thought as much as free it. "We need . . . to look as closely as possible at what differing things might be considered to constitute metaphor under different historical, cultural and geographical circumstances," Punter said (p. 40). He supplied the example of a passage from the Nigerian writer Amos Tutuola in which a king seeks the aid of his people to clear a corn field. It is the king's command that "all the people, spirits and terrible creatures of the island" join together in the task (p. 120). The protagonist relates that "one fine morning, we gathered together and went to the corn field, and cleared it away." Punter asked after the "we" of the passage. It would seem to comprise not only "people," but "spirits and terrible creatures." Is the "we" metaphorical? To a non-mythological sensibility, spirits are not meant to be taken literally. Yet the cultural context of the story suggests that it is not possible to say that Tutuola meant them any other way. "The attribution of metaphor" to the story, Punter said,

> becomes indissolubly linked with assumptions about cultural supremacy; it would . . . be only a so-called primitive people who could accept such a concept literally. Indeed, we might also say that the very thought of *thinking literally* is usually, in our culture, a gesture of dismissal; we are not supposed to think literally, for to do so betrays an unawareness of the slipping and sliding possibilities of language. (p. 121)

Punter alerts us to our tendency to equate the literal with the sensible and the metaphorical with the imaginary. Our mechanistic sensibility asks us to process Tutuola's field clearers in a "this *means* that" analytical reduction, the very logic of the similarity and comparison approaches to metaphor. But Tutuola is inviting us to stick to the image. Invoked by the king, the imaginal figures exhibit an effect: though they may evade our sensibility, they are capable of clearing the field. In Hillman's (1979b) terms, they qualify as "ab-senses" (p. 54), a turn of phrase from *The Dream and the Underworld* cited elsewhere by Punter. Like dream figures, the field clearers are tangibly present though physically absent. Like denizens of the underworld, they are cryptic, but possessed of the latent power of any buried energy. They are imaginally literal and literally imaginal.

Punter's explication of the "we" in Tutuola's story signals that metaphorics can congeal into the very fundamentalism it seeks to replace. The prying open of the literal to reveal the *poietic* force enabling imagination to roam across the manifold in reflective judgment—to bloweth where it listeth—is not an end in itself. To make it so would, in an archetypal sense, take the imaginal *eidos* as a thing seen, but not also as a way of seeing; it would, in a deconstructive sense, invert the opposition literal/metaphorical without revaluing the inherent hierarchy. If a metaphorics is to be true to Nietzsche's demand of an authentic philosophy that it embrace an open-ended intention for more life, it must, as Hillman (1975) said, see through even itself.

Notes

1 Metaphor's emergence as a worldly construct from the chrysalis of Aristotelian categorization appears to gain its impetus from the very designation *poiesis* within which the classical theory places it. Categorical thinking, understood in terms of the conceptual metaphor Categories are Containers, thus finds itself disturbed from its own depths.

2 Black's article, which enabled theorists to throw off the Aristotelian mantle—a paradigm *shift*—was originally published in the *Proceedings of the Aristotelian Society*. It is as though Hermes was at work (at play?) upon the very threshold of the modern view, disturbing settled theory from within. "Shift" as "mantle" raises a question of supplementarity. Commenting on Kant's use of the term *parergon* to refer to decorative elaboration (one of Kant's examples is drapery on a statue; we might say Aristotelian metaphor), Derrida (1987) asks how a thing that is already complete can be said in any way to be elaborated. He proposes that *parerga*, though seen by Kant as supplementary and extrinsic, unavoidably point to inherent incompletion. In addition to drapery, Kant explains *parerga* with the example of a picture frame. It is, of course, precisely the framing of experience that Black—using the exact term— puts into play in his theory of metaphor.

3 The expression is suggestive of David Bohm's (1980) theory of the implicate order, raising the question whether the production of meaning in language might be described as a collapse of the metaphoric wave function. Indeed, Bohm advanced a theory of language as "an undivided field of movement" in which words are not "indivisible atoms of meaning" but "convenient markers in the whole movement of language" that are "lifted into attention" from a comprehensive flux by an "attention-calling function" of mind.

5

DERRIDA AND RICOEUR

This chapter explores two variations on the theme of philosophy's opening to metaphor. They represent the far reaches of the topic as explored in the work of Jacques Derrida and Paul Ricoeur. The chapter follows, in somewhat simplified form, the comparison of Derrida and Ricoeur by Giuseppe Stellardi (2000). The two thinkers grapple with the question of whether philosophy has a discursive regime apart from metaphor (Ricoeur) or whether metaphor is the inescapable a priori of philosophical thinking (Derrida). At its most basic level, the distinction is one between "determinacy" and "dynamism," terms applied by Joel Weinsheimer (1991) in his rendering of a Gadamerian metaphorics. Weinsheimer demonstrated that Gadamer's approach to the crisis of foundationalism positions him in a rich aporia between Derrida and Ricoeur. In the wake of idealism's crest, Gadamer (1981) said, the speculative tradition cannot but admit of "an inner affinity for spellbinding multiplicity," although "the exigence of reason for unity remains inexorable" (p. 19). Gadamer's intertextual position enables Weinsheimer (1991) to deliver a state of the union for the speculative tradition in which dynamism and determinacy do not hang separately. "Neither kind of discourse," he said, "is self-interpreting" (p. 183). Recalling philosophy's interrogative imperative that finds itself repressed every time a philosopher believes himself to have penned the last word, Weinsheimer said speculative discourse by its very definition "does not content itself with the obvious, or cling to received wisdom" (p. 183). Rather, "in the speculative concept, the twin claims of the one and the many are already active" (p. 184).

The Ricoeur–Derrida debate indicates how far scholarly opinion about metaphor and philosophy has come. The notion that these differences of kind, philosophy and metaphor, have little to do with each other has given way to its inverse in which it is possible to view a deep interrelationship and even to speculate that philosophy is a form of metaphorical expression. Ricoeur–Derrida is also edifying for the thematics of the present project because it brings us to the possibility of a theory that applies metaphor to psyche. As Saussure's differential linguistics became generalized to account for structures of meaning placed under investigation by adjacent disciplines, so too can the assessment of metaphor as a semantic operator espoused by early theorists such as Richards and Black carry over to a metaphor-theoretical assessment of psyche.

Some remarks are in order on two of Derrida's terms of art, *logocentrism* and *pharmakon*. The epoch of metaphysics, which encompasses all of philosophy including, and beyond, poststructuralism, is designated by Derrida as logocentric. He meant the term to identify the privileging by speculative reason of itself as the singular means of access to truth. Such accessibility is predicated upon rational thought and the (spoken) word, as the transparent and unmediated vehicle of truth. In this hypothesis, logos *finds itself* in the company of being and as being. But in his exegesis of philosophical texts, Derrida discovered that the presupposed unity of truth and mind or word is problematized by an accompaniment already within the consanguineous origin. There are traces in presence of mind, so to speak, of an absence, of that which is not present but may have been and which still exerts doubt. The production of philosophy's "outside," the concept suspended beyond the play of signifiers, requires the suppression "within" philosophy of differential priority.

As Nietzsche made clear, there is an extant forgetting—of metaphor—already always within the memorialized concept. In Derrida's paradigm, the purity of all origins is obviated by the return of the repressed. Logocentrism requires the arbitrary hierarchization of concepts in which one term, reason, is associated with the beginning, origins, truth, reality, purity, and ultimacy, whereas a second, unmentionable term, say, the carnal or the imaginal, dares not speak its name, and becomes subordinated. Similar to Hillman's valorization of depth rather than ascendance, soul rather than spirit, Derrida inverted hierarchies of privilege, elaborating each consequently revenant—he would say *spectral*—value. He allowed himself to follow the play of the inversion wherever it might lead. Derrida's project was to uncover arbitrary moralizations by attending to what we might see as the psychopathology of the hidden or repressed term, the Freudian slip showing in the philosophical tradition. If psyche might be defined in terms of differential relation, we can say that what is "written in the soul" (Plato, *Phaedrus*, §276) is a prior *writing*.

The dyad most emblematic of Derrida's critique is writing/speech. The opposition is exemplified by a single word, *pharmakon*, which Derrida (1981) extracted from the text of the *Phaedrus*. The dialogue unfolded outside the city walls along the banks of the Ilissus, an uncustomary venue for Socrates, who preferred not to leave the city—for his teachers, he said, were men, not nature—but nevertheless a site to which he had been enticed—not without a hint of double entendre—by the promise of a glimpse of the scroll hidden under Phaedrus' cloak. Upon the scroll was written the text of spoken remarks by the Sophist Lysias about the nature of love and desire between those pedagogical and erotic figures known to the Greeks as *erastes*, the mature male lover, and *eromenos*, the beautiful youth who was the object of his passion. The interlocutors discussed the twining topics of erotics and discourse in this riverine habitat, which, Socrates informs the reader, is the identical spot, or so legend had it, where the play of the nymphs Orithyia and Pharmacia was disrupted by Boreas, the north wind, who carried Orithyia over the edge of an abyss and to her death. Pharmacia's fate still evidently undecided, it was she who was taken up by the dialogue that ensued.

In brief, Socrates' argument to Phaedrus is that only through the immediacy and presence of speech, and not the attenuated and errant mode of writing, can the *erastes* plant the seeds of wisdom in the soul of the *eromenos*. Recounting the myth of Thoth, concerning writing's rejection by Thamus, the mythical king of Egypt, Socrates calls writing a *pharmakon*. Thoth offered the gift to remedy forgetfulness. But Thamus rejected it as poison to memory. "Poison" and "remedy" can be rendered by the same word, *pharmakon*. Though writing was dismissed as poison, Derrida documents the alternative meaning. The term became, for deconstruction, the paradigmatic case of that diaphanous weave in the text of philosophy where ambiguity shows through the threads of the argument. It represented the point of alterity already present within the identity of the concept under promulgation.

"If the *pharmakon* is 'ambivalent'," said Derrida (1981), in much the same mode of expression with which analytical psychology might refer to the collective unconscious,

> it is because it constitutes the medium in which opposites are opposed, the movement and the play that links them among themselves, reverses them or makes one side cross over into the other (soul/body, good/evil, inside/outside, memory/forgetfulness, speech/writing, etc.). It is on the basis of this play or movement that the opposites or differences are stopped by Plato. The pharmakon is the movement, the locus, and the play: (the production of) difference. It is the *differance* of difference. (p. 127)

Logocentrism, then, refers to that unavoidable halting of differences necessitated by the writing of philosophy. Precisely *what* becomes halted is metaphor, the nature and logic of which is to favor the movement and play of difference. *Where* it becomes halted is in the binary opposition, that 180-degree aspect stipulated by both hermeneutic (poststructural) and uroboric (archetypological) circumambulations in which "two ideas," as Dr. Johnson dubbed the terms of the metaphoric equation, might interact *vis-à-vis*. Metaphoric interaction, however, becomes arrested by the inertial "centrism" operating upon whichever term of the opposition serves as figurehead for "logos," that is, indubitable cogito, foundational reason, or analysis—the definitional determinate that, as we have seen, Hillman (1983b) critiqued as "this *means* that" (p. 58). On the other hand, said Derrida (1981), were we to cultivate an awareness of the "alternately or simultaneously" "beneficent or maleficent" tension inherent in the logocentric term, that is, *pharmakon*, we might discover the substance of "cryptic depths refusing to submit their ambivalence to analysis, already paving the way for alchemy" (p. 70).

The alchemical domain, Jung would say, is that of the unconscious. In turn, the unconscious, to the extent that the archetypes by which it is known are fundamentally metaphorical, might be said to be a domain of metaphor. Yet, to extrapolate from Cazeaux's (2007) problematization of philosophy's spatial metaphors, in which he argued (in my view, Hermetically) that metaphor is a "disrespecter of domains" and cannot be reduced to a spatial conceptualization, we might be brought to refer not solely to metaphor, but also to the unconscious, as a *pseudo-domain*, a conceptual placement that at once marks a displacement.

The *pharmakon*, both poison and remedy, is the outstanding example of the double-edged nature of concepts. Derrida was insightfully attuned to covert meanings inherent in any conceptual claim. He brought shadow into play in all analyses by maintaining an awareness that any certainty involves a tensional relationship with a binary opposite. "Derrida's discourse," Stellardi (2000) said, "is often and at all levels openly metaphorical ('under tension,' one might say, in the sense of the modern notion of metaphor)" (p. 69). Stellardi's critique involved the discussion of these tensional doublings that typify Derrida's approach to the relationship of metaphor and philosophy. The doublings, which we will get to shortly, distinguish the deconstructive event from what Stellardi termed "the classic style" of the exposition of the philosophy/metaphor problem. The classic style, Stellardi said, rests upon two lexicographical suppositions: First, that there is such a thing as a philosophical "text" consisting of "the sum of written works traditionally assigned to the discipline named 'philosophy'"; and, second, that such works necessarily qualify as "a *type* of text, a literary genre or a methodic procedure which, by its fulfilling certain requirements and corresponding to a certain form, is recognizable as 'philosophical'" (p. 71).

The classic style can be understood as an entailment of the conceptual metaphor Categories are Containers identified by Lakoff and Johnson (1999). The metaphor assumes an inside and an outside, in this case of knowledge. It functions as a containment *fantasy* (to employ a term of art from imaginal psychology), constituting a circumscribed disciplinary domain for philosophy proper and, beyond it, a poetics of mind from which philosophical thinking distinguishes itself. It was Derrida's desire to problematize the distinction. Stellardi (2000) described "the system of expectations" prevalent in the classical view as one in which philosophers "used, subdued, and employed metaphor to the advantage of philosophy" (p. 71). Metaphor was "an object of research, classification, and systematization within a discourse that concerns and contains it, that establishes its place and its right without being itself affected by it" (p. 71).

Derrida's (1982) reordering of these priorities was spelled out in his seminal essay, "White Mythology," in which he sought to establish metaphor as the basis of metaphysical thought, inverting the hierarchy in philosophy that set the abstract concept upon a pinnacle and consigned the "rhetorical instrument" to the forgotten depths, securing the primacy of the former. Derrida plays upon the meanings of "white," whose paleness might be equally pure and pallid. A *white* mythology, in Derrida's reckoning, is bloodless and morbid, even a specter that feeds upon a living host. No longer florid, it is like a dried flower pressed in the leaves of a book. Philosophy has been the place where metaphor goes to die, left recumbent in the sepulcher of the concept. "These dead metaphors," said Stellardi (2000) of straitened analytical language, "in their whole constitute metaphysics as a sort of white mythology, that is, a conceptual edifice whose difference from common mythology is its discolored presentation, which hides its shameful origin" (p. 73). Philosophy is in this (dis)respect ashamed of its parentage in metaphor. By denying metaphor, metaphysics covers over the scandal of its beginnings in the way perhaps that a morally ambiguous event lies behind every great fortune. This view of philosophical truth draws upon Nietzsche's metaphor of the effacement of the proper:

> Truths are illusions which we have forgotten are illusions; they are metaphors that have become worn out and have been drained of sensuous force, coins which have lost their embossing and are now considered as metal and no longer as coins. (Nietzsche, 2006, p. 117)

The truths have lost their ability to bear an image, to represent with relief the metaphorical transformations of the psyche.

As usual wherever a deconstructive reading takes place, the inversion of the hierarchy (e.g., metaphysics/metaphorics) is accompanied by a revaluation of its terms. Revaluation brings out the unacknowledged signifiers buried in each term. In a depth psychological sense, the occurrence of deconstruction integrates shadow elements. The two-step process of inversion and revaluation demonstrates the condition of undecideability underlying apparently definitive signifiers, what amounts to their Hermetic duplicity or Dionysian androgyny. In the instant case, metaphor sloughs off its designation as "stylistic element," an epiphenomenon, and reveals itself as philosophy's wellspring and recovered other. The relationship of metaphor and metaphysics, Stellardi (2000) said, "begins to become irreparably ambiguous"; the "exterior tool [metaphor] is now to be discovered (albeit in disguise) at the very heart of philosophy, as an essential part of its mechanism" (p. 73). Archetypally, the consequence would appear as a resurgence of mythos; poststructurally as the qualification of logos as mythos. Were the paradigm to shift deconstructively, said Stellardi, "philosophy's striving to affirm itself as rational thought, in opposition to mythic thought, would be annulled or severely impaired at its very root" (p. 73). Logos would take up a decentered position within the semantic universe. A less uncanny destructuring would be difficult to imagine were it not for the history of Copernican revolutions of the *axis mundi*, paradigm shifts beginning with that of Copernicus himself to those of Kant and Freud.

The "irreparable ambiguity" at the heart of Derrida's re-visioning of philosophy can be understood in terms of the *coincidentia oppositoria* native to deconstruction, dispositions that mark it as a child of Hermes. These oppositions are either and both "binary" (the poststructural argot) or "compensatory" (the archetypal argot). Stellardi (2000) alluded to at least three such doublings: (i) deconstruction's stance akimbo, so to speak; its "double posture concerning the philosophical tradition"

(p. 72) in which it aims to disentangle the possibilities of thought from the rule of the concept yet equally recognizes that a conceptual regime is inevitably part of speculative metaphysics; (ii) a "double movement" of libido in which "philosophy takes possession of metaphor, assimilates it, interiorizes it, makes it into a concept" yet also "ends in being submerged by metaphor's uncontrollable tow," that is, having repressed or split off that which is antithetical, philosophy discovers that "the outside, and the beyond are already present, already at work" within (p. 72); and (iii) a "double position" or simultaneity of "broadening and lessening" in which interiorized and buried metaphor, once it is brought to the fore, creates a fuller, more colloquial philosophical voice capable of "invading neighboring genres," producing a democratization of disciplines that, for philosophy, results in a "reduction in its own privilege, function and direct link with being and truth" (p. 77).

These doublings convey the nuances of poststructural and specifically deconstructive positions regarding the metaphysical tradition. Deconstruction has been misunderstood as an assault that seeks to delegitimize philosophy by making linguistic farce of its assertions to cogent truth claims. In fact, Derrida's concern with the recondite, and paradoxical, consequences of philosophical language was meant not to reduce any logocentric edifice to rubble, but, on the contrary, to maintain and even restore to new significance the pellucid constructions of the philosophers. Derrida was at the same time exploiting instances of contradiction inherent within philosophical systems and conceding the inevitability, though not the incontrovertibility, of the systems he placed into question. Deconstruction is a story differently told, but it does not seek to expunge the old tale. Philosophy's resistance to its latent deconstructive tendency expresses the frustration of the Apollonian imperative, yearning for precision of understanding, in its encounter with Hermetic "double talk" (Hillman, 1983a, p, 35). The phrase refers to the allegorical (Freudian) and metaphorical (Jungian) hermeneutics of the dream. Both "start off saying one thing as if it were another" (p. 35), but the allegorical irony focuses on conceptual opposition (latent/manifest), and the metaphorical irony not on the opposites themselves but on the tensional relationship between them, "a throwing together of two dissonants into a unique voice" (p. 35). The distinction makes a crucial deconstructive insight. Deconstruction is precisely the acknowledgement of dispositions. It is not concerned with verity of narrative, but with varying narratives, in particular as to their impacts. It is not a question of adequation to singular truth, but of metaphoric ambi-valence. Metaphors, Hillman said, have a "peculiar unity" (p. 35). Metaphoric unity consists in the strangeness of interaction, not in its resolution. "We are composed of agonies, not polarities," Hillman said, in an invocation of the tragic sense (p. 40). Metaphorics, then, is an epistemology that at all events must take itself contingently.

We can here apply the axiom of imaginal psychology's own repurposing of metaphor, and say that Derrida *sees through* the logos of metaphysics to its metaphoric horizons, pursuing constructs of seemingly determinate meaning to further, and unintended, or unforeseen, possibilities. Both deconstruction and psychologizing are concerned with coincidence, the interplay of synchronous structures, especially those that are literalized or retired from circulation. In any discourse, deconstruction and psychologizing are at all times underway. This claim is not a psychologism (though awareness of the tendency is not uncalled for); it does not entail the reduction of all discourses, including deconstruction, to psychology. It is a re-visioning, a discernment of the overlooked dynamism of the subtext—a reading, Hermetically put, between the lines. Psychology "may be going on best where it is noticed least," Hillman (1975) said,

> as in "negative learning," as an underground interior reaction of "dissonant learning" in which the sourness of the student eats through the established positive statements, corroding their face value, yielding an acerbic learning that is against what is given, a countereducation. (p. 133)

Alchemical effacement of metaphysical positivities, occasioned by awareness of their counterindications, describes a deconstructive concern with interiority. "[I]n order to be itself," said Geoffrey Bennington (1993), in a passage on the place of the (Freudian) unconscious in Derrida's work, "a subject must already relate to itself as to an other. Identity comes only from alterity" (p. 143). And neither is any "deep identity . . . a more secure [literal, absolute] substratum" (p. 144).

"Placed inevitably within the epoch" of logocentrism, said Stellardi (2000), "the deconstructor endeavors to promote the recognition and proliferation of the signs of alterity" (p. 72). The linguistic circumstance that allows for such propagation, touched upon in our discussion of the cognitive turn, is called by Derrida (1981) *dissemination*. It is now possible to expand upon the earlier reference, and to note that what dissemination casts abroad are instances of syntactic novelty. It tests the limits of linguistic structure at the expense of expected, and even polysemic, meaning, putting into play new and often strange—uncanny—allusions. In short, it indicates a *poietic* manner.

Niall Lucy (2005) credited dissemination with being "textually inventive" to the point of "linguistic exuberance" (p. 30). What Lucy discerned in Derrida's way with words is the moment-to-moment possibility of linguistic deviance. A "falsity of narrative appears in the gap between aesthetic order and the sheer facticity of life," Lucy said, locating dissemination both hermeneutically and phenomenologically. Dissemination places into *tension*—that catalytic, and Hermetic, distillation of the interaction theory—not solely semantics, but syntax. It has a destabilizing effect on syntactical structure, the grammatical suppositions that uphold "semantic privilege" (Stellardi, 2000, p. 76). Dissemination assists an imaginal awareness by disentangling meaning from the suppositions of dominant truth claims. It entails the recognition that although at any time we are within an epoch of thought that presents itself as comprehensive, we can distinguish impulses of mind it has failed to contain. As a writerly gesture, it is typical of Hillman's often puckish prose, in which it takes the form of his deliberate infusion into psychology of the exuberant imaginal attitude of the *puer aeternis*. Even in its name, it indicates the very Hermetic crossroads—anciently marked by the ithyphallic *herma*—where a cognitive turn leads to a metaphorical, imaginal mode of philosophical consideration, which is precisely the point of disagreement between Derrida and Ricoeur.

Ricoeur's objection to Derrida's metaphorics asks whether its stylistic, syntactical, and semantic dissemination leaves anything philosophical in its wake. "The question is," Stellardi (2000) said, "Is there an essential difference between philosophical discourse and poetic discourse?" (p. 78). Ricoeur's (1975) own re-visioning, consistent with the modern theory, overturns categorical metaphor. But unlike Derrida's more radical move, it stops short of shattering the vessel and scattering its shards. Ricoeur (1975) broadened the site of metaphoric operation, extending it first from the noun to the sentence, a tenet of the modern theory. As we have seen, theorists have transferred metaphor—they have re-conceptualized transference—from the encapsulated substantive to sentential interrelation. In a second step, Ricoeur built on the element of contextuality in the modern theory by extending the metaphoric purview from the phrase to discourse in general. With this expansion, Stellardi (2000) said, "The semantic theoretic milieu is abandoned to make room for a hermeneutic point of view" (p. 79). Ricoeur's double move suggests a reconceptualization of metaphor's classical expulsion. The rhetorical landscape beyond philosophy's ideal city-state is no longer a domain of ostracism, but the contextual *pseudo-domain* that makes philosophy possible. We can recall that even as companionable speech asserted its libidinal priority over the written scroll, Socrates had found repose outside the city walls. At the mythic origin of unmediated presence, a carrying over, the *metapherein*, has already taken place.

The remapping of inside and outside links Ricoeur and Derrida. For Derrida, Stellardi (2000) said, the outside is "already at work" in philosophy (p. 72). But Ricoeur (1975) took exception to the move on Derrida's part that extends metaphor to a usurpation of philosophical privilege. He retracted implications of modern metaphor theory for philosophical discourse, setting out "to recognize in principle, the *discontinuity* that assures the autonomy of speculative discourse" (p. 258). Ricoeur, Stellardi (2000) said, did not wish to conflate "centered and well-regulated polysemy" (p. 80), which brings forth speculative meaning, with a disseminative practice that overruns what Ricoeur called "ordered extensions of meaning" (p. 261).

Ricoeur (1975) argued that analogies employed to characterize being represent a distinctly different sort of analogy than that at work in poetic discourse. As Stellardi (2000) put it, for Ricoeur:

> Transcendental analogy takes place only on the basis of a difference with regard to poetic resemblance. This difference is the very gesture that founds speculative discourse, after which it remains necessary to accomplish a further leap toward a concept of the unity of Being totally independent of analogy itself. (p. 81)

The analogical difference that founds speculative analogy, in Ricoeur's estimation, is the instantiation of metaphor *within* speculative analysis. Ricoeur's critique involved the assertion that Derrida merely superimposed the opposition proper/figurative onto that of visible/invisible (empirical and temporal versus ideal and eternal), thereby assuming a philosophical posture toward metaphor based in the standard binary of sensible and intelligible. Ineluctably, "metaphysics . . . seizes the metaphorical process in order to make it work for the benefit of metaphysics" (Ricoeur, 1975, p. 294).

The discontinuity of analogy represented by metaphysics leads definitively beyond analogy in a further leap Ricoeur identified as the creation of "a proper sense in the spiritual order out of an improper sense coming from the sensible order" (p. 292). Stellardi classified this transition as a dialectical overcoming, and said that, for Ricoeur, "only this independence of the content (spiritual meaning) from its carrier (in this case, worn metaphor) makes philosophical discourse (including deconstruction) possible at all" (p. 86). For both Derrida and Ricoeur, it seems, the denaturing by which metaphor, in its infinite suggestiveness, founds a determinate concept, becoming what Stellardi (2000) called "lexicalized," a dead metaphor, or "usual" metaphor (p. 85), may be the condition of the possibility of a metaphysics. It constitutes a threshold at which metaphysics walls itself off from metaphorics, protecting the predilections of reason from an upsurge of dissemination. "That there are philosophical terms," Ricoeur (1975) said, "is due to the fact that a concept can be active as thought in a metaphor which is itself dead" (p. 293). We have witnessed philosophy's express reliance upon the denaturing of metaphor, that is, metaphor's conceptual abstraction, in Socrates' stated preference for the environment of the city where the (Apollonian) abstractions of culture prevail over the (Dionysian) ambivalencies of nature.

For Ricoeur (1975), the possibility of a philosophy based in usual metaphor, and specifically its ability to make ontological claims, requires a redress of the modern theory. As he rehearsed the move from denomination to sentential context to discourse, he distinguished the analogical break and the dialectical overcoming as critical moments that ensure the possibility and the necessity of the autonomy of metaphysical speculation. Without this discursive autonomy, the ontological purposiveness of metaphysics becomes vitiated. The broadening of metaphoric process from Aristotelian denomination, in which metaphor was understood as the application of a name to an object that it did not normally signify, to sentential context in which, as Stellardi (2000) put it, "the minimal complete meaningful unit" (p. 79) is the phrase rather than the noun, entails a lessening of ontological presuppositions. In the context of the sentence, the semantic mechanism is no longer the strict signification of the word/object relationship, but a contextual predication that, Stellardi said, expands or loosens the possibilities inherent within the copula *is*.

Contextual predication, a Dionysian loosening of the absolute mode of ontological assertion, has the effect, Stellardi (2000) said, of retracting the "denominative deviance" or categorical misapplication presumed under the classical theory to mere "predicative impertinence" (p. 79). Yet this abatement from deviance to impertinence is still a first step de-literalization of the attribute of falsity. In the further theoretic extension, from the phrase to the discursive context, Stellardi said, "the point of insistency" (p. 79) bifurcates:

> Metaphor is now founded on a double reference: a first degree reference to reality, and a second-degree reference of a poetic nature. The metaphorical power plays in the space between those two limits, and must be understood not in the form of a rhetorical figure centered on the word, or as a semantic impertinence internal to the linguistic code, but rather as the redescription of reality within the space of one of many possible "modes of discourse": the poetic discourse. This type of discourse requires its own structure and activates its own specific kind of truth: a tensional truth. (p. 79)

Rewinding this theoretical development to assert an ontological primacy for philosophical method, as Ricoeur desires, produces a chain of inference that appears to rein in the slippage of falsity, but that cannot evade it: contextual deviance → sentential impertinence → (tensional) *truth*. The false has still managed to predicate the true.

This duplicity of the contemporary theory lies within the analogical process whereby conceptual form gives way to depths of underlying metaphoric dissemination. But with Ricoeur's (1975) assertion of dialectics, the metaphoric enunciation refers to two distinct vocabularies. "On the one hand," Ricoeur said, "speculative discourse has its condition of *possibility* in the semantic dynamism of metaphorical utterance [but] on the other hand speculative discourse has its *necessity* in itself" (p. 296). The distinction Ricoeur wishes to maintain, said Stellardi (2000), is that "between the metaphoric implicit and the conceptual explicit" (p. 87). Ricoeur's retention, or interpolation, of the "dialectic of speculative and poetic" (p. 388) is what sets him apart from Derrida. The tensional space separating, as Stellardi put it, "the referential limits" of "reality" and "the poetic nature" does indeed implicate poetic discourse, but only as one kind of discourse. It "does not," Ricoeur said, "bar [speculative discourse] from beginning in itself and from finding the principle of its articulation within itself" (p. 300). It is the "capacity of distantiation inherent to language," Stellardi said,

> that makes possible the autonomy of one level of discourse, *intellectio*, from another, *imagination*. . . . Metaphor appertains to *imaginatio*; on the contrary, the conceptual order, because of its own ability to form a system, is capable of freeing itself from the play of double signification, and therefore from metaphoric tension. (p. 88)

Ontology retains its philosophical imprimatur despite the metaphoric dynamism underlying speculative discourse because, Ricoeur (1975) said, "The *necessity* of this discourse is not the extension of its [poetic] possibility. . . . Its necessity proceeds instead from the very structures of the mind, which it is the task of transcendental philosophy to articulate" (p. 300).

The distantiated order of things, the *intellectio*, reflects the image of Apollo; it countenances the referential limits of "reality" that Stellardi (2000) juxtaposed with the poetic nature. The slipping away of ontological certainties in the succession from denomination to predication and again to discursive context is stanched by Ricoeur (1975) in the distinction between possibility and necessity. He was content to let the former rest in the Dionysian or disseminative space of metaphoricity, but the latter, necessary and sufficient *reason*, he was compelled to wall off. His strategy to certify the autonomy of speculative discourse (or, to the extent that metaphysics cannot be said to be monolithic, speculative discourses) was to circumscribe it. Such circum*scription*, a *written* boundary, instantly conjures Hermes, god of writing. Circumscription can be had only with the application of the hermetic seal, which in any event is a vacillating threshold. Of willful necessity, circumscription may assert the autonomy of the Apollonian dominant but it nevertheless, and simultaneously, incubates the possibility of the shifting paradigm.

Derrida's response to Ricoeur's criticism that, as Stellardi (2000) put it, "concept lives in metaphor's death, and not in its 'white' disguise" (p. 86) was delivered in lectures published as "The *Retrait* of Metaphor." Derrida's (1998b) choice of the word *retrait* was a reference in two senses to Heidegger. For Heidegger, a defining trait of being, as we have seen, is that aspects of a world are disclosed only as others are simultaneously veiled—an intrinsic and originary self-effacement of pure presence. Heidegger's project also entailed the retreat of metaphysics insofar as it had failed ontologically. Heidegger desired a treatment of ontology that would explicate being not in the purity of its essence, but in the vagaries of its existence. He parted philosophical company with Husserl, who was concerned with a phenomenology of Being, to instead develop a phenomenology of situated beings; the former tending to idealism and the latter to empiricism.

Heidegger did not undertake a study of metaphor, though he used it freely ("Language is the house of Being"), and in later years his principal interest was with what Stellardi (2000) called "the poetic nature." Heidegger's (1991) dismissive statement, "The metaphoric exists only within metaphysics" (p. 48), harkens to the classical theory in which philosophy is the archon of all thought, taking metaphor into itself and legislating its statutory purview. To the extent that a correction of ontology's exposition requires the retrenchment of metaphysics in its earliest possible pre-Socratic moment when being yet may have had non-idealist viability, metaphor as well must be placed into retreat.

The Heideggerian withdrawal of metaphysics is, then, what Derrida (1998b) termed "withdrawal-of-being-or-of-metaphor" (p. 118). Heidegger, Derrida said, attributed a principal circumstance of the failure of ontology, the *epoché* of being—or in Stellardi's (2000) words, its "suspensive retreat" (p. 94) in the face of idealist investigation—to "the vast structural process" of the "history of Western metaphysics" (Derrida, 1998b, p. 116). The structural process, Derrida said, is one that "*would present* an (interlaced) series of guises, of turns, of modes, that is to say, of figures or of tropical aspects which we could be tempted to describe with the aid of rhetorical conceptuality" (p. 116). That a description of the metaphysical structure is apparently dependent upon "rhetorical conceptuality" led Derrida to assert, said Stellardi (2000), that "inasmuch as being can only be named in a metaphoric/metonymic swerve, metaphysics not only deals with and construes the concept of metaphor, 'it would itself be in a tropical position with respect to Being or the thought of Being'" (p. 94). Discontinuous analogy, of the kind Ricoeur proposed as necessary to metaphysical speculation, is in this view a conceptual guise, another swerve of the conceptual/metaphorical tropism.

For Derrida, the trait that distinguishes the distantiation (or proximity) of figure and concept, poetry and speculative thought, Stellardi (2000) said, is "the limit, the margin, the mark" that refers to both but "does not belong to either" (p. 98). It is neither concept nor metaphor, he said:

> If such a trait were something, it would be something older than both [thinking and poetry], their common origin, while remaining singular and different. But it is not original, nor is it derived; it opens a differential drift, it opens the very possibility of naming in language, and therefore is not "itself namable as separation, neither literally, properly, nor metaphorically." (p. 98; internal quote is from Derrida)

With this construal of Derrida's advance to the frontier of metaphorics, Stellardi brings out the Hermetic quality, a differential equation that relates the values of an unknown function. "The trait is retreat," Stellardi (2000) said. "The trait is therefore nothing" (p. 99). Notwithstanding its vanishing act, the "trait" is not to be assimilated ontotheologically to a *deus absconditis*: "It is not an autonomous agency, original in respect to the two that are separated and allied by it; it is nothing; it does not appear itself, it is *structurally* in retreat" (p. 98; emphasis added). The distinguishing trait of philosophical production, then, is the retreat of structure, its reversal and revaluation. It is *in effect* the backwards shoes of Hermes, a poststructural archetypology.

In its deconstructive mode, Stellardi (2000) said, philosophy "risks its own point of foundation" (p. 103), the indubitability of what Ricoeur (1975), in defense of a metaphysics autonomous from metaphorics, called "the mind itself reflecting upon itself" (p. 296). At the fissile core of philosophy, deconstruction encounters the "double-blind" in which philosophy has been envisioned. The task is to affect a re-visioning, to deepen paradox, to relativize the decree of "no exit" with the possibility of a double posture, a double movement, a double position. "The point of foundation," said Stellardi (2000), "is philosophy's blind spot, where its domination is suspended and visibility is impaired through excessive proximity, and where a massive return of what was supposed to be under control remains a constant possibility" (p. 75). The danger, in Hillman's (1997b) view, is that "epistemology loses its ability to correct its own bright blindedness by making radical paradigm shifts" (p. 52). Yet philosophy's foundation is a metaphoric *hermaion* at the intersections objective/subjective, mind/body, presence/absence, and *res cogitans/res extensa*. In exchange for the loss of sacred cows, logocentric symptoms of an insistent purity, deconstruction offers what Suzi Harvey (2000), as noted, called a hidden music that is released with the death of the literal, a lyric treatment. Indeed, at the moment when nausea might have inhibited action, it was a ragtime tune, "Some of These Days," that allowed Sartre (1964) to mark the exit from aversion with a version of loss.

PART II

Metaphor in imaginal psychology

In the remains of our exposition we now move toward a theory of metaphor as might be derived from Hillman's work by demonstrating the metaphoricity of key concepts in imaginal psychology.

6

SOUL

Hillman's (1978b) re-visioned psychology places an "emphasis on the making of 'soul' rather than 'self'" (p. 207) so as to be transparent to its root metaphor, psyche.[1] Immediately at the inception of *Re-Visioning Psychology*, Hillman (1975) associated soul with metaphor, locating both as border phenomena that obtain between matter and mind, but go wanting in the Cartesian reduction. The "modern view," he said, "imagines a universe divided into living subjects and dead objects. There is no space for anything intermediate, ambiguous, and metaphorical" (p. 1). The re-visioning Hillman sought is a compensatory, depth psychological vantage on the literalisms of "modern consciousness" (p. 3). He asked that we look again at the mythical persons of the Greek imagination that inspired the work of Freud and Jung to discern what they might tell us about the perspectives of the gods themselves. He took seriously the motive force of the imaginal figure much in the same sense that Harold Bloom (1998), as we saw earlier, was able to say we cannot be certain whether Hamlet or Shakespeare wrote the play.

"*Our desire*," Hillman (1975) emphasized, "*is to save the phenomenon of the imaginal psyche*" (p. 3). The salvational intent links the desire of the imaginal psychologist to the Romantic quest of the knight errant, who rides on horseback. "The horse-body," said Marie-Louise von Franz (1999), "carries the soul" (p. 71). And so the knight errant, in Hillman's (1975) words, "follows fantasy, riding the vehicle of his emotions; he loiters and pursues the anima with his eros, regarding *desire* as also holy; and he listens to the deviant discourse of the imagination" (p. 161; emphasis added). Imaginal psychology's pursuit is not of soul as an object of desire, but as a process of desiring—of soul, psyche, or anima as "this peculiar and paradoxical intervening variable" (p. xvi). The quest is not for truth, but for the perspectival process that leads to expressions of truth.

As a phenomenological enterprise, imaginal psychology sees through the eyes of Psyche. It brackets suppositions that might hypostasize meaning in order to attend to how the soul interprets itself. The aspect of hermeneutic interpretation relativizes that of phenomenological presentation to make of imaginal psychology a hermeneutic phenomenology. The soul may present itself in innumerable ways, but it is never in itself present, only so in concert with what it points to, depicts, or amplifies. "First of all," Hillman (1975) said, problematizing origination, the soul is "a perspective rather than a substance, a viewpoint toward things rather than a thing itself" (p. xvi). It is "that mode which recognizes all realities as primarily symbolic or metaphorical" (p. xvi). In other words, there is no purity of soul; it is relational and ironical, ever something other. It is always already *like* whatever is ready-to-hand. "Though I cannot identify soul with anything else," Hillman said, "I also can never grasp it by itself apart from other things" (p. xvi). "Its meaning," he said, "is best given by its context," which it in part generates (Hillman, 1997b, p. 44). The soul understands and experiences itself in terms of the phenomena with which it intersects by enabling epistemological conditions, the interpretive structures of mind. If psyche is anything, it is that vanishing moment of intersection in which particulars become mutually contaminated, their integrity wounded, and in whose wake there is a world. The moment when an archetype, or interpretive mode, fails in its function of contextualization, or, to apply the term from metaphor theory, its function of *interaction*, and fixes events to its self-identity, is the moment when soul-making grinds to a halt. The soul's logos, its native idiom, metaphor, then gives over to reaction formation; the imaginal faculty reduces to "pure" reason.

Purity, and reason, in Hillman's re-visioning, are fundaments not of soul, but of spirit. In the relation between the two, we encounter the binary opposition, the differential structure, which supplies imaginal psychology with its point of deconstruction or poststructural departure. In the Hermetic double move that indicates a deconstructive occurrence, Hillman reversed the hierarchy spirit/soul in which the primary term is valued over the supplementary one, and allowed the natural proclivities of the supplement to emerge from their former repression. He then followed the supplementary qualities as they led into perspectival terrain beyond that made viable by the hierarchy. In contradistinction to spirit, which sees as if from on high, clearly—and monomaniacally—soul is the perspective that sees from within and below. "The spiritual point of view always posits itself as superior, and operates particularly well in a fantasy of transcendence among ultimates and absolutes" (Hillman, 1975, p. 68).

The same is true of the analytical point of view, which strives for ever more definite particulars. The preponderate attribute is literalism; the metaphoric *pseudo-domain* is absent. The re-visioning of psychology removes the corrective lenses of the analytical and the spiritual points of view, dissolving single-pointed focus and letting be the distortions of psyche's own astigmatic perspective:

> [T]he relationship of psyche with dream, fantasy, and image . . . the soul's connection with the night world, the realm of the dead, and the moon . . . images of "lunacy" . . . circular reasonings, where retreats are as important as advances . . . [give] a metaphorical sense to life. (Hillman, 1975, p. 68)

The spectre of metaphor, the nature and logic of the in-between, moves into view: "By having its own realm psyche has its own logic—psychology—which is neither a science of physical things nor a metaphysics of spiritual things" (p. 68). Psyche's logos is a poetics of interstice, of "the welter of phenomena and the flow of impressions" (p. 69), a phenomenology of interaction.

The nature of psyche's metaphoric interaction with the physical and the spiritual is polysemic and open-ended; it is, to draw upon Heraclitus (535–475 BCE), depthless. Notable for making the first association of psyche with *bathys*, depth, Heraclitus heralded the belated advent of depth psychology. "You could not discover the limits of soul," Heraclitus wrote, "even if you traveled every road to do so; such is the depth of its meaning" (as cited in Hillman, 1975, p. xvii). It is in part this passage that allows Hillman to assert that the "dimension of soul is depth (not breadth or height) and the dimension of our soul travel is downward" (p. xvii). Soul's depth is a metaphoric indicator that the direction taken by meaning-making leads through ideas that we understand in terms of depth, such as darkness, death, wisdom, seriousness, melancholy, solidity: elements of experience that evoke the tragic sense. In a critique of Hillman's theory of the pathologizing function of the psyche in her work on Dionysian consciousness, Susan Rowland (2017) says of the tragic form of stage drama that: "[T]ragedy here is metaphorical knowing. It forces us to accept fiction as fiction, and yet also as intensely real" (p. 149). Drawing out the interdisciplinary tendencies of literary theory and archetypal psychology, she says, "Tragedy is therefore the fundamental drama of the soul" (p. 152). Yet the notion of *bathys* also sees through the tragic to the comedic by carrying the connotation of *ludicrous*: the deep is also the far-fetched. The metaphoric psyche is a *magister ludi*, language games being a special case, as noted earlier, of a larger metaphoric articulation of the world.

In an imputation of the trickster, the soul seems not averse to ludicrous or asinine depictions of itself. Indeed, the authoritative version of the Psyche myth, which Hillman (1978c) proposed as imaginal psychology's alternative to Oedipus, comes to us as an episode in *The Golden Ass* by Apuleius (125–180 CE). The tale tells of a man who has been turned by misfortune into a donkey, and wanders the world in search of an Ovidian metamorphosis, a divine revelation. He seeks, by the grace of the gods, to regain, or perhaps to accept, his humanity. Along the way, the misshapen traveler has the occasion to hear a story in which a beautiful young woman, Psyche, becomes the beloved of the god Eros. He visits her only at night, and as so often is the case in such stories, she is made to understand that were she to look at her lover, great sacrifice would be exacted (recall how Zeus beseeched Semele not to ask that he reveal himself). Being all too human, she lights a candle against the darkness, and for an instant beholds a beautiful youth who promptly vanishes, seemingly forever. But! There remain redemptive ordeals in the offing, and their successful completion causes the lovers to be reunited, and confers immortality upon Psyche.

The myth allows Hillman to make the central argument of his re-visioned psychology, that the psyche, though it suffers, is not an illness in search of a cure, but a figure of beauty, and mortality, in search of love. The love in question is not a generalized romantic love; it is not Christian love, neither *caritas* nor *agapé*; it is not the enfolding feminine love of Venus, or Aphrodite (who strives to retain Psyche in her own unindividuated train). The love that Psyche seeks is creative love, the mode personified by Eros. Psyche's volatilization, her transformation, not without agony, from ingénue to immortal, is brought about by Eros. It is Eros as creative/destructive lover who tempers Psyche. Soul-making, then, is precisely this libidinal pursuit, the agon of creativity. Rather than seeking to cure the soul's sufferings, Hillman thought, psychology would do better to quicken those same creative urges, bringing forth into the earthly vale the labors of love. To call the world a vale of soul-making, Hillman said, "imagines the tribulations of life as contributions to soul" (Hillman & Ventura, 1992, p. 50).

Yet there is something unmistakably deviant about this love. It appears to have, Hillman (1978c) said, "a double aspect" (p. 74). Like all archetypes, which are "structured with two sides, so their dynamics are ambivalent" (p. 75n), Eros is daimon and demon, compelling and inhibiting (p. 74). He is "both direct, like fire and arrow, and indirect, like the wreathed garland, also [his] symbol" (p. 75). We get a sense of a specific style of ambi-valence by the terms Hillman employed to describe the double aspect of Erotic creativity. Eros, we learn, is intermediary, interfering, intervening, interrupting, redirecting, suddenly shifting, deceptive, frustrating, devilishly duplicitous, hermaphroditic, ithyphallic, Mercurial. "This spirit of resourceful inventiveness and creative intelligence," Hillman said, is "inherited from his father, either Poros [expediency] or Hermes" (p. 90). At the back of the proposed myth of an imaginal psychology, the soul's pursuit of and suffering for creative love, which Hillman called "the creative paternal principle in our psychology" (p. 49), we are not surprised to glimpse Hermes, the absent father.[2] We might conclude that to understand and experience one another, Psyche and Eros require metaphoric transposition, the carrying over of one to the other.

The placement of their story amid the adventures of a human donkey wandering abroad in the syncretic religious and intellectual environment of Hellenism—a *vas* of fermentation for transgressive, mutually contaminated religious forms—reflects the logic of metaphor. In his poem "Thinking of a Relation Between the Images of Metaphors," Wallace Stevens (1990) wrote: "To the unstated theme each variation comes . . ." (p. 277; ellipses in original). Other than the cosmogonic sympathies wrought by metaphor, there is—to borrow from Pascal—only eternal silence. Descending, as the Gnostics imagined, the ineffable passes through a semantic prism, bending to heterodox meaning. The resulting ambiguities are cause for reason's discomfiture, but Psyche cannot find creative expression in the brittle argot of the literal. She requires metaphoric interaction with an erotics of deviance.

The notion of ambiguity is critical, as Plato (1963) already knew 2,500 years ago, when Socrates told Phaedrus: "To say what [soul] really *is* would require a long exposition of which only a god would be capable; but it is within human power to say more briefly what it is *like*" (§246; emphasis added). In other words, we would create an ontology of soul in vain; soul is more amenable to a metaphorics. *Like* metaphor, soul is an ambiguous phenomenon; it is the very phenomenon *of* ambiguity. Hillman indicated as much, saying of soul that it is an "unknown component" (1975, p. xvi) and a "deliberately ambiguous concept" (2004a, p. 28). Each attempt at explanation, he said, corresponds to an "archetypal constellation," or "a statement about the soul by the soul," averring

> that the soul is a harmony or a multiple and varied unity, that it is born in sin, that it is divine and immortal, that it is a quest for meaning or self-knowledge, that its essence is life and warmth, that its essence is death, that it is structured in three or more parts which enjoy a *psychomachia* in a strife of oppositions, that it is in enigmatic relations with the body, that it is fundamentally an element like air or water or a vaporous mixture of them. (Hillman, 1975, pp. 126–127)

This plethora underscores the soul's metaphoricity, and metaphor as the soul's "own language" (Hillman, 1983a, p. 32). Hillman does not associate imaginal psychology with any specific constellation of the soul's identity. His interest is with the backcloth against which such positivities come into resolution. "Each moment of blackening," Hillman (1997b) said, "is a harbinger of alteration, of invisible discovery, and of dissolution of attachments to whatever has been taken as truth and reality, solid fact, or dogmatic virtue. It darkens and sophisticates the eye so that it can see through" (p. 49).

The elliptical quality of soul, its productive excesses of "antimatter," are characteristic of Hermes. By situating his *scienza nuova* within soul, and making a sustained investigation into what soul wants, how it functions, the nature of its expressions and impressions, Hillman (1975) entered into deliberate engagement with the boundary conditions of the Hermetic. Soul, he said, "makes *differences* between ourselves and everything that happens" (p. xvi; emphasis added). In deconstructive terms, the moment of differentiation is also a moment of deferral. Hillman termed it the "reflective moment" (p. xvi). It takes place perhaps at that very *hermaion* or "point of foundation," where, as Stellardi (2000) said, "a massive return of what was supposed to be under control remains a constant possibility" (p. 75).

The idea of soul as the reflective moment in which difference stands out leads to Derrida. The word "psyche," as Derrida (2007) pointed out in an essay of the same name, can refer in French to a full-length, double-sided mirror that rotates on its stand (image as psychic fulcrum). Derrida said of this mirror and this mytheme that it is "the pivoting speculum that has come to relate the same to the other" (p. 20). In an economy of imagination, the mirror image is the token of exchange. Embossed with a backing of quicksilver, the mark of Hermes, god of commerce, it carries a recircular guarantee, which repeatedly places new value into use. The very coinage *soul*, which Thomas Moore (1989) called "that odd word" (p. 5), circulates as legal tender in disparate psychological economies, indicating it as a medium of exchange and a forfeiture of the literal. It places into question the notion of subjectivity by "requiring us to see the other within the self," as Niall Lucy (2005) said of the Freudian unconscious (p. 128). Its usage amounts to a play of signifiers. We cannot escape the ontotheological overtones—soul, Hillman (1975) said, "has a religious concern" (p. xvi)—or its materialist overtones, *the* soul as a thing with a corporeal or ethereal location. It has been expressed ironically in "the fundamental psychological teaching of the Buddha" as *anatman*, "no soul" (Epstein, 2013, p. 9). This formulation contemplates soul as the "unknown component" (Hillman, 1975, p. xvi). Perhaps it comes as close as any term to rendering a polyvalent, destructured meaning, soul as *skandhas* or aggregates, "a conglomeration of parts" (Epstein, 2013, p. 10), or as a constitution of images. Ultimately not susceptible to definition, soul can be understood in the Heideggerian-Derridean sense as a term under erasure, to be written with a line drawn through it, ~~soul~~, indicating its incomplete presence—a particularly Hermetic convention.

The imaging of soul as a root metaphor, Hillman (2004a) said, "attempts two things":

> to state the soul's nature in its own language (metaphor) and to recognize that all statements in psychology about soul are metaphors. In this way, soul-as-metaphor leads beyond the problems of "how to define soul" and encourages an account of the soul toward imagining itself rather than defining itself. (p. 32)

Manifesting as a typical de-literalization, Hillman's achievement was to re-vision the objectified concept, seeing soul instead as "an imagining *activity*" (p. 19; emphasis added), or a "*mode* which recognizes all realities as primarily symbolic or metaphorical" (Hillman, 1975, p. xvi; emphasis added). It is to the cultivation of this symbolic sense that we turn next.

Notes

1 I will tend to use the terms *soul, the soul, psyche,* and *anima* somewhat interchangeably, though not without the recognition that these variants are given with their own expressive tendencies. The first term tends to add a religious coloring; the second a materialist one, the soul as a thing; the third a Greek mythological or, alternatively, a modern medical connotation, and the last a Latin taxonomic and Jungian structural cast, the anima as a person of the collective unconscious or the soul of world, *anima mundi*.

2 Freud and Jung both said that psychological health required grappling with a desire for the mother, whether literally in terms of the Oedipus complex, or metaphorically in terms of the lure of the night sea journey into darkness and depth to be spiritually reborn. In either case, the father is absent. Based on the Psyche myth, Hillman (1978b) proposed Eros as psychology's absent father.

7

IMAGE

Hillman drew the imaginal idea of psychology from two sources: Jung, who said that "image *is* psyche" (CW 13, par. 75), and Henry Corbin, for whom the *mundus imaginalis* constituted an interzone between spirit and matter. By emphasizing image, Hillman hoped to discern a perspective that could be called the soul's own. Imaginal psychology sees psyche not as an object, but as a creative process. The unconscious becomes an animating principle, "the imaginal power of the psyche" (Hillman, 1978c, p. 7). This de-objectification is an attempt to revert from "the egoization of the psyche" to an articulation of the psyche's own logic, seen as *poietic* and agonistic. The reformulation of psyche-logos as aesthetics frees the unconscious from its analytic metaphorization in which it is understood from the perspective of the ego's persistent urge to solve problems, cure illness, and bring all matters into productive alignment.

This chapter will explore Corbin's evocation of image as it has been explained by Tom Cheetham, a principal scholar of Corbin's work, and inquire into the pragmatic application of the imaginal theory. On the latter course, we will proceed in the manner of the *bricoleur* (but have we not already?) by piecing together a thematic diversity on fiction, the nature of possibility, Gnosticism, and the Romantics.

The sense of the imaginal as third term or middle way as derived by Corbin from Sufism lends instrumentality to Hillman's critique of the modern worldview. It furnishes a medium by which insight can be had into the function of mind that modernity elides: the singular quality of psychosomatic interaction that is soul's alone and not attributable to spirit or matter. *Imaginal* is a neologism coined by Corbin for a transformational realm of being avowed by Sufi mystics. Cheetham said Corbin considered the imaginal to be the very interstice neglected by the modern view, the gap in analysis. Cheetham (2012) summarized the view as follows:

> [B]etween the sense perception and the intuitions or categories of the intellect there has remained a void. That which ought to have taken its place between the two, and which in other times and places did occupy the intermediate space, that is to say the Active Imagination, has been left to the poets. (p. 17)

For Corbin, as for the Romantics in general, the imagination is, in Cheetham's words, "an organ of perception" (2012, p. 17) that enables an awareness of religious phenomena. As I have used the term, *religare* is a re-visioning of the bin(d)ary opposition, or fixed perspective, as a Hermetic *pseudo-domain*, an interstitial carrying over whereby positivities are experienced or understood in terms of one another.

As Corbin conceived of it, the *mundus imaginalis*, or imaginal world, Cheetham (2012) said, is "a realm of real being, an objective world" and not merely "a diaphanous and subtle version of the physical world" (p. 18). It is a locus of creativity with ontological agency capable of "healing the [Cartesian-Kantian] rift between thought and being" (p. 20). Corbin, Protestant theologian and scholar of Sufism, said that by cultivating our receptivity to the reality of the *mundus imaginalis* we "make ourselves capable of God" (Cheetham, 2012, p. 19).[1] In imaginal psychology, though, the imaginal becomes de-literalized and secularized to refer not to a transcendent domain, but, as Hillman (2004a) put it, to "imaginative phenomena that are transcendent to the world of sense in their value if not their appearance" (p. 15). While the value for Hillman is in part "theophanic" (p. 15), it is not objectively so as it is for Corbin. "[O]bjectivity," Hillman said, "is itself a poetic genre" (p. 15). The value instead abides in the "virtuality or potentiality which is always more than actuality and its limits" (p. 15). The value of the imaginal idea is in its potency to revalue "such bases as: biological instinct, eternal forms, numbers, linguistic and social transmission, biochemical reactions, genetic coding, etc." (p. 15), in other words, the limits of any fixed idea. It is, as Michael Ventura said, "a place where literal life and mythical life meet" (Hillman & Ventura, 1992, p. 27).

Integral to producing the effect of the *mundus imaginalis* as conceived by Corbin is the interpretive act of *ta'wil*, "a central concept of Shiite hermeneutics," which refers to an act of reading or apprehending the symbols of the imagination that "transforms the soul" (Cheetham, 2012, p. 14). In Corbin's words, *ta'wil* is:

> the mainspring of every spirituality, in the measure to which it furnishes the means of going beyond all conformisms, all servitudes to the letter, all opinions ready-made. . . . [It is] a procedure that engages the entire soul because it brings into play the soul's most secret sources of energy. (Cheetham, 2012, p. 21)

This interpretive function of "the entire soul," might also serve as a description of the poststructural shift away from literalism. Quoting Corbin, Cheetham (2012) said: "The action of ta'wil 'is essential symbolic understanding, the transmutation of everything visible into symbols'" (p. 21). "Conformisms" are surpassed by re-visioning the literal in symbolic terms, the principal phenomenon owing to the nature and logic of metaphor, and the means by which events seen imaginally are "transcendent to the world of sense in their value." Citing Corbin's assertion that the act of *ta'wil* carries "sensible forms back to imaginative forms," Hillman said of *ta'wil* that it amounts to the art of reading life (Hillman & Ventura, 1992, p. 62).

Corbin associated symbolic language with what he saw as the "lost speech" of the religions of the Book. "The true meaning of the Book" in the Abrahamic religions, he said, "is the interior meaning, hidden under the literal appearance" (Cheetham, 2012, p. 25). Speech that is lost to the literal is, in a Nietzschean sense, the forgetting of metaphor. "It is the function of the ta'wil as spiritual hermeneutics," Cheetham said, "to recover this lost speech" (p. 25). The logocentricity in Corbin's conception of lost speech, its suggestion of ontotheological presence, undergoes a re-visioning in imaginal psychology, which would place the emphasis in "spiritual hermeneutics" on the element of continual interpretation, or metaphorization, rather than the recovery of spiritual absolutes. If I have so far made a reasonable case for the association of the archetypes of the collective unconscious with the nature and logic of metaphor, we will be able to see indications of a metaphorics in the *mundus imaginalis*—though it is doubtful Corbin would accept the term *pseudo-domain* to describe the milieu of images. Let us follow Hillman (2004a) in saying that "the *mundus archetypalis* is also the *mundus imaginalis* . . . a distinct field of imaginal realities requiring methods and perceptual faculties different from the spiritual world beyond it or the empirical world of usual sense perception" (p. 15). The imaginal world, relegated to poets and mystics, becomes lost to reason. Its esotericism is a function of the blinding light of literal conformisms. It would be unconcealed only by the alethic art of memory, a passage into the darker textuality—the *thesaurus inscrutabilis*—of the unconscious, whereby phenomena are already always symbolic, metaphoric, and interpretive. The integration into imaginal psychology of the *mundus imaginalis* establishes its psyche-logos as a hermeneutic phenomenology, employing phenomenon as interpretive mechanism. By providing the "method and perceptual faculty" for a phenomenology of image, imaginal hermeneutics seeks to understand and experience actualities symbolically; it memorializes metaphor, recovering the differential language, *writing*, lost to ego consciousness.

"Phenomenology as unveiling the hidden," said Cheetham (2012), "*is* exegesis" (p. 58). With this distinction, we are brought back, methodologically, to Apuleius (2011). Psyche's unveiling of Eros caused him to vanish. He had been hidden in darkness, and she could not be sure of him. Her uncertainty caused her to light a candle, and then he was gone. The paradox of soul is that it couples with desire, but the *interaction*, to use Black's term, is a *tensional* one; it maintains a double posture or double position that does not resolve into one term or the other, but is ever in between. Congruent with Hillman's (1987) construal of *archetype* noted earlier, the soul-making, or meaning-making, process is neither daylit nor darkened, but "a continual dawning" (p. 12)—and setting—that is ungraspable by certainty. You cannot hold a candle to it, cannot *identify* it or identify with it, as we do when our epistemologies become fundamentalisms, because its salvational desire depends upon perception of the shadows. The imaginal process describes a *glancing* movement—psychological and philosophical reflection as perpetual *de*flection from, or re-visioning of, fixed values.

Corbin proposed the term *icon* in juxtaposition to *idol* to distinguish the conditions of mediacy, called by Cheetham "dialogical realities" (2012, p. 5), from that of certainty. In an echo of Foucault's analysis of the sovereignty of perspective, the touchstone for which is his critique of Diego Velazquez's 1656 painting *Las Meninas*, Cheetham likened certainty to "the space of a Renaissance painting" in which "the lines of perspective disappear into infinity" (p. 5). Cheetham contrasted the sovereign fantasy of "external, objective reality" with the "dialogical reality" of the *mundus imaginalis*, by virtue of which, he said, "the lines of perspective converge on the person engaged in dialogue with the reality of the symbol displayed" (p. 5). Perspective so conceived is manifestation of the symbolic. "All things are images," Cheetham said, "and an image can be viewed as an icon if only we ourselves are transformed into imaginal persons—persons who can see imaginal realities" (p. 186), or, in Hillman's formulation, "psychological citizens" (Hillman & Ventura, 1992, p. 125).

The value of imaginal transposition as "virtuality or potentiality" relates the function of the *mundus imaginalis* to a realm of *possibility* in a Heideggerian sense. For Heidegger (1962), possibility was an existential state, the "primordial and ultimate" ontological characterization of *Dasein* (p. 144). Kant searched for the understanding's conditions of possibility, but for Heidegger (1962), the condition of possibility was the basic state of *Dasein*. "[U]nderstanding is the kind of Being of Dasein in which it is its possibilities as possibilities," he said (p. 185). *Dasein* is the ongoing possibility of its own being. It is the encounter with its *thrownness*, its state of already always being in a given world. Possibility is a descriptor of perspectival emergence, or (though Heidegger would not have put it this way) metaphoric enaction. Heideggerian possibility shares a significance with *ta'wil*. Corbin, Cheetham (2012) noted, was Heidegger's first French translator. From Corbin's perspective, said Cheetham, "*Being and Time* is a moment in a cross-cultural conversation that includes that central concept of Shiite hermeneutics, ta'wil" (p. 14). In terms of therapeutic value, the *mundus imaginalis* is the organ of the possibility of the symbolic life. It is the extant state of transposition—and in that respect is Hermetic.

The fulcrum of possibility as I use it here is the image. "For Corbin," Cheetham (2012) said,

> the primary function of the imaginative faculty of the "soul," in his sense, is hermeneutic—and so hermeneutics is fundamentally imaginative. Images unfold and reveal symbolic meanings in such a way that we are transformed by them in *our* mode of being. (p. 198)

Image is a fundamentally interpretive, and therefore transformative, phenomenon. "An image is not a picture. It is a psychosomatic event," Cheetham (2013) said. Like the *complex*—an image, Hillman (2004a) said, is "a complex datum" (p. 21)—an image constellates a nexus of charged impressions and *occasions of experience* (a term used by Whitehead (1978) to indicate both dynamism and interaction) that are expressive of the psyche and, in turn, work upon the psyche to produce "*our* mode of being," that is, the *perspective* within the already always world that we, individually, *are*. We can recall that for Hillman (1975), soul is "first of all, a perspective" (p. xvi). It is an existential situation, an *anima*ted Heideggerian possibility.

Hillman's (1983a) emphasis on the *mundus imaginalis* for its formal value, that is, for the way it shapes an occasion, can be understood in terms of its therapeutic capacity to generate healing fiction. Psychoanalytic possibility is made up of the state of therapeutic interaction—tension—that exists between *literal*, genuinely felt, circumstances presented at the start of every hour and the *literary* demands of plot and narrative made by those same lived circumstances. The psychoanalytic approach to reality exposes the transference of the affective truth of the world from fiction onto history, establishing a clearing for *poiesis*. In Freudian free association, said Adam Phillips (2014), "History begins to sound like fiction" (p. 6). Depth psychology, and imaginal psychology in particular, re-approximates history/fiction with a deconstruction. When it is re-visioned in terms of the poetic basis of mind, "fiction" becomes the condition of possibility for case history. The imaginal becomes the a priori of the historical. It does not ensconce itself as noumena, but, in a *quasi-transcendental* or de-literalized sense, as differend, the border of unfolding phenomena. Hillman's central contribution to psychology is the amplification of the history/fiction deconstruction. In perhaps his preeminent description of soul, an expression of the way in which synchrony impacts diachrony, Hillman (1987) said: "Without the sense of soul, we have no sense of history. We never enter it. This core of soul that weaves events together into the meaningful patterns of tales and stories recounted by reminiscing creates history" (p. 6).

If Richard Rorty was correct to say that philosophy can be taken as a literary genre, then was Hillman also right when he made the literary claim for psychology? The answer may turn upon the nature of the imaginal life urged upon us by Corbin, who was, said Cheetham (2013), "a master of fiction." Invoking the Romantic tenet that the fundamental epistemological faculty is not reason, but the imagination, Cheetham said, "Fiction is the repository of all knowledge and all truth," and is "the only possible means of expressing truth." In a Romantic sense, psychology's telltale significance has to do with its cultivation of the *poietic* faculty missing from what Harold Bloom (1970) called the "tradition of intellectual error that began with the extreme Cartesian dualism, and that progressively learned to devalue contact between the self and others, the self and the outer world, the self and the body" (p. 7). The trajectory of Romanticism, said Bloom, "is from nature to the imagination's freedom" (p. 6). The major Romantic poets—Blake, Wordsworth, Coleridge, Keats, Byron, and Shelley—were far from merely expressing an elegiac desire for spiritual merger with something more elemental than themselves. They would have regarded such a move, Bloom said, as "the despairing surrender of the imagination's autonomy" (p. 6). Their vision was not to extinguish themselves in nature, but to stand out unfettered against its backdrop. They sought the dialogical relationship valued by Corbin. Their move "downward and inward," Bloom said, was not toward unity with nature, but toward "a wider consciousness" (pp. 10–11).

Bloom (1970) said the reaction of the Romantic poets to the circumstances of cultural alienation "in a reductive universe of death, a separated realm of atomized meanings, each discrete from the next" was to pose the question, "How can a poet's (or any man's) life be one of continuous allegory?" (p. 8). The Romantics sought meaning in the portrayal of life as symbolic story, heralding Nietzsche's assertion of life as a work of art. In a reference to Freud on the narcissism of aesthetic pleasure, Bloom said: "The deepest satisfactions in literature, in this [Freud's] view, comes from a release of tensions in the psyche" (p. 3). That which is released—unbound by "metaphoric substitution," to restate Derrida's trope on the binding of Isaac noted earlier—is the pent-up imagination.

Such a move is precisely Hillman's. The psychology Hillman sought to advance was grounded in the characterization of the symbolic life story as *soul*. He invoked the gods not theologically, but in the *poietic* recognition that human consciousness is made in their images, indeed is bound up (*religare*) with those images. The *poietic* binding is what Bloom (1970), invoking another trickster figure preoccupied with the vagaries of the boundary, saw as the Promethean quest of the Romantics. "In Romantic quest," Bloom said,

> the Promethean hero stands finally, quite alone, upon a tower that is only himself, and his stance is all the fire there is. . . . The creative process is the hero of Romantic poetry, and imaginative inhibitions, of every kind, necessarily must be the antagonists of the poetic quest. (p. 9)

As Richard Tarnas (1995) said in his *Prometheus the Awakener*, "Prometheus is the channel of the creative impulse within every psyche" (p. 113). He has his dual antagonists in the fundamentalisms of the Cartesian consciousness, materialist and spiritualist alike. The Promethean move peculiar to imaginal psychology is the incitement of a metaphorical way of knowing. "All those tendencies which impel us to know," said Gaston Bachelard (1964) in *The Psychoanalysis of Fire*, can be placed together "under the name of the Prometheus complex" (p. 12). Here we have knowledge not as epistemology, but as gnosis. Gnosticism, Bloom (1982) said, implying a certain errancy, is a mode of "*antithetical* knowledge, which means of knowledge both negative and evasive, or knowledge not acceptable as such to epistemologists of any school" (p. 56). The evasive mode is, of course, that of Hermes, who, as Trismegistus, is patron of the Gnostic revelation.

Bloom (1982) noted a chain of associations pertinent to the plurivocal character of this study. Gnosticism was explicated by its preeminent scholar, Hans Jonas, in terms of Heideggerian hermeneutics. Heidegger, Bloom noted, "fostered the capable critical school of Deconstruction," which has "touched its limit" of interpretability—reached an unbridgeable gap, or *aporia*—in "the tracing of any poem's genuinely epistemological or negative moments" (p. 56). The way across the gap, Bloom said, is a Gnostic or kabbalistic[2] criticism, which would cease to strive for truth and would instead "ask what it is that we can come to know when we read poems" (p. 56). Jonas (2001) provided the answer sought in the Gnostic striving, but before we arrive there, I want to problematize Bloom's (1982) point about the limits of deconstruction. *Tracing* is in fact the very move that deconstruction does make to follow the negativity of poetic thought. It is by the *trace* that one finds a way down into the *aporia*, the metaphoric abyss, that metaphysics strains to cover with ontotheological presence. As Rodolphe Gasché (1986) put it, *trace* is "an originary tracing and effacement" (p. 186). That is, *trace* is a doubling in which presence and absence are conjoined, an alethic unconcealing. In Jungian terms, it is an *enantiodromia*. In this sense, deconstruction is already Gnostic or kabbalistic. It seeks to know, as Bloom (1982) said of Gnosticism, "negative Creation in the Abyss" (p. 57), which we can also characterize as the *possibility* of *Dasein* in the thrown environment of the fallen world. Derrida (2007) is careful to indicate the impossibility of escape from the ontotheology of presence while at the same time pressing that the "interest" of deconstruction is precisely in the "experience" of just this "impossible" (p. 15).

We can return to Jonas for the basic Gnostic perception, that "the 'what' of the knowledge contains the explanation of its own origin, communication, and promised effect" (as cited in Bloom, 1982, p. 57). Such an explanation, Bloom (1982) said, is the definition of the poetic sublime, the awe and terror, or uncanny and *daimonic*, in the experience of artistic creation. *What* the Gnostics seek is the *experience* attendant upon aesthetic creation, a healing fiction. "One need but read each literal sentence of one's life metaphorically," Hillman said (1983a, p. 48). We can ascribe the practical effect, or felt *affect*, of the *mundus imaginalis* to its evocation of the aesthetic endeavor of lived experience, life as art—a value that, as noted, Hillman (2004a) said lies in a "virtuality or potentiality which is always more than actuality" (p. 15). This superabundance, as we have seen from Kant, Nietzsche, Derrida, the contemporary metaphoricists, and wary critics, such as Ricoeur, is intrinsic to the nature and logic of metaphor. We will recall from Kirk Pillow (2001) that Kant's aesthetic idea is a "presentation of the imagination" that "spurs open-ended reflection" (p. 199). In the manner of the interaction theory, it invites the unheard-of perspective. Kant's (1987) anticipation of the turn toward interaction, the fully creative, "strong" form of metaphor, proceeds in part from his assertion that the imagination "as a productive cognitive power . . . may even restructure experience" (p. 182), the hope and claim of any psychology.

But before we conclude our inquiry into image, a question remains. Does the experience of the sublime take us to origins, to their "explanation," as Jonas (2001) averred? In what sense can we say, as Hillman does, that the image is primary? Interpreting a fragment from Valentinus about the fear and awe of the angels when they came to behold Adam, Bloom (1982) said that the sense of the aesthetic sublime "that falls upon sculptor and poet, according to Valentinus, when they behold the statues and images that they have fashioned in the name of a 'god'" (p. 52) can be explained by the Gnostic idea of the preexistent Man. "The angels were terrified," Bloom said, because "they realized that a greater power of freedom of expression than they enjoyed thus belonged to Adam, who by sharing in the name of preexistent Anthropos stood over them in hierarchical rank and stood before them in priority of genesis" (p. 53). Here we have a primogeniture that also obtains in the poetic basis of mind.

In his study *Poetic Diction*, Owen Barfield (1973) proposed an originary metaphoric reality in which "the earliest words were not, as they appear to be at present, isolated and detached from thinking and feeling" (p. 85). Barfield viewed as a projection of analytical consciousness the notion that poetic diction is a late development: "Men do not *invent* those mysterious relations between separate external objects and between objects and feelings or ideas, which it is the function of poetry to reveal" (p. 86). Rather, "these poetic and *apparently* metaphorical values were latent in meaning from the beginning" (p. 85). Barfield supposes a richer metaphorical consciousness primordially, perhaps even unto prelapsarian innocence, due to the "original unity" (p. 86) of human and world. The earliest speaker "observed a unity and is not therefore himself conscious of a relation" (p. 86). Though one must reject the invocation of *participation mystique* as also a projection by analytical consciousness, Barfield's point is germane as applied to the notion that metaphoric cognition is "originary" *in any moment*:

> Figure and figurative, on the other hand—as long as we disentangle them carefully in our minds from the modern expression "figure of speech"—may justly be applied, owing to the perceptual or aesthetic, the pictorial, form in which these unitary meanings first manifest in consciousness. (p. 88)

For metaphoric consciousness, the poetic basis, or *mundus imaginalis*, "the full meanings of words . . . are flashing, iridescent shapes, like flames" (p. 75). The Promethean appropriation of knowledge has already always taken place, or, put differently, the condition of the possibility of gnosis is the *mundus imaginalis*. "The mind is poetic to begin with," Hillman (2004a) said, "and consciousness is not a later, secondary elaboration upon a primitive base but is given with that base in each image" (p. 21). The origin is displaced from diachrony to synchrony. An imaginal psychology, Hillman said, is "saved from accounting for psychic life in simplistic terms of elementary mechanisms, primordialities of origins, or numerically limited basic structures" (p. 21).

Lastly, but significantly for the Romantic view, there is a Neoplatonic, or transpersonal, deconstruction in the *bricolage* of image as imaginal psychology would assemble it. "The image," Hillman (2004a) said, "is a self-limiting multiple relationship of meanings, moods, historical events, qualitative details, and expressive possibilities" (p. 21). These *skandhas*, so to speak, are "independent of subjectivity"—they "claim their own reality" (p. 19). The *how* of the imaginal, pieced together in the quilted nature of these paragraphs, is *sui generis*: "Images come and go (as in dreams) at their own will, with their own rhythm, within their own fields of relations, undetermined by personal psychodynamics" (p. 19). The usurpation of pure reason in the necessity of analogy finds a corollary reversal and revaluation in the psychology of image. "[T]he mind is in the imagination rather than the imagination in the mind," Hillman said. This expression of the Romantic-Neoplatonic-transpersonal perspective reverses the reason/imagination hierarchy and revalues it to assert a mutual implication—a metaphorics—in which each term is unavoidably *bound* up with the *other*. With an imaginology, Hillman suggested, "The noetic and the imaginal no longer oppose each other" (p. 19). We are thus brought to a psyche-logos that applies the nature and logic of metaphor to re-vision our inaugural concern with the binary opposition.

Notes

1 All quotations from Corbin are as cited by Cheetham.
2 Bloom's (1982) reference is to Lurianic kabbalah, the negative doctrine of God's withdrawal from the world, understood as having left fragments, shards, of a catastrophically shattered divine consciousness. See Hillman (1975) on the "necessary activity of the psyche, which constructs vessels and beaks them in order to deepen and intensify experience" (p. xviii).

8

RE-VISIONING

This chapter is organized around the set of ideas used by Hillman (1975) in *Re-Visioning Psychology*, his most comprehensive argument for replacing an analytical psychology with an aesthetic psychology, or a creative discipline that is "closer to the arts, to writing, to painting, and making music" (p. 40). To portray his subject, psyche, he elaborated upon four themes: personifying, pathologizing, psychologizing, and dehumanizing, each of which occupies a chapter of the book. The chapters "lay out four ideas necessary for the soul-making process" (p. xv), the opus that draws out the imaginal depth of experience. I take each of the four modes of soul-making to be expressive of the nature and logic of metaphor, the basis of the proposed poststructural archetypology. By this conjunction, I mean much the same as Hillman (1981) did by *polytheistic psychology*. Reversing and revaluing the priority that analytical psychology assigns to unity, integration, and wholeness over and above multiplicity, breakdown, and fragmentation, Hillman preserved the "imaginal, mythical mode" (p. 119) of awareness whose reality is strenuously resisted by the fixity to which monotheistic (egoic) consciousness is prone.

As against analytical psychology's priority of centering, represented by reverence for the mandala, Hillman (1980) juxtaposed the metaphorizing impulse of Dionysian "loosening, setting free, deliverance, dissolution, collapse, breaking bonds and laws, and the final unraveling as of a plot in tragedy" (p. 162). The last syllables of *analysis*, Hillman (1980) noted, are *lysis*, "loosening." Dionysus, he said, "was called *Lysios*, the loosener" (p. 162). As "the archetypal dominant expressing life itself" (p. 158), his "metaphorical field" (p. 162) is a "composite of differences" (p. 161). Disentangling Jung's conflation of the shamanism of Dionysus with the nativism of Wotan, Hillman distinguished the therapeutic suffering-through of Dionysian dismemberment from the inchoate "eruption" (p. 158) of Wotanic disintegration. Centering in the Self, he said, may be an appropriate reaction formation against Wotan, but not Dionysus.

In the sense that soul-making is a function of the imagination, the four principles of imaginal *lysis* in *Re-Visioning Psychology* can be understood as categories of the imagination, which was how Jung identified archetypes (CW 9, I, par. 89; CW 11, par. 517–518), but with a significant difference. "For Hillman," said Michael Vannoy Adams (2008b), "the archetypal is not a category but a consideration—a perspectival operation that an individual may perform on any image" (p. 109). "*Archetypal*," Hillman (1989a) said, "refers to a move that one makes rather than a thing that is" (p. 26). The archetypal operation is a matter of "hearing [the image] metaphorically," that is, of sensing its value by sounding out or "experiencing [its] unfathomable analogical richness" (p. 26). Following in this vein, we can understand the expressive mode of the principles to involve a double move, that of a hermeneutic phenomenology, which is both interpretive and descriptive.

The move reflects Hillman's (1975) view that the soul "deepens events into experience" (p. xvi), and that, as Thomas Moore (1989) said, "It is image that is experienced, not literalism" (p. 15). Let us take the designations used by Vannoy Adams, "consideration" and "perspectival operation," to indicate the phenomenological imperative that seeks to describe images on their own terms. Let us take Hillman's designations "hearing metaphorically" or "experiencing unfathomable analogical richness" to construe images as inherently interpretive. On this basis, we can evince a hermeneutic phenomenology expressive of the nature and logic of metaphor, a metaphorics that, like Hermes, sees through the descriptive carapace to its interpretive depths. Hillman's soul-making principles provide the psychological method necessary to make the critical distinction that keeps "literal belief and metaphoric attitude apart" (Hillman, 1981, p. 119). They denote the lyric descantation of a poststructural archetypology.

Personifying

The radical consequence of claiming psychology for aesthetics is the recognition, Hillman (1975) said, of "my own metaphorical existence—that I too am a personification whose reality depends on something other than my own will and reason" (p. 49). That is, I am a literary, not a literal, expression of the drives that are at work in me, the metaphors, figures, images of my psychological make-up: "The literalisms into which we constrict our drives hold us faster than do the drives themselves" (p. 46). To understand ourselves as metaphorical expressions of drives saves us from the "desperate clutching literalisms" in which we become "more pornographically sexualized than our sexuality, more aggressively power-driven than our ambition, more hungry and dependent than our needs, more masochistically victimized than our suffering requires" (p. 46).

The metaphoricity of the self stems from an axiom of depth psychology. As Hillman (1975) put it:

> Therapy works through the paradox of admitting that all figures and feelings of the psyche are wholly "mine," while at the same time recognizing that these figures and feelings are free of my control and identity, not "mine" at all. (p. 31)

Hillman's innovation was to express this axiom completely. In order to establish the paradox that the images of the psyche are autonomous of the ego, Hillman insisted on their personhood. He broke new ground with the aid of a conceptual metaphor, Words Are Persons (p. 9): "To give subjectivity and intentionality to a noun means more than moving into a special kind of language game; it means that we actually enter into another psychological dimension. The noun takes on consciousness, it becomes personified" (p. 1). The move is a form of animation. In the same sense in which animism discerns the living presence of soul, *anima*, in the distinct events, creatures, and places of the nonhuman world, Hillman would have us seek out distinct subjectivities behind the experiences and descriptive discourses of our lives. Further, in a relativization of ego, it is not we who characterize such circumstances, but the circumstances that characterize us—as if out of a quantum indeterminacy these transpersonal discourses, fictions, and fantasies manifest particular qualities of *color*, *flavor*, or *spin*. Hillman sought to reanimate the concepts and vocabularies of literalized modern consciousness with a personifying infusion from the "metaphorical imagination" (p. 11).

A re-visioned psychology seeks its personifications in the prima materia of depth psychology, the classical myths. It takes mythological phenomena on their own terms, seeing through the eyes of allegorized figures. Drawing on classical scholarship, Hillman (1975, citing a text from the Warburg Institute) said the Greeks and Romans

> personified such psychic powers as Fame, Insolence, Night, Ugliness, Timing, Hope, to name but a few. These were regarded as "real daemons to be worshipped and propitiated and no mere figments of the imagination. And, as is well known, they were actually worshipped in every Greek city. To mention Athens alone, we find altars and sanctuaries of Victory, Fortune, Friendship, Forgetfulness, Modesty, Mercy, Peace, and many more." (p. 13)

These designations of the religions of antiquity, Hillman said, indicate "the necessity of personifying for the mythic perspective" (p. 16). If we are to hold such a perspective—and we do so for the therapeutic value it lends to individual and culture—we are obliged to personify: "To understand anything at all, we must envision it as having an independent subjective existence, capable of experience, obliged to a history, motivated by purposes and intentions. We must always think anthropomorphically, even personally" (p. 16). The mode of consciousness that personifies events and qualities is called by Hillman, after Unamuno, "mythopeic" understanding (p. 16).

The therapeutic value in the anthropomorphic move is its effect upon the emotionally charged collection of images and ideas that constitute the complexes of the psyche. Invoking the *via regia* to the unconscious, Hillman (1975) said,

> When a complex is imagined as a distinctly separated entity, a full "person," equal to my notion of ego in intentions, mood, and willfulness, then my relations to my complexes will be as in a dream where they are no more or

> less real than the dream "I." . . . What was once an affect, a symptom, an obsession, is now a figure with whom I can talk. (p. 34)

Herein lies the reparative importance of personification for both individual and society. The understanding of complexes as persons "can change the very being of a complex" (p. 34). This conjecture may be said to derive from the worship of personified concepts in the Greek temples, which we might see as monuments to the transformative potential of the idea that daemons need not be seen as "mine." The mutability of the personified complex indicates a metamorphic possibility rhapsodized by Ovid. The poet's summoning of "bodies in mind" sounds a quintessential ode to the tangibility, and psychological significance, of the personified concept.

The metaphorization of qualities in terms of subjectivity leads to another purchase upon the "tractable" soul (Hillman 1975, p. 14, quoting Plotinus): it is multiple. "Personifying," Hillman (1975) said, "means polycentricity, implicating us in a revolution of consciousness—from monotheistic to polytheistic" (p. 35). The move to polytheism refers to a prior, formative deconstruction, that of the spirit/soul opposition. In the conventional hierarchy, the merits of *soul* have been repressed. The inversion of the terms serves to realize and aggrandize the worth of the supplementary term. The generalization of the newly esteemed term affiliates it with attributes that in the conventional hierarchy have been devalued. Formerly valued attributes are affiliated with the now-relativized primary term. Hillman (1975) assimilated the literalization of the concept in its monotheistic fixity to *spirit*. As against this single-mindedness, the personified concepts of the classical pantheon constitute a psychological pluralism. This latter view he affiliated with *soul*. He departed from the otherworldly certainty of spirit for the ambiguity and density of poly*vale*nt metaphoricity, that is, for the Keatsean "vale." *Soul* became an earthly phenomenon. In the polytheistic disposition of imaginal psychology, "the theological reality of the Gods no longer seems paramount, as they become more psychologically evident in the images and myths of our lives," he said (p. 168). The gods are "bound to the actualities of the secular, where myths are daily taking place" (p. 168). *They* are bound to *us*, not we to them. Unlike a theology, an imaginal psychology does not manifest belief in gods. Rather, Hillman said,

> the Gods are *imagined*. They are approached through psychological methods of personifying, pathologizing, and psychologizing. They are formulated ambiguously, as metaphors for modes of experience and as numinous borderline persons. . . . The soul cannot *be* [emphasis added] except in one of their patterns. (p. 169)

Here again we observe the relativization of ontotheological presence entailed by the logic of metaphor.

With Hillman's (1975) philosophy of mind, we awaken, as if with Dante, in a dark wood. We are no longer confidently in the bright lands of metaphysical essences or scientific positivism. We have become sojourners among the worldly and personified qualities that, borrowing from Heidegger, we could call the *Existentalia*, the very factors that qualify our facticity. "*A God*," Hillman said, italicizing, "*is a manner of existence, an attitude toward existence*" (p. 130). As a religious attitude, personification offers the insight that we are not diachronically destined to overcome the vagaries of existence and our natural surround, but are a synchronic consequence of it. It substitutes the absolutes of our spiritual strivings with the attributes of our animal natures. The leap of (polytheistic) faith Hillman asked us to take is one from the heights of monotheistic exceptionalism into the deep of an animistic world we have come to regard as having been scientifically, culturally, and theologically surpassed. It is an ego death in which the perspective of the personal "I" is relativized by other psychological components with their own motive force and personality.

In conversation with Sonu Shamdasani, Hillman said,

> The task is not to get the answer, the answer is who is dominating my mind, so that's my basic question, who is determining my point of view. It's like a deconstructive "I." . . . The real answer is "Why is that my question?" (Hillman & Shamdasani, 2013, p. 56)

The journey to a psychological pluralism is a *metapherein*, or Hermetic carrying over, a portage across the Lethic boundary from metaphysics to metaphorics where the personifications native to classical consciousness might be recollected and *re-called*: "Today we are so unconscious of these persons that we call their realm the unconscious. Once they were the people of the imagination, as the unconscious was once the imaginal realm of *memoria*" (Hillman, 1975, p. 36). The journey to pluralism is a return, with Apuleius (2011), to a different city-state, the "city that was home to Psyche" (p. 87), where anima was passionately pursued.

Personification thus furthers a re-visioning by compensating for the astringency of modern consciousness. It implies "passionate engagement" with the world: "We do not ask: 'Are things alive or dead?' or 'Are Gods real or are they symbolic projections?'" (Hillman, 1975, p. 16). Such questions indicate the epistemology of "pure" reason. What Hillman called for in its place is "an epistemology of the heart, a thought mode of feeling" (p. 15). The disposition—that is, displacement—of reason called for here is entailed by the deconstruction of what is perhaps the principal binary opposition of the metaphysical tradition, logos/pathos. Feeling is revalued and its particular logic followed into a mythopoeic terrain of understanding. The density of this terrain is forbidding. Dionysian rather than Apollonian, it conceals, as Francis Yates (1966) said, the tortured precincts of the *metaphorica*. "Philosophy," Hillman (1975) said, "works wholly with words, so it must bring their complexities into rational order" (p. 10). But philosophy is not the only field of words. As Plato knew, on the other side of *ratio* there lies *oratorio*. Analysis inevitably gives way to *poiesis*. Philosophy's canalization of words, a bulwark constructed to sustain the principality (an ideal city-state) of the rational mind, overflows its banks. In the realignment whereby one conceptual metaphor, Words Are Things, gives way to another, Words Are Persons, the *topos* of psychology shudders and forms anew.

The black earth of the suddenly Mercurial terrain, which we have mapped as metaphor on the interaction view or as the syntactic novelty of *dissemination*, is both rich and treacherous. "We waver," Hillman (1975) said of the imaginal *terra nova*, "between delusion and prophecy, between visions and illusions" (p. 36). Upon these shores we are presented with the challenge to stick to the image, to attend to the figure as it reflects our predilections and to let the native culture "speak as it appears, as personified" (p. 37). We are made aware of our tendency for uncritical identification with our interpretive screens, avoiding a literalism that merely substitutes idols of rationality for idols of the imagination. We are asked to embody, and thus to concretize, the view that "we, too, are ultimately a composition of images" (p. 41). Hillman calls upon us to struggle with "the semantics of allegory, metaphor, model, paradigm, and symbol" (p. 35). He asks, in a poststructural vein, that we come to terms with the extent to which we are made of discourses, vocabularies: "Although these aspects of the imaginal are defined in the textbooks of rhetoric and psychiatry, the definitions have not affected the tissue of experience in which these imaginal events remain webbed together" (p. 37). We must, Hillman said:

> dissolve the literal belief in persons by repersonifying them into metaphors. Then personality may be imagined in a new way: that I am an impersonal person, a metaphor enacting multiple personifications, mimetic to images in the heart that are my fate, and that this soul which projects me has archetypal depths that are alien, inhuman, and impersonal. (p. 51)

The Hermetic treachery of the conceptual metaphor Words Are Persons is in the encounter it forces upon "the familiar ego" (p. 55), an engagement with the alien and the uncanny in our make-up, those psychological aspects which the "I" labels symptoms and over which it has scant control.

Personifying also explains the advent of the soul's discourse, psyche-logos, in the domain of medical science; it leads to the discomfiture, the dis-ease of the ego. "I must insist," Hillman (1975) said, "*that this movement of consciousness into psychological reality is experienced first as pathological*" (p. 35).

Pathologizing

Following an animating postulate of analytical psychology—Jung's insight that "the gods have become our diseases" (CW 13, par. 54)—Hillman (1978b) said: "[T]oday it is to our pathologies we must look for finding the Gods" (p. 50). Patricia Berry (2008) emphasized the inherently homeopathic nature of this Jungian postulate in terms that, in our context, evoke Derrida's depiction of Socrates as *pharmakos*, simultaneously poisoner and healer. "It is one of those curiosities about archetypes," she said, "that they appear just as easily pathologically (abnormally) as they do normally. . . . [I]n one and the same archetypal pattern lie both the pathology and its therapy" (p. 27). The idea of the double-sided archetype indicates how the gods may be felt as demons harrowing the house of the ego from beyond its monotheist dominion. "Mythology presents pathology," Kerényi and Hillman (1995) said, simply (p. 98). The authorial intentions that inscribe our lives onto the world do so seemingly without regard to the perfectionism of the ego:

> [W]e fail, and cannot see why we go wrong or where, despite high hopes and good intentions. We are unable to set matters right, to understand what is taking place or be understood by those who would try. Our minds, feelings, wills, and behaviors deviate from normal ways. Our insights are impotent, or none come at all. Our feelings disappear in apathy; we worry and also don't care. Destruction seeps out of us autonomously and we cannot redeem the broken trusts, hopes, loves. (Hillman, 1975, p. 56)

This is phenomenological description of the psychological kind. The symptom, Hillman said, "is a demonstration of a life force. . . . In my symptoms is the soul's deepest desire" (Hillman & Ventura, 1992, p. 158). Hillman is not here *explaining away* after the fashion of medicine or theology, but bracketing suppositions to let the observed phenomena fully emerge: "Were we able to discover its psychological necessity, pathologizing would no longer be wrong or right, but merely necessary, involving purposes which we have misperceived and values which must present themselves necessarily in a distorted form" (p. 57). A re-visioned psychology must allow the pathologizing function of the imagination to find its footing without impediment by fantasies of cure, improvement, or growth: "It is the genius of psychology to get it wrong, to disturb, pervert, dislocate, misread, so as to lift the repression of the usual sense" (Kerényi & Hillman, 1995, p. 98).

As we saw above, the mythological basis of Words Are Persons invokes a second conceptual metaphor, Gods Are Perspectives. Working from the thesis of a poetic basis of mind, let us say that pathologizing, the "genius" of psychology, its *daimon* or driving force, is a misprision. We encounter the term in Harold Bloom's manifesto of literary criticism, *The Anxiety of Influence* (1997), in which he credits misprision, the "strong" or "creative" misreading by poets of their predecessors, as a *poietic* factor with which the young poet establishes his own voice, emerging from the shadow of the masters. In Bloom's schema, six "revisionary ratios" expressive of misprision enable the poet to make his own mark in the tradition. The ratios, which we have no need of specifying here, account for the emergence of new poetic language with a recalibration of the balance of influence between received wisdom and novelty. Taken as form of misprision, pathologizing poetically "gets it wrong" to re*verse* and revalue the analyzed psyche. Hillman (1975) said, "The psyche uses complaints to speak in a magnified and misshapen language about its depths" (p. 82). Its pathologized "manner of telling, a way in which the psyche talks to itself," he said, constitutes "metaphorical language" (p. 82).

Psychopathology on an imaginal model "seeks to understand the soul's disorders as snarled communication, or as disrupted social nexus, or as frustrated spiritual fulfillment" (Hillman, 1975, p. 56). Interaction—to use the term of art from modern metaphor theory—that finds itself thusly complexified is compensatory to the untangling of truth sought after by spiritualism or materialism or to the rational order reflected in the language of metaphysics, whose syntax is denatured, pulled taut, clarified. "Philosophical thinking," Hillman said, in an iteration of the post-structural critique of metaphysical propriety, "must speak in terms of purity. Its abstract asceticism is part of the puritan dignity of the philosophical style itself" (p. 131). By contrast, the poststructural linguistics of the psyche is indeterminate. It fails in any absolute way to connect signifier to signified. In a Saussurean sense, no ultimate connection is established between sound and idea, or, in a generalized sense, between image and concept. The pathologized logos of the psyche destabilizes, *undermines*, the foundationalism of signifier/signified. Its implications remain in the *pseudo-domain* of metaphor:

> The psyche uses many languages for describing itself. We see these best in dreams because they are the best model for the actual structure of the psyche. Dreams tell the soul's tales in person and they also use the language of animals and landscapes, much as the Gods told of their different archetypal qualities through persons, animals, and landscapes. . . . The psyche is using a particular metaphorical language system. (p. 83)

This language system is "detailed and concrete" (p. 82). "The soul may speak of itself as a desert, an island, an airport. It may be a cow or a tiger" (p. 82). Dreams may use body parts or family members or other specific images to convey psyche, but none of these are actual; all are metaphorical. The psyche does not say, for example, that it *is* a landscape. It says, rather, that in this instance it is *like* a landscape. Psychological language is not expressive of an ontology or an epistemology, but of a hermeneutic phenomenology. Each psychological self-description is already always interpretive. It requires no analysis in terms of the categories of the understanding because the categories of the imagination have already supplied the interpretive mode. The metaphorical *pseudo-domain* sticks to the image—sticks to the signifier.

Metaphorical language is pathologized because of its ability to move. The *pathos* of the image, Hillman (1975) said, causes us to "start up, afflicted, haunted through the day, psychologically on edge" (p. 83). Pathologized images, "the idiot child, the boy with infantile paralysis, the figure with queer psychotic eyes or on the operating table having her womb cut out" (p. 82), particularly move the soul:

> We are afraid, we feel vulnerable and in danger; our very physical substance and sanity appear to be menaced; we want to prevent or rectify. Especially this last seizes us. We feel protective, impelled to correct, straighten, repair. For we have confused something sick with something wrong. (p. 83)

The use of *sick* here is an irony; the sick is the normal: "[N]orms are the delusions" that differentiated parts of the psyche ascribe to one another (p. 88). They do, however, serve a purpose. "If there were no literalism," Hillman said, "how would we recognize the metaphorical symbolic perspective?" (p. 87). Still, "to understand the metaphorical language of pathologizing we may not look at the twisted in terms of the straight, the failed in terms of the ideal, the dying in terms of life" (p. 87). To do so "sets up a polarity" (p. 87) without revaluing the terms.

The body, too, is a site of metaphorical enactment. Medical diagnoses, Hillman (1975) said, can be de-literalized: "We may no longer make a cleavage between organic pathology and psychopathology, following the old Cartesian division between physical and mental" (p. 80). Organic sickness, of the body or the body politic, admits of pathologizing as well as pathology. Communicating symptomatically, "the psyche is telling us about its lacunae, its gaps and wasteland" (p. 89). Through symptoms, gods speak *in absentia*. The absences sacrificed to our sense of presence inscribe themselves into consciousness, in painful reminder of our animal nature. Pathologizing compensates the "spiritual vision of the perfectibility of man" (p. 89), the fantasy of unlimited progress, the diachronicity of history, and the triumphalism of presence, whether in this life or the next. "Pathology," Hillman said, "always leads into new unknowns" (Hillman & Ventura, 2002, p. 124). Pathologizing therefore "forces the soul to a consciousness of itself as different from the ego and its life—a consciousness that obeys its own laws of metaphorical enactment in intimate relation with death" (Hillman, 1975, p. 89), or, to de-literalize, with "transience" (Hillman & Ventura, 1992, p. 118).

There will be more to say about imaginal psychology's metaphorization of death (its "dead" metaphor) in the section on dehumanizing. Let us at the moment point to Hillman's (1975) view that "pathologizing is present . . . most profoundly in the individual's sense of death, which he carries wherever he goes" (p. 70). The sense of death, he said, is often mythologized in depictions of "the night world [which is] the realm of the dead, and the moon" (p. 68). We recall from the myth that Dionysus, who Nietzsche identified with the metaphoric imperative, was born again in the night world of Hades, a domain of seeming lunacy, which quality in turn provides raw material for psychological consideration. The Dionysian mode of seeing through literalisms to their metaphoric provenance leads to deeper, Plutonic riches. It is this imaginal method of attaining depth that Hillman called psychologizing.

Psychologizing

To psychologize, as Hillman (1975) uses the term, is to reflect upon the paradigms that structure our lives. Psychologizing is the soul's "native activity" (p. 116), and reflection the soul's "first habitual activity" (p. 117). But unlike epistemological speculation, psychological reflection is not concerned with the nature of mirroring in the sense of seeking to establish by rational or empirical propositions how the mind manages to represent the world. Rather, it is concerned with seeing through, the subtitle of Hillman's chapter on psychologizing and the primary term of art in imaginal psychology.

As we have seen with help from Derrida, an image of psyche is a mirror image, or alter ego, the specular reversal whose quicksilver backing gives us the compensatory revaluation, or invention of the other. What Hillman is concerned with in psychologizing is not so much the reflection *in* the mirror as a reflection *upon* the mirror. Psychologizing involves "analyzing not only our personalities and psychological material, such as dreams and problems, but the ideas with which we regard our personalities and psychological material" (Hillman, 1975, p. 127). Psyche is therefore self-reflective, that is, its purpose is Self-regard in the Jungian sense of the Self as developmental goal, and in the imaginal re-visioning of the Self as immersed in the textual play of signifiers not suspended in an ontotheological beyond. Hillman considered seeing through to be a "deconstructive method" (Hillman & Ventura, 1992, p. 121) He occasionally employed a line from Auden, "We are lived by powers that we pretend to understand" (Hillman & Shamdasani, 2013, p. 41). These vital powers are the ideas with which we regard. They are perhaps the Heideggerian tools ready-to-hand for the work of regarding. The *phenomenon* of soul-making—for, like deconstruction, soul-making is an event or occasion that happens and is made to happen—entails reflection upon these same powers: "This psychological questioning, this *reflexio* which turns ideas back upon themselves in order to see through to their soul import, makes soul" (Hillman, 1975, p. 127). Further, the nature of a psychologizing reflection is metaphorical: "*Through psychologizing I change the idea of any literal action at all—political, scientific, personal—into a metaphorical enactment.* I see the act and the scene and stance I am in, and not only the action I am into" (p. 127). The gloss on re-visioning offered here—that to see through in the metaphorical manner of an imaginal psychology involves an awareness of the point of view that brings the observed phenomena into focus—recalls an axiom from Christina Howells (1998) cited in "Toward a poststructural archetypology" at the beginning of this volume. Poststructuralism, she said, "asserts that truth claims are ultimately dependent on the discourse or conceptual scheme from which they emanate" (p. 2). As a transvaluation of structures, deconstruction, which Hillman (1983b) also called "destructuralizing" (p. 57), proves consanguineous with soul-making.

Psychologizing presses upon us the deconstructive desire for the "experience of the impossible," that is, the hope for the arrival of alterity in the medium of the same. Deconstruction does not hold out hope in the diachronic sense of a messianic arrival, but in the synchronic sense in which re-visioning is the condition of possibility extant in every moment. It is from such a vantage of "virtuality or potentiality" that we can see through. Psychologizing requires of us that we see *how we see* rather than establish the propriety of any particular mode of seeing, which in all events will share the fate of Ozymandias. Even the meta-idea that we might profitably discern the ideas by which we construct or co-create our world reflects, or hermeneutically circles back, upon itself. It acknowledges its provisional nature rather than "crediting itself with more value than all others, and in opposition to them," a move that Hillman (1975) said is symptomatic of the decadence of ideas (p. 115). Psychological reflection, the awareness of "the stance I am in," is a de-literalizing move that emphasizes "metaphorical enactment" (p. 127). Were we to take literally "the insights of psychologizing," they would "harden into systematic arguments, becoming solid and opaque and monocentric," leaving us with "a new metaphysics . . . the metaphysical position of psychologism" (p. 133).

The metaphoric effacement, wearing away, of metaphysical literalism destructures the binary opposition that would maintain the "puritan dignity" of the philosophical idea. It gets at the infrastructure. "*Psychologizing goes on whenever reflection takes place in terms other than those presented*," Hillman (1975) said:

> It suggests an interior, not evident intention; it searches for a hidden clockwork, a ghost in the machine, an etymological root, something more than meets the eye; or it sees with another eye. It goes on whenever we move to a deeper level. (p. 135)

In this formulation of reflection, the phrase "a term that is other than what is presented" problematizes presence. Like Derrida, Hillman appears to be auguring the experience of alterity in contradistinction to the metaphysical apotheosis of a "beyond" that is nevertheless immediate, and exempted from interpretative truth. The insight of a psychology that "sees with another eye" follows the same therapeutic, and methodological, arc as a deconstructive philosophy. It looks to the underlying assumption. "Because they express ideas," Hillman (1975) said, "complexes have philosophies in them and can be worked upon philosophically" (p. 132). If philosophies and psychologies can be seen as elaborate metaphoric translations, both deconstruction and imaginal psychology are special cases of metaphor's nature and logic. "The question of deconstruction," Derrida (2007) said, is "through and through *the* question of translation" (p. 2). Like metaphor on the interaction theory, psychologizing seeks to translate into nonobvious terms what Derrida called "onto-logic" (p. 5), in which being is rendered opaque by analysis. Deconstruction sees "through and through." As Derrida emphasized, it "*deconstructs itself*" (p. 4).

Both Derrida and Hillman were master readers. They were adepts in a divination that reads between the lines for "an interior, not evident intention." The questioning of *textual* imperative for its formal influence marks re-visioning as an inter-view (the title of Hillman's published conversations with the pseudonymous Laura Pozzo). The hermeneutics of psychologizing was depicted by Hillman in evocatively cosmogonic terms. In the beginning, Hillman (1975) said, there is "the psychological moment," which he describes as "a moment of reflection, wonder, puzzlement, initiated by the soul which intervenes and countervails what we are in the midst of doing, hearing, reading, watching" (p. 140). The moment is a "a little flicker, a slow dawning, a lightening flash," but once "the clarity has itself become obvious and transparent, there seems to grow within it a new darkness, a new question of doubt, requiring a new act of insight penetrating again toward the less apparent" (p. 140). The moment expands, "becomes an infinite regress which does not stop at coherent or elegant answers" (p. 140). It follows a logic of Self-overcoming: "The process of psychologizing is not satisfied when necessary and sufficient conditions have been met. . . . It is satisfied only by its own movement of seeing through" (p. 140). When we psychologize, "we penetrate or try to bring out, expose, or show why we believe that what lies behind or within is truer and more real, powerful, or valuable than what is evident" (p. 140). In the process of reading for subtext we are "appealing to an ultimate hidden value that can never fully come out but must remain concealed in the depths in order to justify the movement" (p. 140). The positing of a concealed structure links psychologizing to Ricoeur's "masters of suspicion," Freud, Marx, and Nietzsche, who eschewed the literalisms on the surface of intellectual life for their recondite associations.

"The sense of in-ness," Hillman (1975) said, "is fundamental to all psychologizing. The soul draws us through the labyrinth of literalisms ever inward, realizing itself through retreat. The retreating nymph is a perennial anima image in myth" (p. 174). Significantly, however, the unconscious as well must be seen through to perceive the quality that, employing Heidegger, we can call its *equiprimordiality*. "The unconscious," Hillman (1975) said, "is merely a tool for deepening, interiorizing, and subjectifying the apparent" (p. 141). The activity of seeing through destructures even the ideational tool, ready-to-hand, with which we destructure, or see through: "Should we take the unconscious literally, then it too becomes a husk that constricts the psyche and must be seen through, deliteralized" (p. 141). We can recall Max Black's (1962) observation that the principal subject of the metaphorical equation is "seen through," or seen *by means of*, the "screen" of the secondary subject (p. 41). In this sense, the unconscious is the screen that metaphorizes the insighted image. It must be taken as "a mode of seeing through events," not merely "a description of events" (Hillman, 1975, p. 145). "Without the idea of the unconscious we could not see through behavior into its hidden unknowns," Hillman said. "But," he added, in a warning of analytical psychology's own blind spots, "we do not see the unconscious" (p. 141). In this caveat about the disappearing act of the unconscious, we catch a glimpse of Hermes. Lacking the hermeneutic, interpretive aspect of seeing through, phenomenological description risks literalization. It is in this way that imaginal psychology can be said to be a hermeneutic phenomenology.

To invoke Hermes is to court errancy. Indeed, we might add to Aristotle's four causal categories, *proximate*, *formal*, *material*, and *final*, a fifth, and, as such, quintessential, category: the errant cause, invoked by Plato (1963) in the *Timaeus* (§47) as the binary opposite of reason. Such a cause would be Hermetic in attitude. "Hermes," Hillman (1975) said, "is the congenital deceiver bringing equivocation into the world with divine authority. He is god of equivocation and he is guide of the soul" who is at work when we endeavor to "speak most deeply" about our souls and "feel the error, the half-truth, the deception in what we are telling" (p. 160). But, Hillman said, "this is not bad faith unless we forget that Hermes works as well through the messages of lies as through truth. No one can tell the whole truth about the soul but Hermes, whose style is duplicity" (p. 160). In a deconstructive formulation on errancy's inevitability, Hillman said, "Reason cannot bring the errant principle or necessity altogether under its control" (p. 159). Errancy's equivocation, Hillman said, is "an *opus contra naturum*, a place where the psyche is speaking against the natural flow of reasonable, predictable expectations, the truth of the way things are" (p. 160). The errant cause is the Nietzschean factor within every moral value that transvalues it, the Derridean factor within every metaphysical system that deconstructs it, the Hillmanian factor within every archetype that sees through it. The errant cause is native to psychology because, Hillman said, psychology

> is not a discipline of truth, as is science or philosophy or theology. From the psychological perspective, lying and telling the truth are invalid categories; both call for psychologizing, and truths more than lies for they are even harder to see through. (p. 160)

If psychologizing follows the deviant path trod by Hermes, then the imaginal psychologist works in the style of the Hermetic archetype of the knight errant. Hillman (1975) characterized this classic literary figure as "an outcast, a renegade wandering like Cain, never quite able to return within the structures of literalism" (p. 161). He "wanders without goal," without seeking metaphysical closure. A "guiding psychopomp," he is "driven to unsettle all forms," all *eidolon* (p. 162). As a Hermetic "mediator betwixt and between," the knight errant makes his abode in a psychological region characterized by Hillman as "the realm of the daemons, of the *metaxy* (the middle region), in between, back and forth" (p. 161). This locus of interaction is the metaphorical *pseudo-domain*, and the circumstance of the knight errant is also the circumstance of metaphor. Excluded from philosophy proper, metaphor finds itself in, or *as*, a *pseudo-domain* oscillating between the sensible and the supersensible. Indeed, as we have seen, it can be understood as that Kantian faculty of subjective purposiveness by which, as Mark Johnson (1981) said, "the imaginative act of reflection is *felt* as adequate to the representations it organizes, even though there are no concepts (or rules) governing that reflective activity" (p. 39). This activity of reflective judgment is much the same as that performed by the inherently metaphorical term *soul* in the project of imaginal re-visioning that destructures the polarity *res cogitans/res extensa*. Concerning psychologizing, Hillman (1975) asked, "Is Hermes the god within it?" (p. 162). Is the Hermetic mode the way of "counter-education," of "negative learning," "destructuring," and the swerving course of metaphor-making? As distinct from the *epoché* of phenomenology, Hillman said, the "polytheistic hermeneutic" of psychologizing "knows no bracketing-out" of standpoints to inscribe "a sacred precinct" around "metaphysical or scientific content" (p. 163). Hermes, the disrespecter of the *temenos* of the other gods (his is the *pseudo-domain*), reflects "the confabulations and circumlocutions or deceptive fictions" of errancy, which, Hillman said, "are ways of making metaphors, for errors and deceptions say 'this' as if it were 'that'" (p. 163).

Psychologizing amounts to an errant quest-ioning of literal textuality—of interpretive arrest—to discern the under-lying, literary, figurative, metaphorical provenance of truth claims. The absolute that offers the most strenuous resistance to seeing through is the literalism of the human. It is part of our Cartesian legacy that we begin and end with ourselves, but our solipsism reaches back further than modernity. Even God is cast as a literal human. And so Hillman is brought to take up the idea of the human as the fourth de-literalization in his imaginal therapeutics.

Dehumanizing

To dehumanize the psyche is to distinguish soul in terms that are at once Neoplatonic, transpersonal, and Romantic as a "universal principle" having "an existence beyond life and apart from the human being" (Hillman, 1975, p. 173). Psyche's humanization, the sense that I "have" a soul, is a reductive move owing to the anthropo-chauvanism of an anti-ecological worldview. Dehumanizing, on the other hand, constitutes a Copernican relativization on the order of Freud's de-centering of the ego. "Man exists in the midst of psyche; it is not the other way around," Hillman (1975) said, "Therefore, soul cannot be confined by man, and there is much of psyche that extends beyond the nature of man. The soul has inhuman reaches" (p. 173). The imagination's predilection for dehumanizing leads to the revaluation of two principles of Enlightenment thought, one rational, or, as Hillman put it, "logical" (p. 173), and one empirical. For centuries, these principles have stood as alternative philosophical foundations worked out by Descartes and Locke respectively to affirm the soundness of the scientific worldview. The priority of rationality puts logical propositions in a position of ultimacy; that of empiricism valorizes sensory experiences. The dehumanizing maneuver refers the realities of thought and sense to a third term, imagination. "In terms of logical priority," Hillman said,

> all realities (physical, social, religious) are inferred from psychic images or fantasy presentations to a psyche. In terms of empirical priority, before we are born into a physical body or a social world, the fantasy of the child-to-come is a psychic reality, influencing the "nature" of the subsequent events. (p. 173)

The investiture of constructive, or world-making, capacity in the human is an entailment of empiricism when it literalizes, as with Hume, states of observation, and of rationalism when it literalizes, as with Descartes, thought itself. The dehumanizing function relativizes the creative effects of *Homo faber*, generalizing *poiesis* to mean a transpersonal exponent formative not only of human works, but of the human itself. It understands the individual psyche to be constituted by the imaginal psyche:

> That the soul is experienced as my "own" and "within" refers to the privacy and interiority of psychic life. It does not imply a literal ownership or literal interiority. The sense of "in-ness" refers neither to location nor to physical containment. It is not a spatial idea, but an imaginal metaphor for the soul's nonvisible and nonliteral inherence, the imaginal psychic quality within all events. (Hillman, 1975, p. 173)

In a further de-literalization, soul is here distinguished from essence and re-visioned as relational process. The participatory sense does not exclude the possibility that social norms may be constructed. Soul, as noted above, is never in-itself present, but is relational in a radical sense, grasped only in context with all phenomena it interpretively engages.

This is not to say that essentialism plays no role in imaginal psychology. Dehumanizing in particular becomes a question of applying Platonism over Aristotelianism to distinguish the "inhuman reaches" of the soul's "existence beyond life." The pivotal factor in this regard is Hillman's (1975) particularly Charonic coinage of *death*. The term is a placeholder for the very principle that psyche, as *metapherein*, carries over the Styx and beyond the human:

> Aristotle's definition of soul as the life of the natural body inseparably bound with individual lives, does not allow enough place for life's other side, death, or for the relationship of psyche with death. . . . When soul is described only in terms of life and that life identified with individuals, there is no way to "dehumanize" soul, no way to approach psyche other than in the biological and analytical ways Aristotle preferred. . . . Just here Aristotelianism neglects what the Platonists remember: psyche is indeed the essence of living bodies, but living bodies are also dying bodies. The Platonists' insistence on immortality of soul was an insistence on the soul's dissociation from life and a priori relation with death. (p. 206)

Hillman couched his formulation in a therapeutics of Renaissance Neoplatonism, pressing the point that death understood symbolically is a concomitant of rebirth. "Revival emerges from the threat to survival" (p. 207) he said, and he invoked the rape of Persephone to bring the point into stark relief:

> Each of us enacts Persephone in soul, a maiden in a field of narcissi or poppies, lulled drowsy with innocence and pretty comforts until we are dragged off and pulled down by Hades, our intact natural consciousness violated and opened to the perspective of death. Once this has happened—through a suicidal despair, through a sudden fall from a smooth-rising career, through an invisible depression in whose grip we struggle vainly—then Persephone reigns in the soul and we see life through her darker eye. (p. 208)

The chain of inference that inscribes death, the "prime metaphor" (Hillman, 1975, p. 153), into the discourse of psychology might be this: Death → Hades → Depth → Soul.

The drowsy fields of Persephone conjure what Pablo Neruda (1990) called "poppy-petalled metaphysics," a delight in metaphysical purity. "What is impregnable," said Hillman (1993), "is also self-satisfied and self-enclosed" (p. 238). Challenging rationalism and empiricism alike, Hillman (1975) employed the Persephone–Hades myth in an archetypal de-objectification:

> Until Persephone has been raped, until our natural consciousness has been pathologized, our souls project us as literal realities. We believe that human life and soul are naturally one. We have not awakened to death. So we refuse the very first metaphor of human existence: that we are not real. We refuse, too, to admit that human reality is wholly dependent on the realities that take place in the soul. To hold that "we are not real" means to let go of all seemingly irreducible objectifications of human personality, whether it be the organic body, the human personality, or subjective awareness (Descartes), and to realize them as fantasies of the psyche. (p. 209)

As if to underscore Hillman's point about the emergence of the de-literalized psyche, as I transcribed the words "human personality," instead of "human" I typed "hymen." As Freud (1960) knew, the psyche notoriously has a sense of humor. By way of such slips and mortifications ("I could have just died!"), it seeks the disintegration, *the death into metaphor*, of the skin-encapsulated ego. Thus, the rape of Persephone, the "hymen personality." For Derrida (1981), as it happens, *hymen*, the tissue that marks the margin of "inside" and "outside," is a term of art that indicates a lack in "man." This lack is an inability to accept the ambiguity of the in-between, what Niall Lucy (2005) called a "tissue of meanings without an absolutely central or proper meaning against which other meanings could be marked off as 'exterior'" (p. 48). As Derrida used it, Lucy said, *hymen* places ontology into question and "outwits dialectics" because of its imperfect quality, indicating by its relational status "the ontology of the margin itself" (p. 48). As with other of Derrida's terms of art, *text, writing, supplement, trace, play, differance, dissemination,* Lucy said, *hymen* is an indication of his concern with originary difference, the deconstructive factor in every ontotheological presence. Lucy cites Hélène Cixous (for the basic deconstructive disposition):

> [W]riting is the passageway, the entrance, the exit, the dwelling place of the other in me that I am and am not, that I don't know how to be, but that I feel like passing, that makes me live—that tears me apart, disturbs me, changes me, who? (cited in Lucy, 2005, p. 42)

Dionysus, the androgyne who we have identified with interstitial, metaphorical reality, was called by the ancients, Hillman (1983a) said, the "divided and undivided" (p. 39). We can recall that he was carried to *term*, articulated, by Persephone.

By suggesting that dehumanizing means to die into metaphor, I mean much the same thing Corbin did when he envisioned the imaginal life. To enter into the *mundus imaginalis* would be to die to the literalisms of rational idolatry. It would be to embrace a metaphoric reality: iconography, the "writing of the image." *Writing* in this sense is *archi-ecriture*. As Christina Howells (1998) said, it designates meaning formation as "differential, a matter of constant referral" (p. 50). To die into metaphor entails a critical stance toward what Howells called "notions of presence and continuity" (p. 51). We find it expressed in Hillman's (1975) Neoplatonic position against "the optimistic humanism of our northern psychology, its uplifting love, its peaks and resurrections" (p. 207). Dying into metaphor moves us instead into "deeper obscurities" and "exotic otherness" (p. 205). It is a species of descent on the model of Hermes Psychopompos. *Dehumanizing*, for Hillman, as *writing* for Derrida, is the principal metaphor for alterity. Both terms amplify the shadow element in the dominant structure. As Hillman (1979b) put it:

> If we do speak in terms of opposites then there is only one absolute material opponent to any position in life, and that is its death. If we now deliteralize that statement, we are saying that "death" is the way through the opposites, that is, it is the self-regulation of any position by psyche, by nonliteral, metaphorical perception. (p. 79)

In our refusal to die into metaphor, to see ourselves "as metaphors and images made by soul, we have each become fastened into a constant forced literalism, ourselves as real, the Gods dead" (Hillman, 1975, p. 209). Lending voice to the basic transpersonal (dehumanizing) insight of Neoplatonic psychology, Hillman (1978b) said, "Gods are indeed fundamental real structures because they are psychically prior to the minds which believe they project them" (p. 159). The reality of the gods as psychological forces makes us "cognizant above all of human limitation" (Hillman, 1975, p. 193). It takes us from a diachronic or teleological reality in which humankind triumphs over its basic nature to a synchronic reality in which our inflated sense of rationality or spirituality is tempered in every moment by the forces of nature that inhere in us and are beyond the suasion of the ego. Hillman perhaps best expressed what he meant by dehumanizing in a comment on philosophy's inaugural assertion of the prospects of wisdom: "When the Delphic oracle or Socrates or a modern analysis exhorts one to 'know thyself,' this knowledge is of human limits, a humanity limited by the powers in a soul that are inhuman and divine" (p. 192).

Having arrived at a polytheistic structuralism demonstrative of what Jung called "the causative effect of analogy" (CW 12, par. 377), that is, the efficacy of the personified metaphors that suffer the shaping of our lives, the inquiry into the imaginal logic of soul-making can come to rest. We are left with but one task to perform. We must cross the threshold into metaphor.

9

FINALLY, METAPHOR

At the start of these explorations, the announced endeavor was to trace what I called the riverine habitat of metaphor in philosophy. "[T]he commonest symbol for the unconscious," said Jung, is water (CW 9, 1:18, par. 40). In a comment on Jung's *this means that* assertion, Michael Vannoy Adams (2004) pointed out that "the 'unconscious' is, of course, an abstract concept, not a concrete image like a specific river" (p. 53). Hillman, said Adams, urged that images of water not be reduced to the unconscious, but specified for their individual qualities. Specification, Adams said, avoids *conceptual essentialism*. Thus far, we have voyaged upon Kant's "broad and stormy ocean," lingered with Socrates and Phaedrus on the banks of the ancient Ilissus, and incanted a perhaps too operatic Mediterranean fantasy, replete with Derrida's "weathered rock monsters," in the key of post-sirenian melancholy. With the amplification of each image, I have hoped to draw out its implications for a theory of the metaphoric unconscious.

We now arrive in Dublin, on the banks of the River Liffey, scene of Hillman's early literary efforts (Russell, 2013). This is how James Joyce (1939) described it in the opening words of *Finnegans Wake*: "riverrun, past Eve and Adam's, from swerve of shore to bend of bay, brings us by a commodius vicus of recirculation back to Howth Castle and Environs." The "commodius vicus of recirculation" refers to the cyclic view of human history (*corso e ricorso*) in the work of Giambattista Vico. Hillman's (1975) theory of metaphor "starts," he said, with Vico (p. 156). In this section, I also rely upon Vico for a point of departure. He serves as a quay of sorts at the confluence where the just mentioned streams of consciousness issue into a re-visioned theory of metaphor.

Vico's work anticipates elements of archetypology and poststructuralism. In his principal work, *New Science* (2001), he proposed a poetic theory of mind in which, said Terence Hawkes (1977), "that which man recognizes as true (*verum*) and that which he has made (*factum*) are one and the same .... When man perceives the world, he perceives without knowing it the superimposed shape of his own mind" (p. 13). As a re-visioning of a seemingly "artless and 'natural'" world of preconceptions, "Vico's work ranks as one of the first modern attempts to break the anaesthetic grip" of the human mind's "permanent structuring process" (p. 14).

Vico's insights implicate metaphor. "What Vico did, primarily," said James Edie (1969), "was to show the primordial importance of 'the verisimilar' or 'the metaphorical' in human thought, and to demonstrate, as a consequence, the impossibility of thinking without employing the mechanisms of metaphorical transposition" (p. 488). Vico's theory of mind consists in three mental faculties, *ingegno*, *fantasia*, and *memoria*. The contributor of meaning in this tripartite schema is *fantasia*, the equivalent of imagination. *Fantasia*, said Marcel Danesi (1993), produces "meaning-making units" (p. 51) that are then stored in *memoria* and organized into comprehensible patterns by *ingegno*—ingenuity or invention:

> Vico made the imagination the focal point of his treatise. He saw it as the mental faculty that generated our rational thought, our languages, and ultimately our cultures. He sought access to its workings, not by means of an Aristotelian or Cartesian-type method of deductive analysis, but through an understanding of the creative products—especially the first myths and the original meanings of words—that the primordial imagination produced. (p. 36)

The operation of *fantasia* is essentially metaphorical. It formulates what Danesi called "iconic signs" that allow the mind to "map mental images onto the beings, objects, and events that the senses had captured, and thus to make associations and connections among them" (p. 50). The iconic signs are, in a sense, fungible. They are not dependent upon instant experience and so they endow the mind with the "capacity to 'imagine' fictional (context-free) beings, objects and events," and thus to create new meaning (p. 50). In this sense, Vico anticipated contemporary metaphor theory, which re-visions merely decorative metaphor as a cognitive force. "Metaphor itself was for Vico an analogue for cognition," Danesi said (p. 41). For Vico (2001), the "poetic logic" of mind by which "passion" may be "attributed" even to "insensate things," renders every metaphor as a "fable in brief" (p. 404).

Drawing upon Vico, Hillman (1975) saw metaphor as miniature myth: "Vico shelters under his superb mind my frequent lack of distinction between myth and metaphor," he said (p. 156). Hillman's integration of metaphor and myth is the *ingegno* of a psychology of life as art. "[*P*]*syche is the life of our aesthetic responses*," Hillman (2004b) said, italicizing (p. 39). The aesthetic approach to metaphor, influenced by Kant and Nietzsche, is also taken by Mark Johnson (1981), who said metaphors are "miniature works of art" (p. 40), by Ted Cohen (1979), who called them "crystallized works of art" (p. 5), and by Kirk Pillow (2001), who said "a creative metaphor counts as a "miniature work of art in its own right; like all art worth the name, it brings together disjoint materials to express a new perspective that transforms our understanding of ourselves and our world" (p. 202).

The basic *poietic* structure is reciprocal relation. "Not only does man create societies and institutions in his own mind's image," said Hawkes (1977), "but these in the end create him" (p. 14). In Vichian terms, the relation extends beyond the sociological by virtue of *universal fantastici*, or poetical characters. Hillman (1978b) said,

> The poetical character, a Hero or a God (or Goddess), becomes the psychic structure by means of which we place events and see how well they conform with their universal types, or archetypes, of the *mundus imaginalis*. The poetical character would be what we call the archetypal image with which events in your or my case history can be compared, the lacunae discovered, and a rectification take place. Archetypal therapy of this sort proceeds by means of "likeness." (p. 159)

The principle of the poetical character, and of each of us as poetical characters, lends a metaphoric conception to the "metaphysical realities to which physical reality conforms" (p. 159).

To the extent imaginal psychology claims metaphysical association, it does so via myth. "Myth seems to offer the only metaphysics (vision and synthesis) that I can imagine for psychology because it is imagined, it is personified, and it always presents itself as fiction," Hillman said (1989b, p. 221). Hillman's psychologizing of metaphysics in terms of myth marks a theory of mind for which *il n'y a pas de hors-texte*, and everything is known *poietically*, interpretively. The hypothesis of *poietic* construction is a function of fictionality, and cannot be taken literally, but only grappled with by furthering, or deepening, the *poiesis*. Hillman's *fiction* is Derrida's *text*. Both re-vision metaphysics as metaphorics. Patricia Berry (2008) pointed to the basic *poietic* idea when she remarked upon "Jung's lifelong battle to separate his ideas from Plato's hypostasized forms as well as from the substantials of the metaphysicians" (p. 158).

Metaphysics as metaphorics leads not to truth, but to paradigm. I use "leads" in a teleological sense. "Our entire practice [of depth psychology]," Hillman (1989b) said at the symposium comparing his work, and Jung's, with Whitehead's, "is filled with *telos* (*aim* is Whitehead's term), including the deconstructive act of seeing through. . . . In the act of deconstruction there is a constructive aim" (p. 219). Berry (2008) clarifies: "Our aim is psyche," she says (p. 157). The final cause in any metaphorics might be understood as a *model*. As we have seen, in Max Black's (1962) formulation, *model* is *heuristic fiction* (p. 228), on the order of the rule of judgment. The aesthetic *alpha* and *omega* of any philosophy is image, figure, model, *likeness*. "The psychological mind makes the given imagistic, fantastic," Hillman said (1989b, p. 219). And: "Everything we know and feel and every statement we make are all fantasy-based, that is, they derive from psychic images" (Hillman, 1975, p. xvii). Every metaphysics is a metaphorics. "We sin against the imagination whenever we ask an image for its meaning, requiring that images be translated into concepts," Hillman said (p. 39), "We do not hear music, touch sculpture, or read stories with meaning in mind, but for the sake of the imagination" (p. 39). When we hear the lingering echo of our metaphoric composition, we apply the teaching of "the alchemical psychologists to let the images work upon the experimenter; we learn to become the object of the work—even an object, or objectified image, of the imagination" (p. 40). We are the metaphysical models, the poetical characters, worked on by the imagination.

That Joyce's novel is informed by the poetical characters of a Jungian metaphorics was established by Joseph Campbell and Henry Morton Robinson (2005). The archetypal content of the *Wake* is abundant. "What archetypes does it constellate?," asked Thomas Cowan (1987). "All of them that I ever heard of" (p. 227). Among the central motifs in this commodius vicus of archetypes is a fable of *senex* and *puer*, the leaden Saturnian patriarch and the lively Mercurial youth. Joyce establishes the twin brothers of the tale, Shem and Shaun, as versions of the *puer*, and their father, HCE, as the *senex*. The theme of *puer* and *senex* is one of Hillman's pervasive tropes. My interest here is not to explicate Joyce, but to explore Hillman's view of this particular archetypal doubling for how the two figures might inform a theory of metaphor produced by a poststructural archetypology. Thus far, I have argued that the figures of Mercury, Hermes, and Thoth personify the metaphorical ecosystem of the unconscious. In addition, I have associated Saturn, the old devil, with the insistent gap in any metaphysical system that makes possible a revaluation of values, to wit: Jung's millimeter—a binary opposition. I assimilate the *puer* to Mercury because among the "personalities" Hillman (1987, p. 23) associated with the *puer* archetype are the Psychopompos, Mercury-Hermes, and the Trickster. The principal association he made to the *senex* is Saturn.

In a lecture on *puer* and *senex* in 1967, Hillman spoke of the generation gap and the distantly approaching new millennium. His purpose was to suggest a reimagining of history from an archetypal perspective. He used the occasion to further the history/fiction deconstruction. Hillman (1987) said: "The historical 'facts' may be but fantasies attached to and sprouting from central archetypal cores" (p. 6). He recalled Jung's observation that the nature of our time is what the Greeks called a *kairos*, the right moment for a metamorphosis of the gods, or what we might now also understand as an Ovidian shift of metaphor in which the gods change form (*morphe*). Such a *poietic* realignment is not of our conscious choosing, but represents a subsidence in the unconscious. Hillman applied Jung's axiom that we are each "makeweights" on the scale of history, and so our varying capacities to perceive the work of unconscious forces influence the quality of the time. He invoked the mythic figures of the Eternal Youth and Father Time to see through the troubles of the epoch to their provenance in the objective psyche.

Our culture is obsessed, Hillman (1987) said, with the "*chroniques scandaleuses*" of "instant history" (p. 7). In what was a prescient analysis for 1967, he diagnosed the social malady as one "where everything that happens to everyone on the public scene must be recorded and what is recorded must be published—and fast" (p. 7). Borrowing from Mircea Eliade, he said we have become addicted to the experience of *profane* time, Eliade's term for a reality lacking in symbolic richness. The therapeutic course, he said, is to cultivate "another archetypal organization of the events from which we suffer" (p. 7). His call is for *another* archetypal organization because the events of our lives and times are already always archetypally structured, though we may be unconscious of it. We suffer from the double blind of literalism; so certain are we of the absolute nature of profane time that we become like the shades on the Lethic Plain, ignorant of any deeper reaches of awareness. "At the same moment that we light the candle" of our understanding, said Hillman, "we also darken the remainder of the room" (p. 12). His formulation *another archetypal organization* might equally mean a different metaphor, a new paradigm, or a variety of world hypothesis. These theoretical forms are not identical, each may entail specific suppositions, yet they are linked by their common indication of perspectival awareness.

The deconstruction of history as a process of fiction must, of course, stick to the image. To the extent that Hillman (1989b) objected to structuralism and deconstruction, it was because he perceived a tendency in these fields to abstract the living sense of the world or what he called "our animal responses" (p. 224). His guiding premise was that "all things are inherently intelligible" (p. 224). At the symposium comparing his work and Jung's with Whitehead's, he said:

> This intelligibility does not depend upon adducing universal physical laws or upon a coherent systematic theology; it is an intelligibility given with the shapes or physiognomy of the world which is afforded directly to our sensate imagination, to us as animals. . . . I wish Whitehead were still around to take down structuralism and the deconstruction that follows it, because they continue this indifference to the actual occasions of the phenomenal world. (pp. 224–225)

To save these appearances, we must instantiate ourselves within an archetypal framing, which is also a mythological and metaphorical framing, one that recovers "the intelligible nature of things themselves" (Hillman, 1989b, p. 225). We encounter Hillman here in post-Kantian reverie, assuaging the schizophrenic modern consciousness by dint of alchemical *unio mentalis*:

> the interpenetration of thought and image, of perceived world and imaginal world, a state of mind no longer concerned with distinctions between things and thought, appearance and reality, or between the spirit that develops theory and the soul that builds fantasy. (p. 156)

This mode is his rhapsody in blue. In an extended meditation on "that sadness which emerges from despair as it proceeds toward reflection" (p. 154), Hillman said, "We have colored this *unio mentalis* 'blue', because the blue we have been encountering transfigures appearances into imaginal realities and imagines thought itself in a new way" (p. 156).

The new way—another archetypal organization—is a voyage via *memoria*. As we saw with Nietzsche, Yates, and now with Vico, memory plays a critical role in the application of metaphor to experience. Nietzsche in particular, as understood by Sarah Kofman (1993), played upon the forgetting of metaphor as an essential element in the formation of the concept. In order to establish an epistemological redoubt, the concept must abandon its disposition upon the shifting metaphorical sands. What gets left behind (in the unconscious) is the archetypal substrate of experience. "For this way of remembering events," Hillman (1987) said of the recovery of soul, "memory needs to return again to its reminiscence of primordial ideas, to its association with the archetypal root metaphors of human experience" (p. 8). To return to metaphor is to fictionalize history in part by personifying; it asks, as Hillman (or Deleuze) did, *who* is "the person in the person prompting the whole endeavor," which archetypal dominant is at issue (Hillman, 2005, p. 64).

The return to metaphor entailed in soul-making is an *epistrophe* on the order of the hermeneutic circle, that is, it supposes that perceptions are not independent of assumptions. By remembering my historical self to soul, I regenerate it in fictional fashion. It becomes, Hillman (1987) said, "an epic process, a Canterbury Tale, eternally valid, historical but timeless" (p. 8). The re-visioning of my individual fictions from a poetic basis of mind effects no less than the re*versing* of history itself that it might be "washed" of literalisms (p. 8). This "immensely difficult" (p. 8) work carries overtones of Heidegger and Derrida. "And each one, anyone, who makes a clearing in his bit of the forest of the past is the hero who redeems time and is the scapegoat who by taking on himself the sins undoes time," Hillman said (p. 8).

The transvaluation of the history/fiction opposition demands the scapegoat. The image figures prominently in Derrida's (1981) treatment of the *Phaedrus*. As we have seen, central to his reading is the binary quality of the word *pharmakon*, which can mean "poison" as well as "remedy." Related to *pharmakon*, Derrida said, is the term *pharmakos*, which carries the various meanings of "magician, wizard, poisoner; the one sacrificed in expiation for the sins of a city" (p. 132n). Plato's condemnation of the trickery inherent in the written letter is delivered by (that trickster figure) Socrates, who was put to death for impiety. Despite Plato's use of the myth of Thoth to establish the ideality of speech over writing's imperfectability, Derrida demonstrated the relationship of writing as *pharmakon*, remedy and poison, to Socrates as *pharmakos*, healer and poisoner, in the sense that both, said Christopher Norris (1987), represented "that indispensable other" that marks the regime of the binary opposition. (p. 42). Heidegger, in *Being and Time*, rethought ontology in terms of flawed temporality. Heidegger's being-in-the-world carries with it a sense that *Dasein* is "a 'clearing, glade' in a forest" (Inwood, 1999, p. 238). A vale of soul-making temporalizes the archetypal *eidos*, returning perceptions to the ground of their assumptions, redeeming time not in diachronic perfectability but in the recognition of the "twisting and turning" (as David Tacey said of Hillman) in a synchronic cosmos. In this redemptive mode, the idea of a vale of metaphor would "twist cosmology itself, reading the ancient cosmologies not merely as straight historical predecessors but also for their psychological fantasies" (Hillman, 1989b, p. 222).

Hillman, however, did more than reverse and revalue history/fiction. In a meta-move that can only be considered poststructural, he revalued opposition itself. "Meaning," Hillman (1987) said, "cannot be sustained by structure and order alone" (p. 21). As David Miller (2008) put it, employing Heidegger's term *Gelassenheit*, both poetry and psychoanalysis—and, as a place where the roads meet, imaginal psychology—enable "a releasement, a nonattachment to meaning" (p. 252); they are "a dying . . . of egoic perspective" (p. 252). From the vector of the poetic basis, in which all elements are uniquely expressible, the perspective that insists on the definitional imperative "this *means* that" is relativized. To think the binary opposition in psychological terms removes it from the paradigm of what Hillman called "disjunctive rationalism" (p. 14). The logocentric hierarchies that so incited Derrida can be seen through in favor of a psychologized meaning. Hierarchization transforms to archetypization. In his poem of incommensurables, "For the Marriage of Faustus and Helen," Hart Crane (2001) began,

> The mind has shown itself at times
> Too much the baked and labeled dough
> Divided by accepted multitudes.
> Across the stacked partitions of the day—
> Across the memoranda, baseball scores
> The stenographic smiles and stock quotations
> Smutty wings flash out equivocations.

In contrast to the stacked partition of the hierarchized opposition, an archetypized opposition maintains a *tension* of equivocation and is in this regard like metaphor on the interaction theory. "The archetype per se," Hillman (1987) said, "is ambivalent and paradoxical" (p. 12). "Both poles of the archetype are necessary and equal" (p. 13). He likened this harmonious tension to the string of the lyre, whose Hermetic invention, we will recall from Noel Cobb (1992), is "co-emergent with the creation of metaphor" (p. 243). A "hidden music" said Suzi Harvey (2000), "will be released with the death of the literal" (p. 3).

"The co-existence of polarity within the archetype," said Hillman (1987), "is both logically absurd and symbolically true" (p. 15). The existential, and existentialist, marriage of absurdity and truth, or absurdity-in-truth, derives from what Hillman saw as the crepuscular element of the depth psychological world hypothesis. Depth psychology's primary opposition of consciousness and the unconscious posits the discrimination of both "out of original twilight states" (p. 12). "Day breaks with the ego," Hillman said. "Night is left behind" (p. 12). The unfolding is simultaneous. "We may not speak therefore of an evolutionary process of light emerging from darkness, an extension of light at the expense of darkness," he said (p. 13). "The light is not stolen from the dark where there is a privation of light; rather the ego concentrates into one pole the divine primordial half-light, thereby also darkening the divine" (p. 13). Here we revisit Jung's struggle with the doctrine of *privatio boni*, or evil as the privation of good. His millimeter, the forehead that will not touch the ground, is an abeyance of the hierarchized polarity. It is a transvaluation that abides in the symbolically true yet rationally—and spiritually—absurd ambivalence of the depth psychological polarity. The light is "stolen," not in an absolute sense in which darkness is deprived and depraved, but in a Hermetic sense that presupposes metaphorical interaction. "It is as if the light were a theft from the penumbra of dawn and twilight, of paradoxical archetypal light," Hillman said (p. 12). And so it is, said Walter F. Otto (2014), that when Odysseus, "in the midst of his wild solitude," approaches the haunt of the sorceress Circe, Hermes appears suddenly, as is his tendency, bestowing an apotropaic herb. "We sense" in Homer's daylit scene, said Otto, "the peculiar twilight mood" (p. 118). The archetypal light is a paradox, an opposition psychologized. "The quality of the polarity, ranging from conflicting antithesis to harmonious co-operation, depends," Hillman (1987) said, "upon the psychological relation between ego-consciousness and the unconscious" (p. 13).

Archetypal antecedence was typified by Hillman (1987) not as original self-presence, but as "prior disorder" (p. 20). He personified the polyvalent ground—an antifoundationalism—as *senex-et-puer*, reflecting "its order on the one hand, its dynamus on the other" (p. 20). This formulation of systole and diastole is no less than "the archetype of the process of life" (p. 32). Each aspect contains positive and negative "valences" (p. 20). When metaphoric ambiguity—one thing in terms of another—is literalized, "when the duality of this ground is split into polarity," and "the complex, now split, loses its inherent tension, its ambivalence, and is just dead in the midst of its brightness, which is its own eclipse" (pp. 20–21), the "alternating valences" fixate into the oppositions of metaphysics. It is the dystrophy of metaphoric tension into the oppositions of metaphysics that invites the deconstructive moment.

To discover how *puer-et-senex* reflects metaphoric transposition, let us recall the descriptors of metaphoric operation (Table 4), discussed in Chapter 4 on the cognitive turn, with the addition, also discussed there, of Lakoff and Johnson's terms *source domain* and *target domain*. My purpose is to suggest an association between

TABLE 4 Terms of metaphoric transference IV

Originator	*Terms*	
Johnson	Two ideas	
Richards	Tenor	Vehicle
Black	Focus	Frame
Black	Principal subject	Subsidiary subject
Beardsley	Predicate	(No correlate)
Beardsley	Extension	Intension
Beardsley	Central meaning	Marginal meaning
Lakoff & Johnson	Source domain	Target domain

puer-et-senex and Dr. Johnson's "two ideas," the feeling tone of the first term being that of the *senex*, and of the second, that of the *puer*. The personification of *senex* as Saturn or Chronos, and *puer* as Mercury or Hermes differentiates these terms from those listed by lending them a characterological profile. For that reason, we turn for our insights to astrology, which, "more than any other field," said Hillman (1987), "provides the best descriptions of character qualities" (p. 16).

In his exposition of the astrological worldview, *Cosmos and Psyche*, Richard Tarnas (2006) interpreted the voluminous phenomenological record compiled by archetypal astrologers and astrological psychologists over nearly three millennia to arrive at the commonly agreed upon traits associated with the figures of Saturn and Mercury. Though it is incautious to reduce the "multidimensionality" (p. 87) of astrological archetypes to a single designation, it is not incorrect to suggest that in general the association of Saturn is to *fixity* and that of Mercury to *flux*. These are borrowings from Michael Ventura (Hillman & Ventura, 1992) that I associated in an earlier chapter with the structuralist distinction between the diachronic and the synchronic. The terms of metaphoric transference tend to express variations of these two qualities. Nietzsche, as we saw, associated fixity and flux with Apollo and Dionysus. My invocation of Saturn and Mercury rather than the Nietzschean archetypes—and moreover, my use of Hermes-Mercury instead of Dionysus to characterize the basic metaphoric impulse to differ and defer—is an attempted escape from the metaphysical binary. As Deldon Anne McNeely (1996) put it:

> Neither rational nor heroic like Apollo, nor swept away in ecstasy and wild abandon like Dionysus, Hermes is the appropriate antidote when we are able to see only the options of being orderly or wild; he becomes a refuge for those who need to become unbound from impasse. He is the grand escape from the double-bind. (p. 91)

We earlier discerned the *trace* of Hermes-Mercury, his presence/absence, in the interpretations of Eros by Hillman and of imagination by Edward Casey. Behind the reflection, or representation, of the metaphysical absolute, lies the tain of the mirror, as Rodolphe Gasché (1986) entitled his study of Derrida, from which we have drawn. To reprise Derrida's trope of psyche as a mirroring function, noted previously, it would not be far afield (that Hermetic *pseudo-domain*) to propose that Psyche's predisposition to an erotics of creativity, her ardor for an imaginal or imaginative re-visioning of her humanity, is the draw we each feel toward the metaphor that provides us with the backing, the tain, that most sustains us, that backs us up. Further, the drawing of the imagination, the image it depicts, is the pull not only of any specific metaphorical absolute that might be the imprint of our individual fixities, it is the draw of metaphor in general. We are drawn to the mirror image, a reversal or othering of the literal. Archetypally, Hermes *is* this being-toward-image.

In Table 5, I list a selection of descriptors selected from Tarnas alongside the terms for the metaphoric equation. It will become apparent that the archetypal descriptors map onto the metaphoric terms. Let us take each pair in turn.

TABLE 5 Terms from Tarnas alongside descriptors of metaphoric transference

	Senex/*Saturn*	*Two ideas*		Puer/*Mercury*
1	To stabilize	Tenor	Vehicle	To transport
2	To concentrate	Focus	Frame	To conceptualize
3	To found	Principal subject	Subsidiary subject	To make sense of
4	To forge	Predicate	(No correlate)	To translate
5	To order	Extension	Intension	To inform
6	To define	Central meaning	Marginal meaning	To mediate
7	To restrain	Target domain	Source domain	To connect

1. STABILIZE AND TRANSPORT. With the initial pair, we have the stabilizing inclination of the *senex* expressed in the term *tenor* (from the Latin *tenēre*, to hold) juxtaposed to the winged cognizance of the *puer*, its ease of flight from idea to idea, expressed by *vehicle*.
2. CONCENTRATE AND CONCEPTUALIZE. The centrifugal tendency of the *senex*, its patient agglomeration of each prodigal increment of temporality into a central meaning, what Hillman (1987) called "in-gathering" (p. 17), is expressed in the term *focus*. The compensatory term *frame* indicates the wider compass described by the *puer*'s self-suspension at the margins and disinclination to touch down—its high wire act—as well as the skill at contrivance, both as improvised arrangement and as duplicity or untruth, by which the *puer* maintains the open structure, frame, of endless possibility.
3. FOUND AND MAKE SENSE OF. The *senex*, Hillman (1987) said, is a "builder of cities" (p. 16). It founds metaphor upon the principal subject of the semantic equation, a principality, in which the *puer*, more jester than king, serves to elaborate an antifoundational meaning, one that is subsidiary, making sense from subsidence.
4. FORGE AND TRANSLATE. The fourth pair is unique for the openness of the second term. The *senex* predicates, establishes quality and attribute, but the *puer*, impossible to pin down in its perpetual vanishing act, seems as if absent. Yet, puckishly, it leaves its *trace* in the predicate, instilling the capacity for disseminative translations, grasping as the wind grasps, in a movement of dispersal.
5. ORDER AND INFORM. The ordering principle of the *senex* qualifies perhaps as metaphor's formal cause; it concresces the semiological structure (signifier/signified) necessary for semantic pertinence. The causative agency of the *puer*, however, is suggestive of an *in*formal cause, relaxing form so as to conform to (ever unstable) semantic content.
6. DEFINE AND MEDIATE. The definitional quality of the *senex* is determinative, that of the *puer* determinable. The *senex* single-pointedly defines a central meaning from which the metaphor can take its departure; the *puer* meliorates through a centripetal effect, leaving traces of meaning at the articulated margins.
7. RESTRAIN AND CONNECT. The *senex* or target domain is the hoary source of meaning in the differential relation, restraining semantics to tradition,

etymology, or diachronicity. This inheritance is re-sourced with an unheard of insolence by the *puer* or source domain. It unbinds meaning from the diachronic absolutes of *arché* and *telos*, marking synchronic connection with disseminative, far-flung, and bathyic possibilities. In the metaphoric equation, neither domain exists independently of or prior to the other. Rather, they deviate from any Self-purity to co-creatively participate in a contaminated *pseudo-domain* or vale of soul-making.

The marriage of *senex* and *puer* is consecrated not on an altar to truth, the metaphysical propensity, but as an *alter*, after the nature and logic of metaphor. Metaphoric consanguinity is a phenomenon of the boundary, the vale of soul-making where diachronicity meets synchronicity. The commonality of boundary to the phenomenology of both figures enabled Hillman (1987) to characterize them at once as "a union of sames" and "a tension of ambivalent opposites" (p. 32). On this reading, *senex-et-puer* represents metaphor on both the comparison theory (like joined to like), in Kirk Pillow's (2001) view, the "weak" form, and metaphor on the interaction theory (dissimilarities forged into new meaning), Pillow's "strong" form. The necessary hardening of metaphor into the concept takes place when union or tension are sundered and a single aspect reified in consciousness. In this eventuality, we might say with Hillman (1987) that "we are split from our own likeness" (p. 34). In other words, we are split from our own metaphoricity (*like*ness). We fail to perceive the catastrophically shattered images of the many gods. Yet, in *likeness*, metaphor's not-quite ontology, there is no overcoming the woundedness of *writing*. It harbors apertures. What we do in imaginal or deconstructive writing with this sense of incompleteness is we "figure it out." In the final analysis, Hillman's *healing fiction* and Derrida's *no outside text* amount to the same thing, they bring the figure to the fore.

The *puer-et-senex* metaphor for metaphor is a *pharmakon* for the metaphysical double-blind, a therapeutics that reinscribes ambiguity into the binary, leaving us, as Hillman (1987) said, "in the soft light of the dusty world," the metaphoric vale (p. 49). In his alchemical inquiry, "The Seduction of Black," Hillman (1997c) brought the unforgiving border of the *senex* and the iterative border of the *puer* into relief:

> Alchemical psychology teaches us to read as accomplishments the fruitlessly bitter and dry periods, the melancholies that seem never to end, the wounds that do not heal to the *status quo ante*, the grinding sadistic mortifications of shame, and the putrefactions of love and friendships. These are beginnings because they are endings, dissolutions, deconstructions. But they are not the beginning as a one-time-only occurrence. (p. 49)

. . . with this *oratorio* to Silenus, a deconstructive delivery, we find ourselves borne again to the rhetorical question that constituted our beginning.

BIBLIOGRAPHY

Adams, M. V. (1992). Deconstructive Philosophy and Imaginal Psychology: Comparative Perspectives on Jacques Derrida and James Hillman. In R. Sugg (Ed.), *Jungian Literary Criticism* (pp. 231–248). Evanston, IL: Northwestern University Press.

Adams, M. V. (1995). Jungians and Deconstruction. *Roundtable Review of Contemporary Contributions to Jungian Psychology, 3*(1), 7.

Adams, M. V. (2004). *The Fantasy Principle: Psychoanalysis of the Imagination*. New York, NY: Brunner-Routledge.

Adams, M. V. (2008a). Imaginology: The Jungian Study of the Imagination. In S. Marlan (Ed.), *Archetypal Psychologies: Reflections in Honor of James Hillman* (pp. 225–244). New Orleans, LA: Spring Journal Books.

Adams, M. V. (2008b). The Archetypal School. In P. Young-Eisendrath & T. Dawson (Eds.), *The Cambridge Companion to Jung* (2nd ed., pp. 107–124). New York, NY: Cambridge University Press.

Aldrich, V. (1958). Pictorial Meaning, Picture-Thinking, and Wittgenstein's Theory of Aspects. *Mind, 62*, 70–79.

Allison, H. E. (1983). *Kant's Transcendental Idealism: An Interpretation and Defense*. Yale, CT: Yale University Press.

Apuleius. (2011). *The Golden Ass* (S. Rudin, Trans.). New Haven, CT: Yale University Press.

Aristotle. (2005). *Poetics and Rhetoric. Poetics* (S. H. Butcher, Trans.). In *Rhetoric* (W. R. Roberts, Trans.). New York, NY: Barnes & Noble.

Austin, J. (1975). *How to Do Things with Words* (2nd ed.). Cambridge, MA: Harvard University Press.

Avens, R. (2003). *The New Gnosis: Heidegger, Hillman, and Angels*. Putnam, CT: Spring Publications.

Bachelard, G. (1964). *The Psychoanalysis of Fire* (N. Frye, Trans.). Boston, MA: Beacon Press.

Bair, D. (2003). *Jung: A Biography*. New York, NY: Little, Brown.

Barfield, O. (1973). *Poetic Diction: A Study in Meaning*. Middletown, CT: Wesleyan University Press.

Barthes, R. (1972). *Critical Essays*. Chicago, IL: Northwestern University Press.

Bateson, G. (1972). *Steps to an Ecology of Mind*. New York, NY: Ballantine.

Beardsley, M. C. (1958). *Aesthetics: Problems in the Philosophy of Criticism*. New York, NY: Harcourt, Brace & World.

Beardsley, M. C. (1981). The Metaphorical Twist. In M. Johnson (Ed.), *Philosophies and Perspectives on Metaphor* (pp. 105–122). Minneapolis, MN: University of Minnesota Press. (Original work published 1962.)

Bennington, G. (1993). *Jacques Derrida*. Chicago, IL: University of Chicago Press.

Berlin, I. (2013). *The Roots of Romanticism*. Princeton, NJ: Princeton University Press.

Berry, P. (2008). *Echo's Subtle Body* (2nd ed.). Putnam, CT: Spring Publications.

Binkley, T. (1981). On the Truth and Probity of Metaphor. In M. Johnson (Ed.), *Philosophies and Perspectives on Metaphor* (pp. 136–153). Minneapolis, MN: University of Minnesota Press.

Black, M. (1962). *Models and Metaphors*. Ithaca, NY: Cornell University Press.

Black, M. (1977). More about Metaphor. *Dialectica, 31*(3–4), 431–457.

Black, M. (1981). Metaphor. In M. Johnson (Ed.), *Philosophical Perspectives on Metaphor* (pp. 63–82). Minneapolis, MN: University of Minnesota Press. (Original work published 1955.)

Bloom, H. (1970). *Romanticism and Consciousness: Essays in Criticism*. New York, NY: Norton.

Bloom, H. (1982). *Agon: Towards a Theory of Revisionism*. New York, NY: Oxford University Press.

Bloom, H. (1997). *The Anxiety of Influence: A Theory of Poetry* (2nd ed.). New York, NY: Oxford University Press.

Bloom, H. (1998). *Shakespeare: The Invention of the Human*. New York, NY: Riverhead Books.

Bohm, D. (1980). *Wholeness and the Implicate Order*. New York, NY: Routledge.

Bracken, C. (2007). *Magical Criticism: The Recourse of Savage Philosophy*. Chicago, IL: University of Chicago Press.

Brentano, F. (1995). *Descriptive Psychology* (B. Müller, Trans.). London, England: Routledge.

Brown, N. O. (1990). *Hermes the Thief*. Great Barrington, MA: Lindisfarne Press.

Bruns, G. L. (1989). *Heidegger's Estrangements*. New Haven, CT: Yale University Press.

Cambray, J. (2009). *Synchronicity: Nature and Psyche in an Interconnected Universe*. College Station, TX: Texas A&M University Press.

Campbell, J., & Robinson, H. M. (2005). *A Skeleton Key to Finnegans Wake: Unlocking James Joyce's Masterwork* (the collected works of Joseph Campbell). Novato, CA: New World Library.

Capra, F. (1996). *The Web of Life*. New York, NY: Anchor.

Caputo, J. D. (1987). *Radical Hermeneutics: Repetition, Deconstruction, and the Hermeneutic Project*. Indianapolis, IN: Indiana University Press.

Caputo, J. D. (1997). *The Prayers and Tears of Jacques Derrida: Religion without Religion*. Indianapolis, IN: Indiana University Press.

Casey, E. (1974a). Toward a Phenomenology of Imagination. *Journal of the British Society for Phenomenology, 5*, 3–19.

Casey, E. (1974b). Toward an Archetypal Imagination. *Spring*, 1–33.

Casey, E. (1976). *Imagining: A Phenomenological Study*. Bloomington, IN: Indiana University Press.

Casey, E. (2001). *Spirit and Soul: Essays in Philosophical Psychology* (2nd ed.). Putnam, CT: Spring Publications.

Cazeaux, C. (2007). *Metaphor and Continental Philosophy: From Kant to Derrida*. New York, NY: Routledge.

Cheetham, T. (2012). *All the World an Icon: Henry Corbin and the Angelic Function of Beings*. Berkeley, CA: North Atlantic Books.

Cheetham, T. (2013, April 13). *Henry Corbin: All the World an Icon* [Lecture]. San Francisco Jung Institute, San Francisco, CA.

Cobb, N. (1992). *Archetypal Imagination: Glimpses of the Gods in Life and Art*. Hudson, NY: Lindisfarne Press.

Cohen, T. (1979). Metaphor and the Cultivation of Intimacy. In S. Sacks (Ed.), *On Metaphor* (pp. 1–10). Chicago, IL: University of Chicago Press.

Cohen, T. (1981). Figurative Speech and Figurative Acts. In M. Johnson (Ed.), *Philosophical Perspectives on Metaphor* (pp. 182–199). Minneapolis, MN: University of Minnesota Press.

Copleston, F. S. J. (1964). *A History of Philosophy* (Vol. 6, Part II). Garden City, NY: Image Books.

Cowan, T. (1987). On Finnegans Wake. In J. Hillman (Ed.), *Puer Papers* (pp. 24–237). Dallas, TX: Spring Publications.

Crane, H. (2001). *The Complete Poems of Hart Crane* (centennial ed., M. Simon, Ed.). New York, NY: Norton.

Culler, J. (1983). *On Deconstruction: Theory and Criticism after Structuralism*. Ithaca, NY: Cornell University Press.

Culler, J. (1986). *Ferdinand de Saussure* (rev. ed.). Ithaca, NY: Cornell University Press.

Danesi, M. (1993). *Vico, Metaphor, and the Origin of Language*. Indianapolis, IN: Indiana University Press.

Daniels, P. R. (2013). *Nietzsche and the Birth of Tragedy*. Bristol, CT: Acumen.

Davidson, D. (1979). What Metaphors Mean. In S. Sacks (Ed.), *On Metaphor* (pp. 29–46). Chicago, IL: University of Chicago Press.

De Man, P. (1973). Theory of Metaphor in Rousseau's "Second Discourse." *Studies in Romanticism*, *12*(2), 475–498. doi:10.2307/25599880

De Voogd, S. (1977). C. G. Jung: Psychologist of the Future, "Philosopher" of the Past. *Spring*, 175–182.

Deleuze, G. (2006). *Nietzsche and Philosophy* (H. Tomlinson, Trans.). New York, NY: Columbia University Press.

Derrida, J. (1978a). *Spurs: Nietzsche's Styles* (B. Harlow, Trans.). Chicago, IL: University of Chicago Press.

Derrida, J. (1978b). Structure, Sign and Play in the Discourse of the Human Sciences. In A. Bass (Trans. & Ed.), *Writing and Difference* (pp. 278–293). Chicago, IL: University of Chicago Press.

Derrida, J. (1981). *Dissemination* (B. Johnson, Trans.). Chicago, IL: University of Chicago Press.

Derrida, J. (1982). *Margins of Philosophy* (A. Bass, Trans.). Chicago, IL: University of Chicago Press.

Derrida, J. (1987). *The Truth in Painting* (G. Bennington & I. McLeod, Trans.). Chicago, IL: University of Chicago Press.

Derrida, J. (1988). *Limited, Inc.* Evanston, IL: Northwestern University Press.

Derrida, J. (1997). *Of Grammatology* (G. C. Spivak, Trans.). Baltimore, MD: Johns Hopkins Press.

Derrida, J. (1998a). *The Derrida Reader: Writing Performances* (J. Wolfreys, Ed.). Lincoln, NE: University of Nebraska Press.

Derrida, J. (1998b). The *Retrait* of Metaphor. In J. Wolfreys (Ed.), *The Derrida Reader: Writing Performances* (pp. 102–129). Lincoln, NE: University of Nebraska Press.

Derrida, J. (2002). *Acts of Religion* (G. Anidjar, Ed.). New York, NY: Routledge.

Derrida, J. (2007). *Psyche: Inventions of the Other* (Vols. I & II). Stanford, CA: Stanford University Press.

Deutscher, P., & Oliver, K. (1999). *Enigmas: Essays on Sarah Kofman*. Ithaca, NY: Cornell University Press.

Donoghue, D. (2014). *Metaphor*. Cambridge, MA: Harvard University Press.

Dosse, F. (1997). *History of Structuralism* (Vol. 1., D. Galssman, Trans.). Minneapolis, MN: University of Minnesota Press.

Eagleton, T. (1990). *The Ideology of the Aesthetic*. Malden, MA: Blackwell Publishing.

Edie, J. (1969). Vico and Existential Philosophy. In G. Tagliacozzo & H. V. White (Eds.), *Giambattista Vico: An International Symposium* (pp. 483–495). Baltimore, MD: Johns Hopkins Press.

Eliade, M. (1978). *A History of Religious Ideas* (Vol. 1., W. R. Trask, Trans.). Chicago, IL: University of Chicago Press.

Eliade, M. (1989). *Shamanism: Archaic Techniques of Ecstasy*. London, England: Penguin.

Ellenberger, H. (1970). *The Discovery of the Unconscious*. New York, NY: Basic Books.

Epstein, M. (2013). *The Trauma of Everyday Life*. New York, NY: Penguin.

Ferrari, G. R. F. (2005). *City and Soul in Plato's Republic*. Chicago, IL: University of Chicago Press.

Foucault, M. (1965). *Madness and Civilization* (R. Howard, Trans.). New York, NY: Pantheon.

Foucault, M. (1988). *The History of Sexuality, Vol. III: The Care of the Self* (R. Hurley, Trans.). New York, NY: Vintage.

Freud, S. (1955). *Totem and Taboo*. In J. Strachey (Trans. & Ed.), *The Standard Edition of the Works of Sigmund Freud*. London, England: Hogarth Press.

Freud, S. (1960). Jokes and Their Relation to the Unconscious. In J. Strachey (Trans. & Ed.), *The Standard Edition of the Works of Sigmund Freud*. New York, NY: Norton.

Freud, S. (1965). *The Interpretation of Dreams*. New York, NY: Avon.

Freud, S. (1966). Introductory Lectures on Psycho-Analysis. In J. Strachey (Trans. & Ed.), *The Standard Edition of the Works of Sigmund Freud*. New York, NY: Norton.

Freud, S. (2003). *The Uncanny* (D. McLintock, Trans.). New York, NY: Penguin.

Friedrich, C. (Ed.). (1977). *The Philosophy of Kant*. New York, NY: Modern Library.

Frye, N. (1964). Preface. In G. Bachelard, *The Psychoanalysis of Fire* (pp. v–vii). Boston, MA: Beacon Press.

Gadamer, H.-G. (1981). *Reason in the Age of Science* (F. G. Lawrence, Trans.). Cambridge, MA: MIT Press.

Gadamer, H.-G. (1989a). *Hegel's Dialectic: Five Hermeneutical Studies* (P. C. Smith, Trans.). New Haven, CT: Yale University Press.

Gadamer, H.-G. (1989b). *Truth and Method* (J. Weinsheimer & D. G. Marshall, Trans.). New York, NY: Continuum.

Gasché, R. (1986). *The Tain of the Mirror: Derrida and the Philosophy of Reflection*. Cambridge, MA: Harvard University Press.

Gibbs, Jr., R. W. (1995). *The Poetics of Mind: Figurative Thought, Language and Understanding*. New York, NY: Cambridge University Press.

Gibbs, Jr., R. W. (Ed.). (2008). *The Cambridge Handbook of Metaphor and Thought*. London, England: Cambridge University Press.

Giegerich, W. (2007). Psychology as Anti-Philosophy: C. G. Jung. *Spring*, 11–52.

Goldstein, L. (1999). *Clear and Queer Thinking: Wittgenstein's Development and His Relevance to Modern Thought*. Lanham, MD: Rowman & Littlefield.

Golomb, J. (Ed.). (1999). *Nietzsche and Depth Psychology*. Albany, NY: State University of New York Press.

Goodman, N. (1968). *Languages of Art*. Indianapolis, IN: Bobbs-Merrill.

Gras, V. W. (Ed.). (1973). *European Literary Theory and Practice: From Existential Phenomenology to Structuralism*. New York, NY: Dell.

Greene, L. (1976). *Saturn: A New Look at an Old Devil*. New York, NY: Samuel Weiser.

Greer, J. M., & Warnock, C. (Trans.). (2010). *The Picatrix*. Iowa City, IA: Adocentyn Press.

Grof, S. (1998). *The Cosmic Game: Explorations of the Frontiers of Human Consciousness*. Albany, NY: State University of New York Press.

Guthrie, W. K. C. (1950). *The Greek Philosophers: From Thales to Aristotle*. New York, NY: Harper & Row.

Hand, R. (1981). *Horoscope Symbols*. Westchester, PA: Whitford Press.

Handelman, S. A. (1982). *The Slayers of Moses: The Emergence of Rabbinic Interpretation in Modern Literary Theory*. Albany, NY: State University of New York Press.

Harris, R. (2005). Translator's Introduction. In F. Saussure, *Course in General Linguistics* (pp. xlix–lii). Chicago, IL: Open Court.

Hartman, G. H. (1981). *Saving the Text: Literature, Derrida, Philosophy*. Baltimore, MD: Johns Hopkins University Press.

Harvey, S. (2000). *Orpheus: Voices in Contemporary Astrology*. Frome, England: Consider Publications.

Hauke, C. (2000). *Jung and the Postmodern: The Interpretation of Realities*. New York, NY: Brunner-Routledge.

Hawkes, T. (1977). *Structuralism and Semiotics*. Berkeley, CA: University of California Press.

Hegel, G. (1998). *The Hegel Reader*. Malden, MA: Blackwell Publishing.

Heidegger, M. (1962). *Being and Time* (J. Macquarrie & E. Robinson, Trans.). New York, NY: Harper & Row.

Heidegger, M. (1978). Letter on Humanism. In D. F. Krell (Ed.), *Basic Writings* (pp. 213–265). London, England: Routledge.

Heidegger, M. (1991). *The Principle of Reason* (R. Lilly, Trans.). Bloomington, IN: Indiana University Press.

Henle, P. (1981). Metaphor. In Mark Johnson (Ed.), *Philosophies and Perspectives on Metaphor* (pp. 83–104). Minneapolis, MN: University of Minnesota Press. (Original work published 1958.)

Hester, M. B. (1966). Metaphor and Aspect Seeing. *Journal of Aesthetics and Art Criticism, 25*, 205–212. doi:10.2307/429393

Hillman, J. (1967). *Insearch: Psychology and Religion*. Dallas, TX: Spring Publications.

Hillman, J. (1975). *Re-Visioning Psychology*. New York, NY: HarperPerennial.

Hillman, J. (1977). An Inquiry into Image. *Spring*, 62–88.

Hillman, J. (1978a). Further Notes on Images. *Spring*, 152–182.

Hillman, J. (1978b). *Loose Ends: Primary Papers in Archetypal Psychology*. Irving, TX: Spring Publications.

Hillman, J. (1978c). *The Myth of Analysis*. New York, NY: HarperColophon.

Hillman, J. (1979a). Image Sense. *Spring*, 130–143.

Hillman, J. (1979b). *The Dream and the Underworld*. New York, NY: HarperColophon.

Hillman, J. (1980). Dionysos in Jung's Writings. In J. Hillman (Ed.), *Facing the Gods* (pp. 151–164). Dallas, TX: Spring Publications.

Hillman, J. (1981). Psychology: Monotheistic or Polytheistic. In D. Miller (Ed.), *The New Polytheism: Rebirth of the Gods and Goddesses* (pp. 109–142). Dallas, TX: Spring Publications.

Hillman, J. (1983a). *Healing Fiction*. Putnam, CT: Spring Publications.

Hillman, J. (1983b). *Inter Views: Conversations with Laura Pozzo on Psychotherapy, Biography, Love, Soul, Dreams, Work, Imagination, and the State of the Culture*. New York, NY: HarperColophon.

Hillman, J. (1985). *Anima: Anatomy of a Personified Notion*. Dallas, TX: Spring Publications.
Hillman, J. (1987). *Puer Papers*. Dallas, TX: Spring Publications.
Hillman, J. (1989a). *A Blue Fire: Selected Writings*. New York, NY: HarperPerennial.
Hillman, J. (1989b). *Archetypal Process: Self and Divine in Whitehead, Jung and Hillman*. Evanston, IL: Northwestern University Press.
Hillman, J. (1992a). *Emotion*. Evanston, IL: Northwestern University Press.
Hillman, J. (1992b). How Jewish Is Archetypal Psychology? *Spring*, 121–130.
Hillman, J. (1992c). *The Thought of the Heart and the Soul of the World*. Putnam, CT: Spring Publications.
Hillman, J. (1993). Concerning the Stone: Alchemical Images of the Goal. *Sphinx: A Journal for Archetypal Psychology and the Arts, 5*, 234–265.
Hillman, J. (1994). Once More into the Fray: A Response to Wolfgang Giegerich's "Killings." *Spring*, 1–18.
Hillman, J. (1996). *The Soul's Code: In Search of Character and Calling*. New York, NY: Random House.
Hillman, J. (1997a). Culture and the Animal Soul. *Spring*, 10–37.
Hillman, J. (1997b). *Suicide and the Soul* (2nd ed.). Woodstock, CT: Spring Publications.
Hillman, J. (1997c). The Seduction of Black. In S. Marlan (Ed.), *Fire in the Stone: The Alchemy of Desire* (pp. 42–53). Wilmette, IL: Chiron Publications.
Hillman, J. (1999). *The Force of Character and the Lasting Life*. New York, NY: Ballantine.
Hillman, J. (2000a). Look Out: Three Occasions of Public Excitation. In D. P. Slattery & L. Corbet (Eds.), *Depth Psychology: Meditations in the Field* (pp. 161–174). Einsiedeln, Germany: Daimon Verlag.
Hillman, J. (2000b). *Pan and the Nightmare* (rev. ed.). Woodstock, CT: Spring Publications.
Hillman, J. (2004a). *Archetypal Psychology: Uniform Edition of the Writings of James Hillman* (Vol. 1). Putnam, CT: Spring Publications.
Hillman, J. (2004b). *The Thought of the Heart and the Soul of the World*. Putnam, CT: Spring Publications.
Hillman, J. (2005). *Senex and Puer*. Putnam, CT: Spring Publications.
Hillman, J., & Shamdasani, S. (2013). *Lament of the Dead: Psychology after Jung's Red Book*. New York, NY: Norton.
Hillman, J., & Ventura, M. (1992). *We've Had a Hundred Years of Psychotherapy—and the World's Getting Worse*. San Francisco, CA: HarperCollins.
Hobbes, T. (1968). *Leviathan*. New York, NY: Penguin.
Homer. (2011). *The Iliad* (S. Mitchell, Trans.). New York, NY: Free Press.
Howells, C. (1998). *Derrida: Deconstruction from Phenomenology to Ethics*. Cambridge, MA: Polity Press.
Husserl, E. (1931). *Ideas: A General Introduction to Pure Phenomenology* (W. R. Boyce Gibson, Trans.). London, England: Allen & Unwin.
Hyde, L. (1998). *Trickster Makes This World: Mischief, Myth, and Art*. New York, NY: Farrar, Straus and Giroux.
Inwood, M. (1999). *A Heidegger Dictionary*. Malden, MA: Blackwell Publishing.
Jakobson, R. (1973). Two Aspects of Language: Metaphor and Metonymy. In V. W. Gras (Ed.), *European Literary Theory and Practice: From Existential Phenomenology to Structuralism* (pp. 119–131). New York, NY: Dell.
James, W. (1975). *Pragmatism*. Cambridge, MA: Harvard University Press.
James, W. (1996). *A Pluralistic Universe*. Lincoln, NE: University of Nebraska Press.
Jameson, F. (1979). Introduction. In J. F. Lyotard (Ed.), *The Postmodern Condition: A Report on Knowledge* (G. Bennington & B. Massumi, Trans., pp. vii–xxii). Minneapolis, MN: University of Minnesota Press.

Jaspers, K. (1962). *Kant* (R. Manheim, Trans.). New York, NY: Harcourt, Brace, Jovanovich.
Johnson, M. (1981). *Philosophical Perspectives on Metaphor*. Minneapolis, MN: University of Minnesota Press.
Johnson, M. (2008). Philosophy's Debt to Metaphor. In R. Gibbs (Ed.), *The Cambridge Handbook of Metaphor and Thought* (pp. 39–52). Cambridge, England: Cambridge University Press.
Johnson, R. (1991). *Transformation: Understanding the Three Levels of Masculine Consciousness*. San Francisco, CA: HarperSanFrancisco.
Jonas, H. (2001). *The Gnostic Religion*. Boston, MA: Beacon Press.
Joyce, J. (1939). *Finnegans Wake*. New York, NY: Faber & Faber.
Jung, C. G. (1979). *Collected Works of Carl Gustav Jung* (R. F. C. Hull, Trans.). Princeton, NJ: Princeton University Press.
Jung, C. G. (1989). *Memories, Dreams, Reflections* (A. Jaffe, Ed., C. Winston, Trans.). New York, NY: Random House.
Kafka, F. (1971). *The Complete Stories*. New York, NY: Schocken.
Kant, I. (1977). *Prologomena to Any Future Metaphysics* (P. Caras, Trans., rev. J. W. Ellington). Indianapolis, IN: Hackett Publishing.
Kant, I. (1987). *The Critique of Judgment* (W. S. Pluhar, Trans.). Indianapolis, IN: Hackett Publishing.
Kant, I. (1996). *The Critique of Pure Reason* (W. S. Pluhar, Trans.). Indianapolis, IN: Hackett Publishing.
Kaufmann, W. (1974a). Translator's Introduction. In F. Nietzsche, *The Gay Science* (pp. 3–31). New York, NY: Vintage.
Kaufmann, W. (1974b). *Nietzsche: Philosopher, Psychologist, Antichrist* (4th ed.). Princeton, NJ: Princeton University Press.
Kaufmann, W. (1992). *Freud, Adler, and Jung*. New Brunswick, NJ: Transaction Publishers.
Kerényi, C. (1956). The Trickster in Relation to Greek Mythology. In P. Radin, *The Trickster: A Study in American Indian Mythology with Commentaries by Karl Kerényi and C. G. Jung* (pp. 173–191). New York, NY: Schocken.
Kerényi, K. (1976a). *Dionysos: Archetypal Image of Indestructible Life* (R. Manheim, Trans.). Princeton, NJ: Princeton University Press.
Kerényi, K. (1976b). *Hermes: Guide of Souls* (M. Stein, Trans.). Zurich, Switzerland: Spring Publications.
Kerényi, K., & Hillman, J. (1995). *Oedipus Variations: Studies in Literature and Psychoanalysis*. Woodstock, CT: Spring Publications.
Kitcher, P. W. (1996). Introduction. In I. Kant, *Critique of Pure Reason* (W. S. Pluhar, Trans., pp. xxv–lix). Indianapolis, IN: Hackett Publishing.
Kofman, S. (1993). *Nietzsche and Metaphor* (D. Large, Trans.). Stanford, CA: Stanford University Press.
Kövecses, Z. (2002). *Metaphor: A Practical Introduction*. New York, NY: Oxford University Press.
Kugler, P. (1990). The Unconscious in a Postmodern Depth Psychology. In K. Barnaby & P. D'Acierno (Eds.), *C. G. Jung and the Humanities: Toward a Hermeneutics of Culture* (pp. 307–317). Princeton, NJ: Princeton University Press.
Kuhn, T. (1993). Metaphor in Science. In A. Ortony (Ed.), *Metaphor and Thought* (2nd ed., pp. 553–542). New York, NY: Cambridge University Press.
Kuhn, T. (1996). *The Structure of Scientific Revolutions* (3rd ed.). Chicago, IL: University of Chicago Press.
Kurzweil, E. (1980). *The Age of Structuralism: Lévi-Strauss to Foucault*. New York, NY: Columbia University Press.

Lacan, J. (1970). The Insistence of the Letter in the Unconscious. In J. Ehrman (Ed.), *Structuralism* (pp. 112–147). Garden City, NY: Doubleday.

Lakoff, G., & Johnson, M. (1980). *Metaphors We Live By*. Chicago, IL: University of Chicago Press.

Lakoff, G., & Johnson, M. (1999). *Philosophy in the Flesh: The Embodied Mind and Its Challenge to Western Thought*. New York, NY: Basic Books.

Lavers, A. (1982). *Roland Barthes: Structuralism and After*. Cambridge, MA: Harvard University Press.

Leary, D. (Ed.). (1990). *Metaphors in the History of Psychology*. New York, NY: Cambridge University Press.

Lévi-Strauss, C. (1967). *Structural Anthropology* (C. Jacobson & B. Grundfest Schoepf, Trans.). New York, NY: Anchor Books.

Locke, J. (1959). *An Essay Concerning Human Understanding*. New York, NY: Dover Publications.

Loewenberg, I. (1981). Identifying Metaphors. In M. Johnson (Ed.), *Philosophical Perspectives on Metaphor* (pp. 154–181). Minneapolis, MN: University of Minnesota Press.

López-Pedraza, R. (2003). *Hermes and His Children* (3rd ed.). Einsiedeln, Switzerland: Daimon Verlag.

López-Pedraza, R. (2007). Post-Jungian Movements: Conversations with Raphael López-Pedraza. *Spring*, 245–276.

Lorenz, H. S. (2004). The Presence of Absence: Marking Postcolonial Spaces. In D. P. Slattery & L. Corbett (Eds.), *Depth Psychology: Meditations in the Field* (pp. 225–243). Einsiedeln, Switzerland: Daimon Verlag.

Lucy, N. (1995). *Debating Derrida*. Melbourne, Australia: Melbourne University Press.

Lucy, N. (2005). *A Derrida Dictionary*. Malden, MA: Blackwell Publishing.

Lyotard, J.-F. (1989). *The Postmodern Condition: A Report on Knowledge* (G. Bennington & B. Massumi, Trans.). Minneapolis, MN: University of Minnesota Press.

Manguel, A. (2007). *Homer's the Iliad and the Odyssey: A Biography*. New York, NY: Atlantic Monthly Press.

Maslow, A. H. (1968). *Toward a Psychology of Being* (2nd ed.). New York, NY: Van Nostrand Reinhold.

McNeely, D. A. (1996). *Mercury Rising: Women, Evil and the Trickster Gods*. Woodstock, CT: Spring Publications.

Miller, D. (1984). On Literalism: The Letter and the Monkey. *Spring*, 151–161.

Miller, D. (2008). Psyche's Poetry. In S. Marlan (Ed.), *Archetypal Psychologies: Reflections in Honor of James Hillman* (pp. 245–260). New Orleans, LA: Spring Journal Books.

Milutis, J. (2013). *Failure: A Writer's Life*. Winchester, England: Zero Books.

Moore, T. (Ed.). (1989). *Blue Fire: Selected Writings by James Hillman*. New York, NY: HarperPerennial.

Moran, D. (2000). *Introduction to Phenomenology*. London, England: Routledge.

Nabais, N. (2006). *Nietzsche and the Metaphysics of the Tragic* (M. Earl, Trans.). New York, NY: Continuum.

Nagel, T. (1974). What Is It Like to Be a Bat? *The Philosophical Review*, *83*(4), 435–450.

Nehamas, A. (1985). *Nietzsche: Life as Literature*. Cambridge, MA: Harvard University Press.

Neruda, P. (1990). *Selected Poems* (N. Tarn, Ed., A. Kerrigan, Trans.). New York, NY: Houghton Mifflin.

Nietzsche, F. (1956). *The Birth of Tragedy* and *The Genealogy of Morals* (F. Golfing, Trans.). New York, NY: Doubleday Anchor.

Nietzsche, F. (1967a). *The Birth of Tragedy and the Case of Wagner* (W. Kaufmann, Trans.). New York, NY: Vintage.

Nietzsche, F. (1967b). *The Will to Power* (W. Kaufmann & R. J. Hollingdale, Trans.). New York, NY: Vintage.

Nietzsche, F. (1974). *The Gay Science* (W. Kaufmann, Trans.). New York, NY: Vintage.

Nietzsche, F. (1979). *Philosophy and Truth: Selections from Nietzsche's Notebooks of the Early 1870s* (D. Breazeale, Trans.). Atlantic Highlands, NJ: Humanities Press.

Nietzsche, F. (2006). *The Nietzsche Reader* (D. Breazeale, Trans.). Malden, MA: Blackwell Publishing.

Norris, C. (1987). *Derrida.* Cambridge, MA: Harvard University Press.

Nuyen, A. T. (1989). The Kantian Theory of Metaphor. *Critical Inquiry, 22,* 95–109.

Ortony, A. (Ed.). (1979). *Metaphor and Thought.* London, England: Cambridge University Press.

Ortony, A. (Ed.). (1993). *Metaphor and Thought* (2nd ed.). London, England: Cambridge University Press.

Otto, W. F. (2014). *The Homeric Gods: The Spiritual Significance of Greek Religion.* New York, NY: Mimesis International.

Ovid. (1994). *The Metamorphoses* (D. R. Slavitt, Trans.). Baltimore, MD: Johns Hopkins University Press.

Pepper, S. C. (1970). *World Hypotheses.* Berkeley, CA: University of California Press.

Pepper, S. C. (1973). Metaphor in Philosophy. In *Dictionary of the History of Ideas* (Vol. 3, pp. 196–201). New York, NY: Scribner's.

Perloff, M. (1996). *Wittgenstein's Ladder: Poetic Language and the Strangeness of the Ordinary.* Chicago, IL: University of Chicago Press.

Phillips, A. (2014). *Becoming Freud: The Making of a Psychoanalyst.* New Haven, CT: Yale University Press.

Pillow, K. (2001). Jupiter's Eagle and the Despot's Hand Mill: Two Views on Metaphor in Kant. *Journal of Aesthetics & Art Criticism, 59,* 193–209.

Pillow, K. (2003). *Sublime Understanding: Aesthetic Reflection in Kant and Hegel.* Boston, MA: MIT Press.

Plato. (1957). *The Republic* (A. D. Lindsay, Trans.). New York, NY: Dutton.

Plato. (1963). *The Collected Dialogues* (E. Hamilton & H. Cairns, Eds., R. Hackforth, Trans.). New York, NY: Pantheon.

Pluhar, W. S. (1987). Translator's Introduction. In *Kant's Critique of Judgment* (pp. xxii–cix). Indianapolis, IN: Hackett Publishing.

Punter, D. (2007). *Metaphor.* New York, NY: Routledge.

Radin, P. (1985). *Primitive Man as Philosopher.* Mineola, NY: Dover Publications.

Richards, I. A. (1981). The Philosophy of Rhetoric. In M. Johnson (Ed.), *Philosophies and Perspectives on Metaphor* (pp. 48–62). Minneapolis, MN: University of Minnesota Press.

Ricoeur, P. (1975). *The Rule of Metaphor: Multi-Disciplinary Studies of the Creation of Meaning in Language* (R. Czerny, K. McLaughlin, & S. J. Costello, Trans.). Toronto, Canada: University of Toronto Press.

Ricoeur, P. (1978). The Metaphorical Process as Cognition, Imagination, and Feeling. In S. Sacks (Ed.), *On Metaphor* (pp. 141–157). Chicago, IL: University of Chicago Press.

Rorty, R. (1979). *Philosophy and the Mirror of Nature.* Princeton, NJ: Princeton University Press.

Rorty, R. (1989). *Contingency, Irony, and Solidarity.* Cambridge, England: Cambridge University Press.

Rorty, R. (1997). Philosophy as a Kind of Writing: An Essay on Derrida. In L. Menand (Ed.), *Pragmatism: A Reader* (pp. 304–328). New York, NY: Vintage.

Rorty, R. (1999). *Contingency, Irony, and Solidarity.* New York, NY: Cambridge University Press.

Rowland, S. (2005). *Jung as a Writer*. New York, NY: Routledge.
Rowland, S. (2006). Jung and Derrida: The Numinous, Deconstruction and Myth. In A. Casement & D. Tacey (Eds.), *The Idea of the Numinous: Contemporary Jungian and Psychoanalytic Perspectives* (pp. 98–116). New York, NY: Routledge.
Rowland, S. (2017). *Remembering Dionysus: Revisioning Psychology and Literature in C. G. Jung and James Hillman*. New York, NY: Routledge.
Russell, D. (2013). *The Life and Ideas of James Hillman: The Making of a Psychologist* (Vol. I). New York, NY: Helios Press.
Ryle, G. (1949). *The Concept of Mind*. London, England: Hutchinson's University Library.
Safranski, R. (2003). *Nietzsche: A Philosophical Biography* (S. Frisch, Trans.). New York, NY: W. W. Norton.
Sartre, J.-P. (1964). *Nausea*. New York, NY: New Directions.
Saussure, Ferdinand de (2005). *Course in General Linguistics* (C. Bally & A. Sechehaye, Eds., R. Harris, Trans.). La Salle, IL: Open Court.
Schopenhauer, A. (1969). *The World as Will and Representation* (E. F. J. Payne, Trans.). New York, NY: Dover Publications.
Scruton, R. (1996). *An Intelligent Person's Guide to Philosophy*. New York, NY: Penguin.
Searle, J. (1981). Metaphor. In M. Johnson (Ed.), *Philosophical Perspectives on Metaphor* (pp. 248–285). Minneapolis, MN: University of Minnesota Press.
Sperber, D. (1992). Claude Lévi-Strauss. In J. Sturrock (Ed.), *Structuralism and Since* (pp. 19–51). New York, NY: Oxford University Press.
Spinoza, B. (1996). *Ethics*. London, England: Penguin.
Stellardi, G. (2000). *Imperfect Thought: Heidegger and Derrida on Philosophy and Metaphor*. Amherst, NY: Prometheus Books.
Stevens, W. (1990). *The Palm at the End of the Mind*. New York, NY: Viking.
Sturrock, J. (Ed.). (1992). *Structuralism and Since*. New York, NY: Oxford University Press.
Sutherland, J. (2013). *A Little History of Literature*. New Haven, CT: Yale University Press.
Tacey, D. (1998). Twisting and Turning with James Hillman: From Anima to World Soul, from Academia to Pop. In A. Casement (Ed.), *Post-Jungians Today: Key Papers in Contemporary Analytical Psychology* (pp. 215–234). New York, NY: Routledge.
Tarnas, R. (1991). *The Passion of the Western Mind: Understanding the Ideas That Have Shaped Our World View*. New York, NY: Ballantine.
Tarnas, R. (1995). *Prometheus the Awakener: An Essay on the Archetypal Meaning of the Planet Uranus*. Woodstock, CT: Spring Publications.
Tarnas, R. (2006). *Cosmos and Psyche: Intimations of a New World View*. New York, NY: Viking.
Townsend, D. (1995). Metaphor, Hermeneutics, and Situations. In L. E. Hahn (Ed.), *The Philosophy of Paul Ricoeur* (pp. 191–209). Peru, IL: Open Court.
Turbayne, C. (1970). *The Myth of Metaphor*. Columbia, SC: University of South Carolina Press.
Unamuno, M. de (1954). *The Tragic Sense of Life* (J. E. Crawford Flitch, Trans.). New York, NY: Dover Publications.
Vaihinger, H. (2009). *The Philosophy of "As If."* Milton Park, England: Routledge.
Varela, F. J., Thompson, E., & Rosch, E. (2000). *The Embodied Mind: Cognitive Science and Human Experience*. Cambridge, MA: MIT Press.
Vico, G. (2001). *New Science* (3rd ed., D. March, Trans.). New York, NY: Penguin.
Von Franz, M.-L. (1999). *The Cat: A Tale of Feminine Redemption*. Toronto, Canada: Inner City Books.
Warminski, A. (1987). *Readings in Interpretation: Holderlin, Hegel, Heidegger. Theory and History of Literature* (Vol. 26). Minneapolis, MN: University of Minnesota Press.

Weinsheimer, J. (1991). Gadamer's Metaphorical Hermeneutics. In H. J. Silverman (Ed.), *Gadamer and Hermeneutics: Continental Philosophy* (Vol. 4, pp. 181–201). New York, NY: Routledge.

White, E. (1999). *Marcel Proust*. New York, NY: Lipper Viking.

Whitehead, A. N. (1978). *Process and Reality: An Essay in Cosmology* (D. R. Griffin & D. W. Sherburn, Eds.). New York, NY: Free Press.

Wilcken, P. (2010). *Claude Lévi-Strauss: The Poet in the Laboratory*. New York, NY: Penguin.

Wittgenstein, L. (1958). *Philosophical Investigations* (2nd ed., G. E. M. Anscombe & R. Rhees, Eds., G. E. M. Anscombe, Trans.). New York, NY: Blackwell Publishing.

Wojtkowski, S. (2008). Deconstructing the Monstrous: An "Ecologically Correct" Approach: From "What Are Dragons For?" to "What Do Dragons Want?" In S. Marlan (Ed.), *Archetypal Psychologies: Reflections in Honor of James Hillman* (pp. 293–314). New Orleans, LA: Spring Journal Books.

Yates, F. A. (1964). *Giordano Bruno and the Hermetic Tradition*. Chicago, IL: University of Chicago Press.

Yates, F. A. (1966). *The Art of Memory*. Chicago, IL: University of Chicago Press.

INDEX

For Product Safety Concerns and Information please contact our EU representative GPSR@taylorandfrancis.com
Taylor & Francis Verlag GmbH, Kaufingerstraße 24, 80331 München, Germany

www.ingramcontent.com/pod-product-compliance
Lightning Source LLC
LaVergne TN
LVHW021128300926
849160LV00010B/907